HITLER'S MOUNTAIN TROOPS

HITLER'S MOUNTAIN TROOPS

JAMES LUCAS

ARMS AND
ARMOUR

Arms and Armour Press
A Cassell Imprint
Villiers House, 41–47 Strand, London WC2N 5JE.

Distributed in the USA by Sterling Publishing Co. Inc.,
387 Park Avenue South, New York, NY 10016-8810.

Distributed in Australia by Capricorn Link (Australia) Pty. Ltd,
P.O. Box 665, Lane Cove, New South Wales 2066.

British Library Cataloguing-in-Publication Data: a catalogue record
for this book is available from the British Library

ISBN 1-85409-079-8

Cartography by Peter Burton.

Designed and edited by DAG Publications Ltd. Designed by David
Gibbons; edited by Michael Boxall; typeset by Ronset Typesetters,
Darwen, Lancashire; camerawork by M&E Reproductions, North
Fambridge, Essex; printed and bound in Great Britain by Hartnolls
Ltd, Bodmin, Cornwall.

Contents

Acknowledgements, 6
Introduction, 9
The Background, 12

1st, 2nd and 3rd Gebirgs Divisions in Poland, 1939, 18
2nd and 3rd Gebirgs Divisions in Norway, 1940, 27
1st Gebirgs Division in France and the Low Countries, 1940, 39
5th and 6th Gebirgs Divisions in Greece, 1941, 47
1st and 4th Gebirgs Divisions in Yugoslavia, 1941, 68
5th Gebirgs Division in Crete, 1941, 72
1st and 4th Gebirgs Divisions on the Eastern Front, 1941, 86
1st and 4th Gebirgs Divisions in the Encirclement Battles around
    Uman, 95
2nd, 3rd, 6th, 6th SS and 7th Gebirgs Divisions in Lappland,
    1941–1945, 104
1st and 4th Gebirgs Divisions on the Eastern Front: Caucasus,
    1942–1943, 129
5th Gebirgs Division in the Volkhov Sector: Leningrad, 1942–
    1943, 136
756th Regiment in Tunisia, 1942–1943, 142
7th SS Gebirgs Division 'Prinz Eugen' in Yugoslavia, 1942–1945,
    144
2nd Gebirgs Division and 6th SS Gebirgs Division 'Nord' on the
    Western Front, 1944–1945, 164
1st Gebirgs Division in Hungary, 1944, and in Steiermark, Austria,
    1945, 173
9th Gebirgs Division in Steiermark, Austria, 1945, 189
Epilogue, 196

Appendix: History of the Army and SS Gebirgs Divisions, 198
Maps, 209
Select Bibliography, 218
List of Contributors, 219
Index, 220

Acknowledgements

THE FACES staring out from the photographs are all of young men who are dead but who do not rest here in the village churchyard. Instead they lie on any one of the battlefields on which the German Army of the Third Reich fought and bled. Some of the faces are those of recruits, posing self-consciously and formal in their new uniforms. Others bear the resolute expression of veteran soldiers who have experienced the full fury of war. A few faces are smiling – records of happier military occasions. These photographs are all that is left to show that these men once lived. Now their bodies lie as far apart as the Arctic Circle, Tunisia, France and the Caucasus mountains.

Two things link them all. First, they were all local men – men from particular villages in the vicinity and, secondly, their arm of service is readily apparent. Each carries on the left side of his cap or on his right sleeve the edelweiss emblem which distinguishes him as a Gebirgsjaeger – a man of a mountain division. To read the details on the plaques below the photographs is to follow the campaigns of the division that recruited here. 'Here' is any village in the alpine regions of Germany or Austria, and most village churchyards have a wall bearing the photographs of those who did not come home to the silent and eternal mountains which they left to go to war.

It is sad that they were all so young – these men who died before they had had a chance to live. Sadder yet is it to see the same family name recorded so frequently on this wall of the dead. Fathers, sons, uncles and nephews who went out to fight as Gebirgsjaeger during the Second World War, following the road trodden by an earlier generation whose men lie on the battlefields of the Great War of 1914–18. The blood-letting of two world wars affected each family in these alpine regions and often destroyed forever a family that had been living here for countless generations.

It is the men of the mountain divisions of the Wehrmacht and the campaigns which they fought that are the subject of this book.

It was nearly half a century ago, during the war, that I first recall meeting the Gebirgsjaeger. This was in Italy during the Gothic Line offensive which raged throughout the autumn of 1944. It is of course possible that, prior to this, I may have come across the Gebirgsjaeger of 756th Regiment when they were fighting in the area of Medjez el Bab in Tunisia where I too was serving, but if so I do not recall this. The Gothic Line battle, fought by 169 (Queen's) Brigade, to capture Monte

Gemmano, had been a hard but fair fight in which our opponents, Jaeger of 100th Regiment, used the terrain so skilfully that we were denied the satisfaction of capturing that key feature. When my battalion marched away from Gemmano after being relieved from the line, we were all aware that our opponents had been soldiers of exceptional skill and undoubted courage. After the war ended I served in the army of occupation in Styria, a province of Austria that had provided Gebirgs-jaeger not only for the Wehrmacht, but also, in former days, for the Imperial Army of Austria–Hungary and then its successor, the Army of the Republic.

In that province I was able to walk the ground – the war in Europe had ended only a few months earlier – on which 1st Gebirgs Division had fought and sacrificed itself so that the bulk of German Sixth Army could escape westwards and out of the clutches of the Red Army. To visit any battlefield is an emotional experience for a soldier. To walk across one on which the relics of the struggle were still lying, on which there was still the evidence of battle and death, was deeply moving. During my years in the Army of Occupation, it was my good fortune to meet former Jaeger, now released from prisoner-of-war camps and returned to civil life. With them I went trekking through the Hochschwab mountains, sat drinking in the rural inns of eastern Styria and was taught to ski by a former sergeant-major instructor of an SS Gebirgs battalion.

Those who live in mountainous areas are neither volatile nor flamboyant, but are generally slow to speak and deliberate in action. In those regions during the years prior to the Second World War, the peasants and their families had led hard lives with few luxuries. They were introspective, clannish people and silent in the company of strangers, but once one was accepted into the family circle, their hospitality was boundless and their friendship durable and loyal. I have been very fortunate to have met Gebirgsjaeger in both war and in peace, am honoured to number them among my friends and to include their stories in this book.

It is, therefore, with grateful thanks that I acknowledge the help of those German and Austrian comrades as well as of Gebirgsjaeger organizations and archives. I further acknowledge the help of other archives, libraries and museums in this country and in America.

There are several friends and colleagues whose help proved so invaluable that they must be mentioned by name. The first of these is Helma Oswald, née Auer, born in eastern Steiermark and who now lives in the south of that province near where the Jaeger of 1st Division began the campaign against Yugoslavia in 1941. Fredi Scheucher, another of my friends from eastern Steiermark, was particularly helpful in the matter of organization tables and other research details. Alf Spiess has been a correspondent for several years now, and while with 1st Gebirgs Division trained for the invasion of England in 1940. To Helmut Herrman, who was a battalion commander in 100th Regiment against which I fought in Italy, I express my most sincere thanks as well as to the celebrated author

Brian Davis for his invaluable advice. To my American friend, Mark Yerger, go very special thanks. As a successful author he is well aware of the difficulties that I would meet in trying to conduct research by letter with archives in his country and has been a source of strength and most generous in supplying material from his own extensive collection.

Those who have been named above represent the many people to whom I owe so much for their help in the book's research and preparation stages. There are others on the production side and these include the Arms and Armour editorial staff and the design team of DAG Publications. No expression of my gratitude would be complete, however, without mention of the debt I owe to my beloved wife, Traude, for her constant support and encouragement.

James Lucas, London 1991

Introduction

TO FIGHT IN THE MOUNTAINS was to go to war in a desert. Not the familiar horizontal wilderness of flat sand, but a vertical and equally arid desert, in which to gain the objective of a mountain peak just a handful of miles distant usually meant a steep descent into the valley and a time-consuming, exhausting ascent – and all the time under fire. Mountains are devoid of comfort and incapable of sustaining human life. One left the protection of the alpine valley and climbed towards the tree line whose pride was soon reduced to gnarled and riven dwarf conifers clinging grimly to the thin and bitter soil. These storm-twisted, stunted trees thinned out to become scraggy bushes and then, past them, ascending higher, there was an area where nothing grew but hardy, coarse grass. Higher still and there was not even grass but just bare rock and shale. On the highest peaks one entered the land of perpetual snow and everlasting ice.

In such inhospitable – hostile is a more accurate word – regions where no people lived and where above a certain level nothing grew, the mountain troops had their battlefield. To fight in such an environment meant that every mouthful of food, every piece of equipment and every round of ammunition had to be portered to the combat zone. In some mountain areas, chiefly in Bosnia, in Yugoslavia, there were no streams, so that every drop of water had to be brought by slow and painful porterage out of the valleys and on to the arid heights.

The infantryman's protection against shell-fire was the slit trench, but in the mountains there was not even that simple cover. One could not dig out of solid rock even the shallowest scrape hole. Instead, a small rampart of rock and stone, a sangar, formed the first primitive shield. But even a sangar held dangers. The impact of a bullet or a piece of shrapnel could break off razor-edged rock fragments to mutilate or blind the man sheltering behind the low wall. To be wounded on the upper slopes of a mountain meant having to be carried by relays of one's comrades, for hours at a time. A personal memory is of the battle for Monte Camino in December 1943, where it took six hours for our wounded to be brought to the Regimental Aid Post – and Monte Camino was not a very high feature.

To overcome the peculiar problems associated with warfare in alpine terrain the German Army's Gebirgs divisions had establishments, weapons and transport quite different from those found in standard infantry divisions. They had few trucks. Instead there were trains of pack-animals, a system that was both practical and efficient. By a bitter irony, however, many of the campaigns which the Gebirgsjaeger fought were on level ground, where the lack of mechanical transport placed the Jaeger at a disadvantage which only their incredible foot marching abilities were able to cancel out. On a tactical plane, the experience of the troops of the Imperial Austrian Army before the First World War had shown that small, all-arms formations were those best suited for mountain operations. Jaeger battalions, therefore, were, self-contained, having their own artillery and pack-animal trains. A regiment co-ordinated the operations of its battalions, usually fielding two in the line and one in reserve or on portering duties. The First World War also provided evidence that a division could exercise effective, tight control over only two and not three Jaeger regiments. A binary division, thereupon, became the standard establishment.

Once again, as with transport, it was found that although a two-regiment structure was the best tactical unit in high country, there were deficiencies when it operated in non-mountainous terrain. There were in the two Jaeger regiments of a Gebirgs division too few infantry to carry out the type of task given to a standard division. The usual solution was to bring on to divisional strength an ordinary line regiment, accepting as unavoidable all the problems associated with such a temporary amalgamation. In the matter of artillery support, too, the Gebirgs establishment was at a disadvantage on level ground. It had too few anti-tank or anti-aircraft guns and the standard mountain artillery pieces may have been light and mobile, but had the disadvantage of being short ranged. Ideal for operations in alpine regions, they were of limited use in other terrain. Surprisingly, there had been little development in the field of mountain artillery since the First World War and the greatest number of pieces in German service dated from that time. Only the 7.5cm 1936 pattern and the 10.5cm 40 (Geraet 77) were of more modern construction. Literally, in the last weeks of the war, a new piece came into service – the Gebirgs Howitzer 45 – and that only with one single formation, the Dachstein Artillery School, serving with 9th Gebirgs Division in the battles on the Semmering.

From the above it can be seen that Gebirgs divisions, fighting in their natural element, were adequately armed and equipped, but that the advantages which they enjoyed when fighting on the heights no longer obtained on other terrain. It was to be the fate of the Gebirgsjaeger that there was so little opportunity for them to demonstrate their unique, alpinist skills. Instead they were more usually employed as assault infantry in conventional battle, a role in which they excelled, but not the one for which they had been trained. Their expertise was misused and their skills wasted.

Gebirgsjaeger fought at both extremes of the Eastern Front; beyond the Polar Circle in the north and, in the south of that vast front, their operations in the Caucasus almost took the war out of Europe and into Asia. There was no campaign during the Second World War in which they did not fight, from Poland in 1939 to Austria in 1945. There, 1st Gebirgs Division stood and held the Soviets at bay so their comrades of

Sixth Army could escape and pass into American and not into Russian prison camps. In Yugoslavia 7th SS Gebirgs Division 'Prinz Eugen', carried out a similar self-sacrificing act, continuing its fighting rearguard action even though the war in Europe had ended days earlier.

These, then, were the Gebirgsjaeger of the German Army who fought the Second World War, some of whose exploits we shall follow in the pages of this book. We shall accompany them in their long and exhausting marches across the plains of southern Poland and launch ourselves with them into the waters of the Aisne, in France. With Dietl's isolated force we shall share the sense of being cut off, and advance with the relief column towards Narvik. In the high north of Norway, in the freezing desert of Lappland, we shall watch the Jaeger as they prepare to open the war against Russia, and go with them into the new campaign. Deep in the south of Europe, in the Balkans, we shall storm the blockhouse defences of Greece's Metaxas Line, thrust into Yugoslavia and traverse the waterless White Mountains of Crete. In Russia we shall follow the divisions into the encirclement battles of the autumn of 1941, and with them climb the mountains in the Caucasus that separate Europe from Asia. With them we shall live through the days of bitter retreat in North-West Europe, in Italy, Hungary, Austria and Yugoslavia. Wherever the Jaeger fought they gained for themselves a reputation for élan in attack and staunchness in defence.

Obviously, in a world-wide conflict which lasted from September 1939 to May 1945, a great many battles were fought in which Gebirgsjaeger took part, but which I have been unable to include for lack of space. For that same reason the actions of certain independent Gebirgsjaeger battalions and regiments cannot be included for what are described are the most important operations fought by the Gebirgs divisions of the German Army and the SS.

Today, fleets of helicopters move large numbers of troops over great distances in a very short space of time. To read of the Jaeger, trudging for hours on end to reach a mountain peak where they will spend days and nights shivering in the bitter alpine cold, as they did during the war, is to glimpse an uncomprehended Calvary of pain and suffering. The soldiers whose exploits fill the pages of this book, endured their suffering in stoic silence, proud to accept the hardness of their lot because they wore the Edelweiss, the badge which set them apart and distinguished them as Gebirgsjaeger, the men of Hitler's mountain troops.

The Background

IT WAS NOT UNTIL the development of the railway network during the second half of the 19th century, that the mountainous regions of Europe became accessible to the tourist and were developed into areas of pleasure through which travellers could journey without fear of rockfall and avalanche. Because the mountains lacked a network of roads and because the region could not support large numbers of people, these inhospitable alpine areas were not ones in which major military operations could be conducted. Then, too, troops prefer to fight on level ground and their leaders planned campaigns that would be fought on flat, open terrain where they would be able to exercise tight control of the battlefield. In time of war defence of a mountainous region had, by custom and usage, been left to small detachments of the native, civil population who were grouped within a loose para-military organization. When their mountain homeland was threatened by invasion, the civilian groups were stiffened by professional soldiers and the whole defence was taken on to the military order of battle. This was the pattern, particularly in Imperial Austria where, upon mobilization being proclaimed, regiments of mountain men were raised and grouped around a cadre of the regular army's mountain regiments; these formations were designated either Jaeger or Schuetzen. In a military sense these terms are synonymous, both implying a type of rifleman.

The men of the Jaeger or Schuetzen regiments knew the ways of the mountains and produced the tactics for a successful defence of their home territory. Being expert marksmen a handful of them could delay, obstruct or even repel an enemy force many times their number. This semi-civilian *ad hoc* method of warfare changed during the middle decades of the 19th century, in line with the changes in many fields, including transport with the invention of the railway, in armaments with the development of weapons technology, politically with the rise of nationalism, and socially in improvements in living and working conditions for the masses. All of these directly or indirectly played their parts in making mountainous regions important in the context of military operations.

Social improvements meant that the masses using the railway network could enter and enjoy the hitherto inaccessible alpine areas and with familiarity these regions ceased to be considered hostile. One consequence of this was that the numbers of people choosing to live there grew while, conversely, the expansion of the railway network liberated from their scattered and lonely villages the inhabitants of otherwise remote alpine valleys.

Politically, Garibaldi's unification of Italy brought increasingly strident demands that Austria's cis-Alpine provinces should be ceded to the newly created state. The Italian Army responded to its government's aggressive nationalism and raised Alpini regiments creating a threat along the mountain frontier which the Ministry of War in Vienna could not ignore. Austria's existing Jaeger and Schuetzen organization was enlarged and the para-military civilian bodies were formalized and improved to meet the demand for increasing numbers of mountain riflemen or Gebirgsjaeger. Alpine frontier regions became sensitive areas to be considered either as routes along which an enemy country could be entered or as channels through which an enemy force might invade. In the case of Austria and Italy the war plans of both countries were based upon battles in the mountains as the first clash of arms. The large bodies of troops which it was believed would be needed for these battles could be brought to the mountains by train because the railway had speeded-up the pace of warfare. The weapons of war were charged with more powerful propellants which lengthened the killing range of rifles or widened the deadly effect of artillery projectiles. Breech-loading rifles and machine-guns raised infantry rates of fire and the rifling of barrels produced standards of accuracy both for hand guns and for the artillery's weapons. The tactics of mountain warfare were changed to meet the changing circumstances, but the fundamental strategy remained the same. In a defence posture a few determined men, native to the area and using modern weapons, could still hold back a force outnumbering their own. In an attack these native Gebirgsjaeger could guide non-mountain units through difficult terrain to attack an enemy and defeat him or else to outflank his positions and compel his retreat. Military operations in mountain areas depended upon an army having on its strength large numbers of men skilled in alpinist techniques.

There was evidence in military history to show how important such men were to an army. During the Russo–Turkish war of 1877–8 the Tsarist forces, which spent less than a week crossing the mountains but which had too few guides to lead them, lost more than ten per cent of their effectives. The lesson of such disasters was not lost upon military staffs, and countries with alpine frontiers and aggressive neighbours, principally Italy, France and Austria, strengthened or expanded their mountain troops organization accordingly. Germany, whose alpine frontier was with Austria–Hungary, a state to which she was bound in military alliance, had no need to create a special Gebirgsjaeger arm of service, but did have an embryo organization.

When war came in August 1914 the principal battlefields were the low-lying countries of Flanders and Russia/Poland, but in 1915 Italy declared war against Austria and fighting flared along the alpine region between those two countries. So urgent was the need on that southern front for skilled mountain men that on 21 May 1915, the first contingents of what was to become the German Alpenkorps assembled in a camp at Lechfeld in Bavaria and were dispatched, only three days later, to the southern alpine front. The Alpenkorps was made up of specially selected men from crack military units drawn chiefly from the Bavaria and Wuertemberg armies. In 1918, Erwin Rommel, who was to become a Field Marshal during the Second World War, won Prussia's highest award, the Pour le Mérite, while commanding a Wuerttemberg Gebirgs-jaeger formation on the Italian Front.

The survivors of the Alpenkorps returned home at the end of the Great War with such an impressive record of service in that conflict that the German General Staff retained cadres of Gebirgsjaeger in the small army of the Weimar Republic. Within the framework of the 100,000-man army which the Republic was allowed to retain under the terms of the Treaty of Versailles, a few sub-units of the former Royal Bavarian Army were entrusted with the task of maintaining the traditions and precepts of the Alpenkorps until such time as a growth of numbers within the German Army allowed for an expansion of the Gebirgsjaeger establishment. That came about on 16 March 1935 when Adolf Hitler not only proclaimed the limitations of the Treaty of Versailles to be null and void, but announced that the armed forces of the Third Reich were to be enlarged by the re-introduction of general conscription. From the Gebirgs organization cadres of skilled soldiers were drawn around whom new mountain units would be formed. These cadres became the officers and senior NCOs of the newly raised Gebirgs formations and they were replaced *en bloc* in the battalions which they had left by mountain-trained Bavarian state policemen. Within a short time a Gebirgs Brigade had been raised by General Ludwig Kuebler, and at the beginning of August 1937, the flow of recruits was sufficient for the brigade, now under the command of General Hubert Lanz, to be expanded to become 1st Gebirgs Division. This became the fount and model for the ten Alpine divisions of the German Army and those of the SS that served during the Second World War.

The composition of 1st Gebirgs Division was, 98th, 99th and 100th Jaeger Regiments, 79th Gebirgs Artillery Regiment and the usual service detachments. The establishment of an infantry division allowed only for two infantry/Jaeger regiments, so the 100th Regiment, being surplus to establishment, was eventually posted, together with one of the Gebirgs artillery battalions, to help create 5th Gebirgs Division in 1940.

From the earliest years of the National Socialist Party it had been Hitler's political ambition to bring back into the Third Reich all Germans living outside its borders. The first step in fulfilling this was the re-occupation of the Rhineland on 7 March 1936, following upon the re-incorporation of the Saarland. But even before these political successes had been gained, Hitler had addressed himself to the incorporation of Austria into the new German Reich. The first attempt to coerce Austria, made in 1934, was thwarted by Benito Mussolini, who brought 50,000 Italian troops up to the Brenner Pass and threatened to use them if Germany made any aggressive move against Austria. By 1938 the power of the Third Reich was greater than that of fascist Italy and Hitler could ignore Mussolini's opposition. In February 1938 he invited the Austrian Chancellor, Dr Kurt von Schuschnigg, to Berchtesgaden and promptly issued an ultimatum to his guest: either von Schuschnigg carry out certain political demands or Austria would be invaded. The Austrian Chancellor capitulated, but upon his return to Vienna sought to negate his acceptance of Hitler's ultimatum by asking the Austrian people to vote for a free and independent nation. German pressure forced von Schuschnigg to call off the referendum, but this came too late and Hitler ordered the invasion of Austria, necessary, as he claimed, 'to restore order'.

On Saturday, 12 March 1938 German troops crossed the frontier. Austria had 'returned home to the Reich' and had ceased to exist as an independent nation. Within days her civil and military instruments of power were absorbed into those of the Third Reich. So far as the German Army was concerned the immediate benefit of this annexation was an increase in the number of divisions on its establishment, and the German mountain troop organization was a principal benefactor when from former Austrian divisions two additional Gebirgs divisions were created and added to the Wehrmacht's order of battle.

A former officer of the old Imperial and Royal Army, Valentin Feurstein, who had commanded the 3rd Division of the Austrian Army of the Republic, was given the task of raising the 2nd Gebirgs Division of the German Army around Austrian alpine and infantry battalions. The 2nd was allocated the provinces of Vorarlberg, Tyrol, Salzburg and Upper Carinthia as its recruiting areas, but the creation of the new division took so long that it was not until December 1938 that the first batch of recruits was taken on strength. From the former Austrian battalions two regiments were formed: Gebirgsjaeger Regiment No 136 (Tyrol), commanded by Colonel Hake, and Gebirgsjaeger Regiment No 137 (Salzburg), commanded by Colonel Schlemmer. The other major formations making up the divisional establishment were 111th Gebirgs Artillery Regiment, 48th Pak Battalion, 82nd Gebirgs Pioneer Battalion, and the Gebirgs Signals and Gebirgs Medical Detachments.

The four battalions of 136th Regiment were stationed in the Tyrol, chiefly in the Innsbruck and Bregenz areas. The 137th Regiment located its units in the province of Salzburg as well as in East Tryol, particularly in Lienz, where regimental headquarters were also located. The artillery regiment garrisoned the area around Hall in Tyrol.

German Army organization laid down that two divisions constituted a corps. The raising of 2nd and 3rd Gebirgs Divisions on 1 April 1938 led to the creation of XVIII Corps (the title changed during December 1941 to include the word 'Gebirgs'.) The headquarters of the newly created XVIII Corps was Salzburg and the first commander was General Eugen Beyer.

During September 1938 2nd Gebirgs Division was posted to lower Austria to be used as a military threat in the political war of nerves that was being waged against Czechoslovakia. When 2nd Division moved to its new area it had as its flank neighbour its sister Division in XVIII Corps,

3rd Gebirgs Division, whose units were deployed along the border of Moravia. The political crisis of that autumn concerned the Sudeten German provinces of Czechoslovakia which, until 1918, had been part of the Austrian Empire. Hitler's determination to bring these millions of Sudeten Germans into the Reich and the methods he threatened to use to accomplish this brought the fear of war to Europe. Czechoslovakia was coerced by Great Britain and France to surrender the Sudetenland, and with Czechoslovakia's loss of that province the Germans gained permanent defensive systems built on the pattern of the French Maginot Line. Hitler's political act had been accomplished without a shot being fired.

The Sudetenland was free and the units of 2nd Division which advanced across the River Thaya reached Znaim and Frein inside Sudetenland without encountering opposition from the Czech Army. The soldiers of the Gebirgsjaeger division, some of whom only months earlier, had been Austrian citizens, entered towns and villages which formerly were Austrian. Small wonder then that the marching Gebirgsjaeger were met not by Czech soldiers but by Sudeten civilians carrying flowers, food and beer. So far as the Sudeten Germans were concerned they, like the Austrians, had come home into the Reich. During the following months the men of 2nd Gebirgs Division lived, worked and trained in deep contentment among the people of that province.

The 3rd Gebirgsgjaeger Division, which was mentioned earlier as having been on the right flank of 2nd Division during the political crisis of August–September 1938, was created out of the former 5th and 7th Divisions of the Austrian Republic. When the amalgamations had been completed the divisional order of battle was: 138th Regiment, three battalions strong and stationed at Loeben in the Steiermark; 139th Regiment, also three battalions strong, stationed at Klagenfurt in Kaernten, and 112th Gebirgs Artillery Regiment, whose three battalions garrisoned the area of Graz, the capital city of the Steiermark. The recruiting areas for 3rd Gebirgs Division were the provinces of Steiermark and Kaernten. It will have been noted that there is a gap in regimental numerical sequence between 1st and 2nd Divisions and that such breaks will also be seen for the other divisions. This break in sequence is attributable to the fact that all the Jaeger were considered to be on the infantry establishment and that standard regiments of the infantry line had been and continued to be raised between the formation of the several Gebirgs divisions.

The Sudeten crisis in the autumn of 1938 was succeeded by a new crisis in March 1939 when Hitler ordered the German Army to march in and seize the remnant of Czechoslovakia. On 31 March 1939, angered by Germany's breach of the Munich agreement, Neville Chamberlain, the British Prime Minister, offered the Polish government in Warsaw a unilateral agreement of assistance which was promptly accepted. France moved to support the British lead and both nations had, in effect, placed the decision whether or not there would be a war in the hands of a third nation – Poland. Furthermore it was an agreement which, in the event of war, could not be honoured by either of the two Western Powers. Neither France nor Great Britain shared a land frontier with Poland; the Polish fleet was bottled up in the Baltic and Allied aircraft did not have the range to support the Polish armies in the field. Hitler's desire for territorial aggrandizement had not been satisfied with the taking over of the fragments of Czechoslovakia and throughout the uneasy summer of 1939 German 'hate' propaganda directed against Poland grew more strident and threatening. The final pointer to the inevitability of armed conflict was the Russo–German Pact of 23 August 1939 whereby the Soviet Union stated her intention to remain neutral if Germany invaded Poland. With this assurance Hitler's last doubt was overcome. There would be no two-front war. The Third Reich did not need to fear the intervention of Russia in the East, while in the west it was clear that neither France nor Great Britain would begin offensive operations to help Poland. They were both committed to a defence strategy, sheltered behind the Maginot Line whose massive fortresses stretched from Switzerland to the Belgian frontier. Poland was an isolated victim.

The crisis deepened throughout the summer of 1939, and there were troop movements across Germany as army divisions and corps concentrated around the long frontier with Poland. XVIII Corps did not become involved in these movements until 19 August when Corps HQ, together with advanced parties from the regiments of both divisions, left their bases and moved to concentration areas in Slovakia. The mass of these two divisions arrived just before the outbreak of war.

The 3rd Division, which began to arrive a few days later than 1st and 2nd, formed the left flank unit and was concentrated around Rosenberg in Slovakia. The 2nd Division in the centre was grouped in the area of Story Shokovec, while 1st Division held the right flank and concentrated around Lubotin in eastern Slovakia. The last days of peace passed in preparation for the war to come. There had already been incidents along the northern and central frontier areas between Poland and Germany, but on 26 August there still had not been the declaration of war that Hitler had planned. Then, on the morning of Friday 1 September, German troops crossed the border following behind the Luftwaffe squadrons which had already begun to destroy the Polish Air Force on the ground. On Sunday 3 September, the British Prime Minister announced that a state of hostilities existed between Great Britain and the Third Reich. For the second time in just over twenty years, the United Kingdom was at war with Germany.

1st, 2nd and 3rd Gebirgs Divisions in Poland, 1939

THE FUEHRER DIRECTIVE on 'Case White' (the code-name for hostilities against Poland), had laid down that the annihilation of the Polish Army was to be achieved by a double encirclement. To bring this about OKW (the Armed Forces High Command) divided the Field Army into two huge Groups: North and South. Although it is the operations carried out by the Gebirgs formations in Fourteenth Army in the latter-named Army Group that are relevant to this chapter, an outline of the strategy of the war and the way in which it developed will set the scene for the part played by the Gebirgs divisions.

The western region of the republic of Poland projected as a blunt salient into the eastern provinces of Germany. OKW believed that Polish military formations within this salient were poised to strike either at the capital, Berlin, or into the industrial areas of Saxony and Silesia. OKW's prognosis was a 'worst possible' situation, but it was false. In view of the geographical situation the best that the Polish Army in the salient could do would be to launch spoiling attacks to disrupt the unfolding of the German war plan. The Polish High Command accepted that because the western salient was outflanked by East Prussia to the north and by both Slovakia and Hungary in the south, it would have to be given up although not without a bitterly contested defence. The Polish Army would then fall back to a succession of river lines, particularly the Vistula and the Bug, on which it was hoped the Germans could be held.

When war came the Polish Army was overwhelmed by the new tactics which the Germans unleashed at the very beginning of the campaign. This was the 'Blitzkrieg', or lightning war, during whose first stages the relentless deployment of bomber aircraft and swift advances by panzer forces would create havoc among the defenders. As it had been planned, so did it occur. Within a few hours on Friday, 1 September, the Luftwaffe destroyed much of the Polish air force on the ground while panzer columns, advancing at a fast speed and without consideration of any possible threat to their flanks, struck deep into Polish national territory from the north, west and south. The task of the panzer mass was to advance far and fast thereby cause such confusion among the Polish forces that the German Army would have occupied the river defence lines of the Vistula and Bug before the slowly retreating Poles could reach them. This was the basis of the double encirclement plan; a pincer movement to the west of Warsaw and one to the east of the capital.

The Germans enjoyed several advantages. Their army had nearly completed mobilization; the Poles had barely begun theirs. This German preparedness ensured that they could put into battle more infantry than the Poles; a ratio of 3.3 to 1. The German Army had numerical superiority in artillery of 4.3 to 1, and in armoured fighting vehicles the imbalance was even more marked. For every tank that the Poles could field the Germans could deploy eight. In the air, too, the Luftwaffe could deploy 1,600 aircraft, the Poles less than a quarter of that number. Nevertheless, despite the advantages of total surprise and the numerical superiority which she enjoyed, it was not an easy victory for the German Army and the act which finally destroyed the Polish nation was the brutal, unprovoked invasion of her eastern territories by the forces of the Soviet Union. The German campaign had lasted eighteen days and it ended with Poland divided between her two aggressors.

The part played by XVIII Gebirgskorps in the campaign against Poland has become indissolubly linked in military history with Lemberg, the objective it had been given. Lemberg (in Polish Lvov) was not only the provincial capital of Galicia, but more importantly the road and rail link of southern Poland as well as the base for the southern group of the Polish Army. The capture of that city would thrust deep into the enemy's southern flank, would interdict his road and rail communications and cut the retreat route of his armies withdrawing – as they surely must – from western Poland. Its speedy capture was vital to the German plan to encircle the Polish Army to the east of Warsaw. The initial problem facing XVIII Corps was to reach Poland for at the outbreak of hostilities the divisions would first have to cross the high mountains which formed the border between that country and Slovakia. Corps' battle plan for the first day of the war laid down that only 2nd Gebirgs Division was to go into action, striking northwards through the Beskides mountains to gain touch with the remainder of Fourteenth Army. Meanwhile 1st Gebirgs Division would march eastwards through Slovakia to the area of the Dukla Pass and would there strike through the mountains and enter Poland. This would give rise to a potentially dangerous tactical situation with 2nd Division moving northwards and 1st Division marching eastwards, leaving a gap between them which would widen the farther that each drove. To cover this dangerous gap, those few units of 3rd Gebirgs Division which were already in Corps area, would hold the line and would be reinforced as and when the other detachments reached Corps' concentration area.

Even when 1st and 2nd Divisions gained touch on Polish soil a further problem would arise. The tremendous distances which the divisions then had to cover to reach Lemberg could only be achieved by long, exhausting foot marches. The location of XVIII Corps, on the deep southern flank of Fourteenth Army, meant that Berger's divisions would have a greater distance to cover than the other formations of that Army and, given the lack of road and rail links in Corps area, that distance could only be covered on foot. The story of the Gebirgsjaeger divisions in the

Polish campaign is, thus, the story of marches from dawn to dusk, repeated day after day and interspersed with fierce and frequent battles against determined defenders. The 2nd Division's start-line was more than 300 kilometres from Lemberg – as the crow flies. The Jaeger, however, would have to scale mountains and traverse hills, natural obstacles whose height and depth would add considerably to the distance that had to be marched. The roads were little more than cart tracks in the soil of the southern Polish plain and the chief recollections of my contributors were of those roads, ankle-deep in sandy dust, the hot, sunny weather and the lack of water on the march.

The strategic plan of Fourteenth Army was for it to take a principal part in trapping the Polish Army in the eastern encirclement. Once the Gebirgsjaeger Corps had captured Lemberg the whole of Fourteenth Army would wheel northwards and drive up past the River Bug on whose banks it would meet the descending pincer of Third Army. When these two jaws met, OKW's plan for the encirclement of the Polish forces to the east of Warsaw would have been accomplished and on the River Bug the Polish Eastern Army would be crushed and destroyed. The Corps Commander summed-up the task facing his Jaeger. 'To reach Lemberg we shall have to march and march, but from Lemberg we shall have to run.' It is with 2nd Gebirgs Division that this account opens and the orders it received directed it to force its way through the mountain barrier of the eastern Beskides and capture the small town of Novy Sandec, sometime between D-Day + 5 and D-Day + 7. At that place its thrust-line was to change from northwards to eastwards, that is towards Lemberg. As soon as 2nd Division reached Novy Sandec, 1st Division was to enter Poland with 99th and 100th Regiments advancing to the west of the Dukla Pass and by the Recce Battalions to its east. Corps anticipated that the Pass itself would be so strongly defended that both time and men would be lost in forcing it. It would be less time-consuming, but for the Jaeger more strenuous, to march across the mountains. At a point to the east of Novy Sandec both Gebirgs divisions would meet and then march side by side towards Lemberg.

Very early in the morning of the day on which war broke out, General Feurstein, whose 2nd Gebirgs Division was concentrated around Bela Spisska, close to the Slovak/Polish frontier, led a reconnaissance patrol into the Dunajec defile. This first mission to be undertaken by Gebirgsjaeger was met with fire from Polish defenders and the patrol suffered casualties; the first of the thousands of Jaeger who were to be wounded or who were to fall in battle during the course of the Second World War. Throughout the next two days the rest of 2nd Division underwent the baptism of fire, the first formation of General Beyer's XVIII Corps to do so. In the campaign 1st Division was to earn its laurels for a tenacious defence although at times surrounded and cut off, while 3rd Division was not needed for the task of filling the gap between its sister divisions. The advance by the 1st and 2nd had been so rapid that they gained touch very quickly and thereby closed the gap between them.

The 3rd was then redeployed to Corps' left wing, to guard against attacks by Polish forces which were now withdrawing to the line of the River Bug. It was an unspectacular role and it was the fate of 3rd Division not to take part in the final victory in Poland. The 3rd was closing in on Lemberg when the order came for it to halt and it was posted to the Western Front where a Franco–British offensive was anticipated.

The other two divisions had, meanwhile, maintained their advance into Galicia and by 11 September were at Sambor, only 80 kilometres from Lemberg. It was on that day that the Corps Commander issued orders for 1st Division to send out a motorized battle group and capture the city by *coup de main*. The battle group was made up of four Jaeger Companies plus anti-tank, pioneer, 15cm artillery and flak detachments.

At the end of this chapter there is an account of what the German Press called 'the storming charge to Lemberg'. This narrative, written by an officer of 1st Division, described the day by day events in undramatic words. And yet, his Division was attempting an operation of great daring. Its battle group was to thrust like a lance through the Polish defences to seize a large and well-defended city. The main body would follow and within hours there would be a German island set within a Polish sea. The account's anonymous author assumed that his readers were familiar with the Polish campaign and with military terminology so his report omits a detail, unimportant to him but essential for us to realize, namely that a flood of Polish units was moving from Przemysl towards Lemberg. The 1st Gebirgs Division which, by 14 September, had reached the northern and western hills around Lemberg, became acutely aware that the enemy forces attacking them from the north and north-west had been massively reinforced by fresh units. The commanders of the Przemysl group formations were determined to break through the Gebirgsjaeger ring so as to reinforce the garrison of Lemberg. The Jaeger, who in the first days had been able to hold the Polish assault, now needed help as more and more major enemy formations, withdrawing from the western salient of Poland, fought to take up positions in the River Bug defence line. But for the Jaeger there could not yet be any relief.

The battle of Lemberg can be divided into two stages: the first, being the thrust by the battle group which reached the outskirts of the city and captured the high ground. The second phase was the period of attack and defence by the main body from 15 to 21 September. On that last day a Polish emissary offered to surrender the town. The Red Army had crossed the Russo–Polish border and this had destroyed any Polish hope of a prolonged defence. The Polish emissary insisted that he would surrender the city only to the 1st Gebirgs Division which had fought and held out against assaults from every direction.

The Russian invasion of Poland held the advantage that XVIII Corps did not now need to force-march as part of the pincer to the east of Warsaw. But the joy at being spared that effort was dispelled by the knowledge that Lemberg would have to be handed over together with the battlefield on which its Jaeger had fought and endured. The 1st Division would have to abandon the city to the Russians. It was a bitter disappointment.

Let us go back in time to the first days of the campaign and follow 1st Division as its parched and tiring regiments advance kilometre after unending kilometre along the dusty roads of Galicia. Let us halt with them to face furious assaults of Polish infantry desperate to drive back the German invaders. Let us accompany No 10 Company of 100th Regiment as it storms forward in a bayonet charge with the words of the German Army song 'Erika' on its lips. Let us share the tiredness, the hunger, the anxiety of being isolated on the hills around Lemberg and the concern about ammunition supplies running out. Share with the Jaeger the nights from whose darkness would storm Poles in suicidal bayonet charges. Cower with them as Polish artillery pounds the slit trench line in barrages to which their own artillery could make only a fitful response and then share the elation at the news that a panzer division was marching south-eastwards to the relief. All this suffering, pleasure, sadness and endurance are contained in the following report, although in true military fashion the writer only touches upon them for he has couched these many experiences in simple and unemotional words.

As has already been mentioned the participation of 2nd Division in the campaign began with the crossing of the Beskides mountains and during their passage the Jaeger of 1st and 2nd Divisions fought against brigades of Polish mountain troops supported by motorized formations. These enemy forces formed the left wing of the Pzemysl group which was itself the deep flank of the Polish Field Army. The Polish defence in the mountains collapsed in the face of the storming assault of Feurstein's division which was soon joined by 1st Division on the plains of southern Poland. They were now ready to open the advance into Galicia. It is at this point that the contemporary narrative begins. The edited and abbreviated account of this thrust for Lemberg by 1st Gebirgs Division was written for a book published by the Propaganda Ministry in 1941. In the words of the subtitle it '. . . gives an idea of the nature of the fighting on the Eastern Front and thus not only records the war with Poland but describes German leadership as well as illustrating the courage of our soldiers'.

'September 12, was a memorable day. The Lemberg operation opened with the bloodless capture of Sambor during the evening of 11th, and at 08.30hrs on the 12th, the divisional commander sent a message to Colonel Schoerner which read: "The task for today – an all-out advance to Lemberg." Captain Merxmueller was directed to form an advance guard which would spearhead the main body of Schoerner's regiment. At 10.00hrs the Captain's column left Sambor-North closely followed by the remainder of the regiment. At a cross roads to the south of Konivszka the advance guard encountered a Company of enemy infantry marching as if it did not have a care in the world. The leading vehicle opened fire with a machine-gun causing the enemy to scatter into the fields on either side of the road. Left on the road were dead and wounded men and abandoned horse-drawn carts. The pace of the drive was increased. On either side of the road groups of enemy soldiers, three, six, ten and often twenty men strong, threw away their weapons and raised their hands. The advance guard raced through Rudki in a cloud of dust with the pace now increased to 60 and at times 70kms per hour. It was expected that the Poles would make a stand at Malovanka, the last major obstacle before Lemberg. At that place the road narrows to a thin strip of land between two lakes. The column built up speed so as to smash through to the town's centre. Enemy machine-gun and sniper fire compelled part of the advanced guard and the whole main body to halt. The first casualties were reported. That fire-fight lasted for one and a half hours and then the road forward was clear again.

'The regimental commander regrouped his units under fire and planned a frontal attack to be mounted by a totally motorized spearhead which was to lead the advance guard and would be followed by regimental headquarters and then a Company of Pioneers. The instruction given to the motorized spearhead was to drive at fastest speed to the objective. Behind it would come a lorried battalion of Jaeger. The whole length of the road to Lemberg was covered with equipment, weapons and abandoned vehicles. On either side of the road Polish soldiers stood with raised hands. Others ran along the roadside ditches towards the German column. The pace of the advance was increased yet again as the trucks raced along the Lemberg road.

'Staff officers standing at the side of the road encouraged the troops racing past them with the cry "Lemberg". Despite their tiredness the Jaeger did not rest until at last Lemberg–West was reached. At that point an intense and well-directed fire was opened from rifles, machine-guns and then from two artillery pieces. The enemy hiding in houses and in defensive positions had only to fire along the main road to be sure of hitting something. Resistance grew. It was clear that the enemy had overcome his initial surprise and was firing from houses and railway wagons and also had snipers hidden in trees. Polish infantry began to work their way forward. Our handful of troops was grouped, together with the regimental Staff, in a few houses in the west of Lemberg. They were determined to hold the ground they had won until the main body arrived. Reports came in that along the line of advance, particularly in Rudki and to the north of that place, there was heavy fighting against Polish groups which had scattered during the advance but which had quickly regrouped. Any question of quick relief to the men cut off in Lemberg had to be given up. The divisional commander, Kuebler and his 1a, managed to reach Lemberg–West during the afternoon and the General ordered all available motorized detachment to thrust for the city. Throughout the 12th September, the mass of 99th Gebirgsjaeger Regiment marched, pausing only to rest for an hour in Grodovice, before resuming the trek to Sambor. The battalions reached the small town at 18.00hrs and took up defensive positions. During the night more and more Jaeger joined them. On 13th September, at 06.30hrs after an O

Group orders were issued that Lemberg was to be attacked from the west and the north-west so as to capture the high ground around Zboiska.

'H-Hour was at 10.15hrs . . . It was important to maintain the pace of the assault for it was noticeable that whenever the Jaeger attack flagged Polish resistance flared up and grew in strength. The attack went in although the Jaeger had been without food for more than a day and were suffering in the intense heat. There was increased sniper activity. Jaeger patrols were struck by well-aimed fire and driven back. Over a telephone link that had been set up, the divisional commander stressed how vital it was to gain the Zboiska heights. Picker's group worked its way in single file through thick bushes and tangled undergrowth, the Jaeger carrying their heavy loads through thick bushes and ravine-like valleys – until at last the column reached a point some 1½ kms south-west of Holosko where the ground opened up. Time was of the essence as it was already twilight. The regimental commander ordered Holosko to be taken quickly and for the advance up the road to Zboiska to be pushed ahead.

'A native Viennese, living in the area, pointed out the quickest route to Zboiska, a rare piece of good fortune because on our 1 to 300,000 maps that route would not have been found. The Jaeger advanced along both sides of the road; No 13 Company, then a platoon of machine-gunners, followed by No 7 Company, part of No 1 Pioneer Company, then a long gap and finally No 8 Company. It is not known where No 2 and No 6 Companies were at that time. Two very surprised Polish officers were captured in the first stages of the assault. In Zboiska No 13 Company successfully stormed a Polish bivouac area although a great many Poles escaped in the dark leaving behind their dead and a great many fully laden ration carts. It became clear that Zboiska could not be held through the night as the Poles had begun a series of well-directed counter-attacks many of which were pressed home to within hand-grenade range. Picker's group was ordered to pull back out of the village and to take up all-round defence positions on high ground which dominated the main road. The darkness of the night made it difficult to carry out those orders and it was not possible to organize a proper defence of the Zboiska heights and Molosko before dawn on 14th September.

'On the morning of that day a defensive battle began on the Zboiska heights and around Holosko, which will be remembered whenever the encirclement of Lemberg is discussed. Schoerner's battle group defended Zboiska, Holoska and the surrounding high ground for eight long days. At first they faced a two-front battle, then this developed into a fight on three and, finally, on four fronts. On three separate occasions the battle group was cut off completely from the Division and from any source of supply or reinforcement. Transports and patrols attempting to use the 5km-long western road came under fire.

'The enemy was vastly superior in number to the German forces and more than 20,000 Polish soldiers and over 100 guns were employed in the defence of Lemberg. Polish units outside the German encircling ring, chiefly from 11th and 14th Divisions, sought to force a way into the beleaguered city and the situation fluctuated throughout every day and night. Regimental headquarters was dug in on the Lemberg firing range and just how close that HQ was to the front lines is shown by the fact that in the south [i.e., facing Lemberg] only 500 paces separated it from the northern perimeter and only 700 paces from the southern. To the eastern perimeter at Zboiska, however, it was a good 1½ hours of walking and to the encircled groups at Holoska about 40 minutes. Under normal conditions that would have required a gentle stroll of no more than 25 minutes.

'On 15th September, there was a particularly dangerous situation when attacks from the north and breakout attempts from within Lemberg were co-ordinated. We know now that some enemy groups were in wireless contact with each other and the enemy artillery was very accurate but then, of course, the gunner officers would have known the ranges to targets around Lemberg to a yard. It was a serious blow to Jaeger morale to be bombarded by artillery fired from behind them. If, for example, Seitz's battalion was fighting off an attack from the north, then the artillery batteries in Lemberg would give to the attacking Polish infantry supporting fire from the south. Crises developed but each was mastered. There was also heavy fighting in the western and southern sectors and often the only artillery support which could be given to Schoerner's group was the fire of one or two batteries, whereas the Poles were often able to concentrate a battery and a half of 7.5cm and a battery of 10cm guns, as well as a number of individual guns of varying calibres and the fire of several fortress artillery pieces which were later discovered to be of 12cm calibre.

'For the commanders the most difficult task was to apportion the artillery support which could be given to a group fighting hard against overwhelming odds. Not all the Jaeger could understand the seriousness of the situation; that they were isolated. Many calls for ammunition supplies, food, for help to evacuate the wounded or for reinforcements had to go unanswered. The positions had to be held.

'On 21st September there was a dramatic change of fortune [the city surrendered]. The battle group had taken 25,000 prisoners, including 150 officers, two of whom were regimental commanders and a number of General Staff officers. In addition to a mass of rifles and machine-guns there were two 7.5cm and one 10cm batteries of artillery. This was, however, only a small amount of the actual booty. On 21st we were ordered to evacuate Lemberg as the city was to form part of the Russian zone of occupation. Then, from the woods of Zuchowice and from the surrounding heights, whole columns of Polish troops came in to be taken captive together with their horses and military supplies.

'The positions had been held despite the enemy's superior forces thanks to the skill of the officers and the toughness of the Jaeger. The realization that we of XVIII Corps had penetrated deepest into enemy territory was a principal reason for our not giving in. The memory of those hard fought days on the Zboiska heights and in the hell of Holosko will always be associated with our brave comrades who laid down their lives for victory.'

To conclude the story of the campaign in Poland, General Kuebler was awarded the Knight's Cross of the Iron Cross, the first divisional commander to be so honoured. The 1st and 2nd Gebirgs Divisions then moved from the Eastern to the Western Front, the 2nd to serve with 3rd Gebirgs Division and the 1st in an independent role. It was already autumn; too late for another campaign to open, but the war was not over and further tests of Gebirgsjaeger fighting skill lay only months away.

2nd and 3rd Gebirgs Divisions in Norway, 1940

I N MARCH 1940 the 2nd and 3rd Gebirgs Divisions, occupying positions in the valley of the River Ahr, expected that they would advance from there to take part in the campaign against France which everyone expected would come next. It did not happen that way. The campaign which opened in April was to be against Denmark and Norway and both divisions were to fight in this new theatre of operations. Dietl's 3rd Division was the first to be taken, and was posted to the concentration area at Doeberitz, just outside Berlin. The 2nd Division was not required in the opening assault and stayed in the Ahr valley.

Planning for the campaign in Scandinavia had begun as early as 14 December 1939 when Hitler, acting on the advice of Admiral Raeder, ordered the preparation of 'Studie Nord' a paper to establish whether an attack upon Denmark and Norway was necessary and practicable. Raeder had pointed out to the Fuehrer that Germany's armaments industry was dependant upon the importation of 11 million tons of Swedish iron ore, Germany's own production being insufficient to meet the demands. The ore reached Germany by one of two sea routes, either from the Norwegian port of Narvik and down the length of the coast of Norway, or via Swedish ports to German harbours in the Baltic. Raeder pointed out that Great Britain also relied heavily upon Swedish ore and was certainly preparing plans to invade Norway. Thereby, she would gain two objectives. Not only would a British invasion cut off the ore supplies to Germany, but from a strategic point of view Britain's occupation of Norway would outflank Germany to the north. A German pre-emptive strike, so Raeder argued, would reverse the situation; Germany would control the iron ore and with the ports of northern Norway under its control the Kriegsmarine would have harbours on the Atlantic seaboard from which commerce raiders and U boats could sail. It would be an impossible task for the British Home Fleet to control the vast length of Norway's coastline.

By a bitter coincidence the leaders of Germany and Great Britain both saw Norway as an objective to be gained and were not only determined upon invasion but had chosen approximately the same date to carry this out. To halt the flow or iron ore Royal Navy warships mined the sea routes, and Britain, together with France, had prepared an invasion force which would attack and capture Narvik. On 5 April Hitler, alarmed by British incursions into Norwegian waters, decided to invade. D-Day for the operation was to be 9 April. Based on Intelligence estimates OKW had concluded that the military forces required for the invasion of both Denmark and Norway need not be large. Denmark, whose northernmost harbours and airfields were needed as bases for the attack upon Norway, was expected to offer no resistance and would be taken out in a matter of hours. Norway, too, was a weak country which had been at peace for nearly two centuries and had a standing army of only 14,500 professional soldiers backed by a militia force that could be expanded to 110,000 men. When the Germans invaded, such was the speed of their assault that the militia was never completely mobilized. The Norwegian Army had no tanks and very few anti-tank or anti-aircraft guns. The whole of southern and central Norway was quickly overrun and only in the region north of the Arctic Circle, between Trondheim and Narvik, was there fighting which, at Narvik, lasted almost from the first day of the campaign until June when Norway capitulated and the Allies withdrew.

Since Narvik lay so far north and the German forces had to be in position on the morning of 9 April, the convoy carrying the invasion force had to sail in before D-Day. The Gebirgsjaeger regiment that was to attack and capture Narvik was Colonel Windisch's 139th, of Dietl's 3rd Division. During the night of 6/7 April, the battalions of his regiment boarded a number of destroyers in Wesermünde harbour and when loading had been completed they sailed into the German Bight where a convoy was forming up. The 'Narvik' destroyer flotilla was then joined by two battleships, *Scharnhorst* and *Geneisenau* and the heavy cruiser *Hipper*. Other units joined the Fleet battle group which left the German Bight and sailed along the western coast of Norway towards Narvik and Trondheim, the principal objectives of the campaign.

It is strange to think that the majority of the Jaeger in that convoy, racing through the April night, had never before seen the sea, and none of them could ever have imagined the misery of being packed like sardines below decks in the heaving and pitching dampness of a destroyer. The journey from the Bight to Narvik was more than 1,200 nautical miles, but although the sea area was dominated by the Royal Navy, the weather was Germany's ally for most of that northward dash. The wind which had been slight to begin with soon rose to Force 8 and then to 9 during the second day at sea. The misery of the Jaeger can well be imagined. Destroyers are built for speed. They are not troopships in which a soldier might sling a hammock and hope through sleep to escape the awfulness of seasickness. In the bowels of the destroyers carrying 139th Regiment – two hundred men in each vessel – the Jaeger lay on the cold, steel decks, soaked to the skin from the pounding waves which swept over the ships and filled the decks with icy water. 'Before we boarded our vessel our CO gave us a short talk on the tasks which lay ahead of us. Then we climbed a steep gangway, took off our kit and went below deck . . . We washed and were given a meal and then chatted for a long time about the new campaign.

'. . . [When we came up] on deck we found that we were already on the high seas. It was a splendid sight to see a long line of twelve ships positioned on one side of us driving through a bright, sunlit sea. A wind blew up and soon high waves rocked our ships. Together with several of my mates I lay down on the deck so that I would be less affected by seasickness . . . A sailor told us that the best thing to do was to sleep if we could . . . The sea was so rough that our quarters were in a terrible mess. Everything that was not nailed or screwed down had been flung about . . . Sleep was out of the question but we managed to doze fitfully now and then . . . In time our ship's pitching and tossing lessened and a sailor told us that we had left the high seas and had entered coastal waters . . .' (Franz Puechler) The convoy had entered Ofotfiord in which Narvik is located. The Jaeger paraded on deck ready to disembark; 1st and 3rd Battalions at Bjervik and 2nd Battalion at the Narvik town pier. There was no sign of the British. The Germans had won the race to be first in Narvik and occupied the area without incident. Not a man had been lost.

The destroyers were detailed to debark their Jaeger at the northern end of the fiord at Elvegadsmoen and at 0500, in a blinding snowstorm, the first troops, packed into assault craft, raced for the rocky shore. The only sign of life in the half light of early dawn was a patrol of Norwegian cavalry who were taken prisoner. During the morning the remainder of 1st and 3rd Gebirgsjaeger Battalions were disembarked and moved into their allotted positions.

By 0600 Dietl had landed, had demanded and had received from the Norwegian authorities the surrender of the town and its military garrison, a battalion of the Norwegian 13th Infantry Regiment. The next step was to secure the area against the Franco–British landing which must soon come in. The difficulties facing the Gebirgsjaeger general were many and increased continually. Three supply ships laden with equipment, including a 15cm gun battery, failed to arrive and it was assumed that they had been intercepted by the Royal Navy and sunk. On that first day 139th Regiment had only the backing of the guns of No 1 Destroyer Group, the 'Narvik' Flotilla, but that protection was likely to be brief – the destroyers were under orders to return to Germany once they had been refuelled. That would be a protracted affair. Only *Jan Wellem*, one of the two fleet tankers, had reached Narvik. The other, *Kattegat*, had been intercepted and sunk en route. The loss of *Kattegat* meant a doubling in refuelling time because *Jan Wellem* could service only two destroyers at a time. Thus it was that the warships and the tanker were still in the harbour at Narvik when, on 10 April, five British destroyers swept into the Ofotfiord and opened fire. Unknown to the Royal Navy part of the 'Narvik' Flotilla had moved higher up the fiord and those ships, alerted by the sounds of gunfire, steamed into action and caught the British between two fires. According to German sources four of the five British destroyers were sunk, but in fact only two, *Hardy* and *Hunter*, were lost. This short-lived victory was the first of several engagements which ended in the loss of all the ten German destroyers.

The situation which faced the German forces in Narvik was terribly clear. With the destruction of the destroyers they were cut off from any relief. The nearest German troops were in Trondheim nearly 1,000 kilometres distant. The Royal Navy's blockade was so tight that no supply ship could reach them. They had no artillery and an Allied attack could be expected at any time. The general decided on a course of action. To substitute for the mountain artillery pieces which had gone down with *Jan Wellem*, he would bring off from the sunken German warships all the naval and anti-aircraft guns. Their own crews would man the ships' guns thus releasing his Jaeger for front-line infantry service. Divers were ordered to recover food supplies from the sunken ships as well as warm clothing and other necessities. The radio set of the destroyer *Diether von Roeder* was brought to shore, repaired and put into service. The extensive food supplies aboard a Norwegian whaler in Narvik harbour were commandeered and added to those in the Gebirgsjaeger ration stores. In place of pack-animals the ore railway was used to transport the heavier pieces of equipment. Then, on 13 April, there was a welcome addition to the garrison's artillery strength. A squadron of eleven Junker Ju 52 transport aircraft landed on a frozen lake and disembarked a battery of 7.5cm guns. That first flight was followed, on such infrequent occasions as the weather allowed, by air drops of food and equipment. The naval gunners had been allotted their task, but there was a sizeable group of naval crewmen who could now be used for other duties. These men, nearly two thousand in all, were formed into battalion-sized groups, to be used in minor military roles until they had become proficient in handling infantry weapons and carrying out infantry tactics. Their training time would be of the briefest and then they would be put into the line, if this became necessary.

Dietl's Jaeger and the ships' crews had soon created a firm, if loose, defensive system which ran from a small promontory at Fagevers round the town harbour as far as the ferry crossing point at Taraldsvik. The defence of this sector was in the hands of 3rd Battalion, 139th Regiment and its commanding officer concentrated his greatest strength and most of the heavy weapons on the Framnes promontory. It would be the task of 3rd Battalion and the heavy weapons detachments to repel any attempt by the Allies to come in from the sea and capture the town. It must be remembered that against the Allies, who could and would reinforce their units, the German force was quite isolated. No reinforcements could be expected and there were so few men to man the perimeter, small though this was, that not a single Jaeger could be spared to guard the south-eastern flank, which ran from the town to the Swedish frontier. The nature of the terrain made it unlikely that the Allies would attack on this sector so its defence could be left to an as yet untrained naval detachment. Dietl was taking a calculated risk in having no military concentration in the south-east, but he had no alternative. He knew that an Allied attack was most likely to come on the northern sector, but although this was the most sensitive area, there were just not enough men to hold it in strength. The defence line, such as it was, was made up chiefly of posts holding two or three Jaeger. The trenches in which they would spend the next months had been blasted or dug out of the mountain rock and were spread so far apart that they were unable to give mutual support. Each trench and each small group would have to fight its own battle. These isolated trenches on the high ground to the north of the Romboks fiord, were occupied by 1st Battalion, 139th Regiment backed by a naval detachment of approximately battalion size.

The land battle for Narvik can be said to have begun on 13 April when a Jaeger group patrolling the iron-ore railway struck a Norwegian battalion. The realization that enemy regular Army troops stood between his forces and the Swedish frontier was worrying and Dietl risked sending out a Company along the railway line accompanied by a home-made 'armoured' train and with a ski platoon to protect the open right flank of the advance. As the Company approached the northern railway bridge the Norwegians, holding excellently sited positions, opened fire. They clearly intended to destroy the railway bridge, and the cutting of that link to the Swedish frontier would isolate Dietl's force completely. To prevent the destruction of the bridge the Jaeger Company commander used his snipers in a dual role. One group kept the Norwegian engineers from placing the demolition charges, while the other sniper group destroyed the charges which had already been placed. In a short but intense fire fight, during which the fabric of the bridge was slightly damaged by the detonation of a single charge, the Norwegian battalion was driven back from the bridge but then swung its attack against the Bjornfell tunnel. The fighting there lasted for two hours, but the Jaeger Company was so aggressively handled that the end of the battle came when a senior Norwegian officer and forty-five of his men surrendered. A further 150 Norwegians crossed the border into Sweden, preferring internment to being taken prisoner. The Jaeger Company had been in continuous action for three days during which it had had to endure appalling weather as well as the attacks of the enemy. But it had been victorious and Dietl could be well pleased with his men. They had cleared the Norwegians from positions between the town of Narvik and the frontier. The immediate danger to the iron ore railway had been cleared.

While this single Company had been removing the threat to the back of Dietl's group, the British 24 Infantry Brigade had landed to the north of Narvik and soon gained touch with Norwegian 6th Division. The first Allied attack came in on 14 April and subsequent attacks put such pressure upon 139th Regiment that Hitler considered giving up Narvik and the surrounding area. He proposed that Dietl's battle group march southwards or else be airlifted out. General Jodl pointed out to the Fuehrer the impossibility of a march southwards because of terrain and weather and also that an airlift could only bring out a fraction of the German garrison. Such an attempt must accept that a great many transport aircraft would be lost and the morale of Dietl's force would suffer as a consequence. Convinced by Jodl's argument Hitler signed an order that Narvik was to be held to the last. This was not to be the only time that the Fuehrer considered giving up the town. Late in May he once again gave Dietl freedom to act on his own initiative and take his men into Sweden, if he thought it necessary. Dietl refused to give up the battle, unequal though it had always been, and even though his men were under terrible Allied pressure. There was no thought of surrender by Dietl or his men.

The greatest part of military activity during the following weeks and months consisted of patrols with short bursts of furious battle when the Allies made fresh attempts to destroy the garrison and capture the town. Otherwise the time passed slowly for the Jaeger and the sailors, with guard duties, fetching rations, improving positions and trying to combat the deadly monotony, the cold and the everlasting hunger. One thing was constant and part of everyday life; the Royal Navy ships, which patrolled the fiords and fired a few rounds into the Jaeger positions. The Allied military forces, having been repulsed in their first attempts, began an operation which led to the town's coming under concerted attack. An assault on the northern sector by a Norwegian battalion came in against No 3 Company of 1st Battalion. The Norwegians advanced under cover of a blinding snowstorm. In poor visibility and camouflaged with snow suits, the Allied troops had gone undetected by the Jaeger who were forced to give ground. The blizzard died away and in the afternoon sunlight the Jaeger could see that the Norwegian artillery was in difficulty. Deep snow drifts had hindered movement and stopped the crews from bringing their guns forward. This could be turned to a German advantage, but already the sun was setting and it was too late for a counter-attack that day. But at first light on the following morning, the 25th, a battle group went in, wading through chest-high snow to reach a road junction. There the heavy weapons detachments moved into position to give supporting fire while the Jaeger shook out into attack formation. They went in and a classic demonstration of fire and movement destroyed the Norwegian artillery unit.

Allied pressure again grew on the northern sector. The attacks by Polish, French, Norwegian and British troops were seldom co-ordinated and could be held, but each fresh assault brought fresh casualties and this constant drain reduced the numbers of Jaeger in the battle line. The Allied commanders, sensing that they could effect no break through to the north, swung the full weight of their military effort to the southern flank and to the small port of Sildvik. There the battle lasted for weeks. Only one Jaeger Company could be spared to strengthen the naval units which were under attack by Polish mountain troops, the type of men who had faced the 1st and 2nd Divisions in the mountains of southern Poland only seven months earlier. Between the opening of the Polish attacks at the end of April until they died away on 28 May, No 6 Company, although suffering losses from each fresh assault, could be relieved from the line for only one brief period of rest. Those few days apart, the Jaeger spent their days in almost incessant battle – but they held the southern flank.

Allied pressure began at last to tell and the Jaeger line was forced farther and farther back. The direction of the attacks soon made it clear that it was the enemy's intention to thrust parallel to the Swedish frontier, reach the railway and to cut off Battle Group Dietl, on the landward side. The Jaeger were determined to hold out, but one position after another was lost and the ring around the battle group tightened as the German perimeter was pulled in time and again. It was a bitter little war fought out almost on a man to man basis on the German side for, as if to compensate for the perimeter's being reduced, the numbers of those killed, wounded or sick was increasing all the time. Not all the defensive positions could now be fully manned and the gaps between each lonely post were becoming ever wider. With so few men there could be no thought of a proper defensive line, but Dietl knew that his men would hold. They would hold although their rations were cut and cut again. They would hold although no hot food was coming forward, and although they could not light fires to keep warm. Despite the steady drain of casualties; in spite of the appalling weather and the awful tiredness that comes from so many nights disturbed by enemy attack, Dietl knew his lousy, exhausted, hungry mountain men would hold. And he was right; they did. Depressed by the suffering that his men were undergoing, the general sent a string of signals asking for reinforcement, but the war in the west had opened and now the Narvik garrison had a low priority *vis-à-vis* the momentous events that were taking place in Holland, Belgium and France.

The successes gained by the German forces in the west did not affect the determination of the Allies to capture Narvik. By this time more than 15,000 troops were in action against Battle Group Dietl, as it was now officially titled, and the perimeter contracted still farther. At 23.00 on 27 May, a flotilla of Royal Navy ships entered Ofotfiord and opened fire on the German positions. Under their bombardment two battalions of the French Foreign Legion carried out an assault landing from the sea, and in the area of the railway tunnels French Chasseurs Alpins stormed forward to cut the railway line. The Allies were determined to destroy this handful of men who were still continuing to resist. Narvik did, indeed, fall to the Foreign Legion and some of the Jaeger Companies fought on; often battling hand-to-hand to force the French back.

Some reinforcements came through at last. The early successes gained by the German paratroops in the war in the west allowed groups of them to be dropped on the Bjornfjell Heights during three successive days: 23, 24 and 25 May. These were followed by two Companies of Jaeger from the 137th Regiment who were parachuted in. Welcome and needed though those reinforcements were, they were too few to defeat the imminent major Allied offensive. The Allied Command had planned this to come in on both the southern and northern fronts, a pincer operation which MUST take out, at long last, the remnant of Dietl's force. Some ground on the southern front was gained, but the deepest penetrations were made on the northern sector reducing the German battle line to a small perimeter around the railway. The southern part of this bridghead was held by a naval group and 2nd Battalion, 139th Regiment. The 1st Battalion, 1st Parachute Regiment defended the railway line, and the northern part of the perimeter was held by 1st Battalion, 139th Regiment. A small force from 2nd Battalion formed Dietl's reserve. It would be wrong to think of the units holding the small perimeter as battalions at full strength. After nearly two months of battle, each was but a remnant and they knew that the Allies would soon open yet another operation to smash them. The Jaeger prepared for this last battle – but it did not come in the fury that they had expected. There was indeed an attack on 7 June on the northern sector of the perimeter, but it was light and easily beaten off. The fighting died away in the north and in the south there was no activity at all, only an unnatural quiet. On 8 June Jaeger patrols returned with reports that the Allies had withdrawn from the Narvik area. The town was re-entered late that night. Narvik had been held.

While part of 3rd Division had been fighting in and around Narvik, the remaining echelons of the division, together with the whole of 2nd Gebirgs, were inactive, a situation which was to change abruptly. On 23 April the units were alerted and ordered to prepare for immediate departure. The issue of cold weather clothing indicated that their destination would be Norway, and that most probably they would be heading for Narvik to reinforce Dietl's hard-pressed force.

Operational orders issued to General Feurstein, commanding 2nd Division, confirmed the destination. These orders read, in part: 'You are to proceed to Trondheim and open up a northern overland route through which you will relieve General Dietl's forces . . . faced by superior enemy forces in the Narvik area . . .' Speed was a critical factor, but given the poor road and rail communications in Norway, it was clear that it would take too long to move the whole division first to Trondheim and thence to Narvik. Feurstein ordered the fighting echelons to move from the valley of the Ahr to Jutland and to proceed by sea to Trondheim. The train would leave for the same destination but would depart from Stettin on the Baltic. The division's 'heavy' formations, that is to say, the guns of 3rd Battalion of the artillery regiment, the anti-tank detachments, the reconnaissance battalion and the motor transport columns were to remain behind in the Ahr. This 'stripping down' of 2nd Division produced, in effect, a large battle group composed of the Jaeger regiments and the light mountain artillery battalions.

The fighting echelons concentrated in Denmark and on 2 May an advance party made up of 2nd Battalion, 137th Regiment, half a battery of guns and a pioneer platoon was transported by air from Copenhagen to Trondheim. The rest of the battle group, including 2nd Battalion, 136th Regiment, an artillery battalion, the divisional headquarters staff and Battalion HQ Group of 136th Regiment, sailed for Trondheim. The small convoy of two converted freighters and two smaller merchant ships escorted by a flotilla of six minesweepers and an MTB, set sail on 30 April.

The convoy had hardly reached the high seas when a British submarine scored a torpedo hit on the transport, *Bahia Castillo*. The other ships, perhaps unaware that the transport had suffered damage, continued to steam ahead in double column with the escorting vessels on each flank. Then the transport *Buenos Aires* was hit and so seriously damaged that her captain ordered the soldiers to abandon ship. Most of the Jaeger battalion were still below decks and had begun to carry out the captain's orders when a second torpedo struck. *Buenos Aires* was taken in tow but sank before she reached harbour. With her went down the regiment's pack-animals and much of its equipment. The damaged *Bahia Castillo* was also taken in tow and was successfully brought back to Frederickshaven.

Meanwhile, as we have seen earlier in this chapter, the situation in Narvik had deteriorated alarmingly. Reinforcements were needed urgently and since these could come neither by sea nor by land, only an air drop could bring Dietl's beleaguered force the men of which it stood in dire need. On 9 May 2nd Division asked for volunteers to form two paratroop Companies to drop in the Narvik area. More men came forward than were needed and those selected were given the briefest of training before jumping outside the town, landing and going into action alongside their comrades of 3rd Division. Luck attended the drop and only three men were slightly injured, but as an example of the losses which were later suffered, in a telegraph message, sent on 3 June, Dietl advised the commanding officer of 137th Regiment that one Company commander had fallen and that nearly one-third of the NCOs and men had either been killed, wounded or were missing.

The remainder of the divisional group, concentrated at Trondheim, had set out to march 1,200 kilometres along the one main road which, in those days, ran through the narrow strip of mountainous country between the sea to the west and Sweden to the east. This single highway restricted the burden of the fighting to the width of one battalion; the one which was carrying out advance guard duties. The first objective on the stretch of the march from Trondheim was the small port of Namsos. From reconnaissance photographs it was clear that part of the Allied force in the area was being evacuated by sea and that those units that could not be taken away by ship had begun retreating north towards Narvik. General Feurstein, determined to overhaul and destroy these enemy elements before they could reach that port, ordered a vigorous pursuit. Although his men carried out forced marches they could not gain touch with the rapidly retreating Allies. Feurstein intended to make a new attempt to bring the enemy to battle, at Mosyoen, a large town on the divisional thrust-line. Again he was thwarted by a combination of strong Allied rearguards and hostile terrain. This was a region of swamp, tundra and bare rocks, described by one former soldier who wrote: '. . . a foretaste of the hardships we were later to meet in Lappland. A thaw set in and very quickly the land which had been frozen only hours before was covered with water. The depth of streams and rivulets increased dramatically, often within an hour or two, making these impassable. And it rained and rained, day and night and almost without pause.'

So as to cause the greatest difficulty to the pursuing Jaeger, the retreating Allies blew up every bridge over the succession of water barriers as they pulled back towards Mosyoen. The problems created by those demolitions can be gauged from Hapnesbro where the bridge had been totally destroyed and the river, now thawed, was in flood; wide and turbulent. A recce group found a place, several kilometres inland, where the river was still completely frozen. A message to the main body urged it to move quickly as it might be possible to cross over the frozen surface at that point. The main body laid a corduroy road over the ice and across this the Jaeger moved slowly on foot and then towed the unloaded trucks across by ropes. It can be truly said that the whole march was an enterprise which stood upon brittle glass. The battalion forming the advance guard was totally unsupported. It was 50 kilometres ahead of the next divisional group, two Companies of Jaeger. Feurstein wondered whether it might not be wiser to halt the advance of the spearhead group and refrain from further advances until the Companies had closed up. His concern was understandable for behind them was a 200-kilometre gap to the next group. These vast distances between detachments gave the division the unenviable reputation of being the 'longest' division in the German Army. Whether to advance without delay or wait for the two Companies to close up was a difficult decision but Feurstein knew what was expected of him. He must reach Narvik. Each day brought for him its own problems, man made or climatic. On one morning a Norwegian ski battalion attacked with such determination that it held up the advance guard for a long time. These Norwegians were not the local militias that could be dispersed without trouble but professional soldiers who fought well and hard and were only driven off with great difficulty. Day followed day of marching along the narrow road, the single lifeline in this desolate and unpopulated region.

At last the advance guard reached Mosyoen where Feurstein had planned to bring the Allies to battle. It was a large village of solid but primitive-looking houses, set in green meadows and fringed with deep forests along the shores of a fiord. On 11 May the divisional commander issued an order of the day which praised the efforts of the advanced guard for having covered the 400 kilometres to Mosyoen in seven days against enemy opposition and demolitions. Feurstein's flexible handling of the situation was demonstrated again only a few days later. Dietl's head-quarters called for the pace of the advance to be sped-up, but when the point unit reached Elsfiord there was a unique problem. There the road north petered out at the foot of a huge ridge of mountains and began again at the village of Hemnes on the far side of the ridge. The Norwegians had always overcome the problem by taking a boat between Elsfiord and the Ronenfiord, at whose end lies the village of Hemnes. The Germans could not solve the difficult problem in the same way. Not only were there too few ships to carry the whole advance guard by sea, but

Feurstein had also learned that British troops were being landed in Hemnes. It was clear that they were there to impede his advance and he decided that a bold move before the enemy had established himself might force him to retreat. How to carry a body of troops from Elsfiord to Hemnes was resolved by using Junker Ju 52 sea-planes. Twelve Jaeger were carried in each aircraft and the Jus swooped over the fiord just as the Royal Navy's ships were steaming away. The Jus touched down on the fiord, taxied to the shore and the Jaeger leaped out to open the battle for the village. A British destroyer which had returned and opened fire on the German troops, was bracketed by shells from a mountain artillery gun, turned and sailed out of the fiord. The Jaeger went on to clear the peninusla, forcing the Allied troops to retreat again.

But there was still a long way to march to reach Narvik; three hundred kilometres of poor road on which, at every opportunity, the British rearguard halted the point unit and continued to delay it. Only when the mountain artillery smothered the enemy positions with shellfire and the Jaeger opened a fresh assault, did the British pull out, leaving behind only the dead and those too badly wounded to be taken away. North of Stien, another milestone on the route, lay the town of Mo and beyond lay the Arctic Circle. For weeks the pattern had been, march and fight, march and fight. Vensmoen, Rognan, Finneda and Hopen were fought for and captured and still the advance was pushed on until the battalion reached Soerfold, the town from which the last thrust would be made to reach Dietl's beleaguered force.

In Narvik the situation had deteriorated badly and Dietl sent out an urgent message saying it was now only a matter of days. Feurstein's division, which had covered nearly 1,000 kilometres on foot, was being called upon for one last mighty effort. There is an analogy here with alpinists who, struggling to reach a peak, make their final effort by leaving behind most of their equipment and drive in skeleton order for the crest. The 2nd Division commander did just that. He issued an order on 22 May: '. . . from specially selected men three strong "Narvik" battalions will be created. Each Company will choose one or two of its best men and form a platoon and each battalion will provide one or two "Narvik" companies which will be led by energetic commanders with alpinist qualifications. Thus, each regiment will have produced a Narvik battalion of 2 to 3 Companies which will be supported by heavy machine-guns, infantry guns, a platoon of mountain guns and Pioneers. Lt-Col von Hengl will command Operation "Bueffel" . . .'

What faced those specially chosen men was a 200-kilometre trek across a wilderness in which there were no roads at all, nor any human life; a region for which no maps existed, in which the magnetic influence of the North Pole corrupted compass readings, and an environment which was totally hostile to man. There was no time to reconnoitre a route. Dietl's needs were too pressing. The land route between Soerfold and Narvik was up and down precipitous slopes, across a glacier and over flooded rivers. In some areas snow lay more than a metre deep, in other places it had cleared leaving bare and icy rock that had to be scaled. One break in the monotony and the muscle-wrenching endeavour would come when Fyelbu was reached. From there the light iron ore railway ran into Narvik. The only other support was that three Ju 52s dropped sufficient rations and tents over the 'Narvik' detachment advance guard for it to create four food stores. The difficulties of the march can scarcely be imagined. To avoid frost-bite which wet boots and clothing would produce, trousers, socks and footwear were removed every time water had to be crossed on foot – and there were a great many streams and rivers. Whole stretches of a day's march were made in thick fog or in pouring rain, but the advance was driven on through the trackless wilderness.

On the morning of 9 June a message was received that made no sense. The signaller was interrogated to see whether he had correctly deciphered the transmission. He had, but the text of the message 'Operation Bueffel cancelled' seemed improbable. The orders which Feurstein had been given had been to reach Narvik from Trondheim within 60 days. Now on the 57th day of the march had come the order to halt it. An explanation for this curious message was soon received. Norway had capitulated and the fighting had come to an end. A group of picked men of the 'Narvik' detachment completed the march and at 13.00 on 13 June, the leader of the 20-man detachment was able to radio that he had made contact with Dietl's forces. On the same day the High Command communique announced '. . . a specially selected group of Gebirgsjaeger which had begun a march on 2nd June northwards from Fauske across a trackless wilderness, gained touch on 13th June with the forces in Narvik . . .'

With the end of the war in Norway 2nd Division concentrated in central Norway and together with 3rd Gebirgs Division and elements of 181st Division formed 'Gebirgskorps Norway'. The commander of the new corps was the recently promoted General Dietl who handed over his division to General Kreysing. The area which the new corps was called upon to control was vast, more than 1,600 kilometres long, and to begin with there were just the units of Gebirgskorps to control it. An SS battalion which came on to strength was soon posted away to Kirkenes. Occupation duties, it seemed, were to be the lot of 'Gebirgskorps Norway'.

1st Gebirgs Division in France and the Low Countries, 1940

A T THE CONCLUSION of the war with Poland 1st Gebirgs Division returned to Germany and spent the winter of 1939/40 training on the Eifel hills. In April 1940 the campaign in Scandinavia opened and the 1st was disappointed that, although the premier division, it had not been called upon to spearhead the operation at Narvik, but at midday on 9 May a telephone code-word put the division at two hours' notice to move. The war in the west was about to begin. Later that day came the executive order to march out to a new campaign, and in the evening of the 9th the columns of Jaeger headed westwards towards Belgium. The regiments marched for 40 kilometres before going into billets for the night. Reveille next morning was well before first light and before it was fully day the regiments were already on the road. Late that night they crossed the Luxembourg border and it was not until they were a long way past Bastogne that a halt was called. The march continued throughout the 11th, and as the division was not in the army's assault wave during its approach march it had met no opposition of any kind nor had there been sight or sound of the enemy.

The war in the west opened finally on 10 May, after Hitler had postponed its opening date several times. The OKW battle plan was to use three Army Groups: North or 'B', Centre or 'A' and South or 'C'. Von Bock's Army Group 'B' was to drive through Holland and Belgium and by destroying the armies of those two kingdoms prevent them from striking into the right flank of von Rundstedt's Army Group 'A'. This Group was to make the principal effort by smashing through the weakly defended Ardennes front and racing across the River Maas. The panzer divisions would thrust out of the bridgeheads which would be established on the river's western bank and head north-westwards, that is to say, into the back of the Allied forces in northern France and Belgium. The role of Army Group 'C' was to defend the western border of Germany between central France and the Swiss frontier. The tremendous successes which the German forces gained in the opening operations of the war in the west gave rise at OKH (Army High Command) to the belief that a supplement to the original battle plan would conquer the whole of France. A fresh plan was quickly produced and the second part of the campaign, known as the Battle for France, was an operation executed as swiftly and as decisively as had been the Battle for Flanders.

The 1st Division was the only Gebirgs formation available at the start of the campaign in France, although 6th Division was raised swiftly enough for it to take part in the final operations in the Vosges and subsequently to serve in the army of occupation. It is with 1st Division that this account deals.

The 1st, marching westwards in bright, early summer weather, had still seen no sight of the enemy. The Jaeger trekked through the verdant countryside towards the Maas and found when they reached the river during the afternoon of the 14th that the French, who might have been expected to defend to the last this important water barrier, had fled. The Maas was crossed and then in the war diary one reads the bald statement '. . . men were drowned in the crossing . . .' I sought an explanation because the division had as yet met no opposition. Its crossing of the Maas was uncontested and yet men had been lost. Why? The explanation was that the leading Companies had crossed by night using a partially destroyed bridge. This raises the question. Why did the men have to carry out so risky an operation at night? There was no urgency about crossing the river and, in fact, the bulk of the division crossed later, and in daylight, using two bridges which army engineers had built. The war diary does not expound on the reason for the night-time crossing which cost casualties.

As 1st Division advanced, the Jaeger saw evidence of just how badly the French had been hit by the weight of the German Army's attack. The roadsides were littered with cast-off equipment, abandoned artillery pieces and there were many prisoners. On 17 May the regiments were still marching without contact with the enemy, but on the 18th 3rd Battalion of Kress's 99th Regiment was involved in a sharp action as it approached the small town of Rocroi. French tank units striking out of the deep woods around Signy and St Michel opened fire on the marching Companies. They went to ground and the battalion's anti-tank gun Company came into action with such speed and fired with such accuracy that the armoured vehicles were forced to retreat. Jaeger patrols combed the Signy forest and returned with a number of undamaged tanks. Among the two hundred prisoners taken during the operation was a divisional commander and four colonels. On the 19th orders changed the direction of the division's advance from west to south-westward and it was directed to reach the canal which connects the Oise and the Aisne; two of the great rivers of France. The divisional task was to form a strong defensive front along the line of the Oisne–Aisne Canal to protect the flank of the panzer divisions as they thrust down towards Amiens.

The French held the canal's south bank in great strength and confronted 1st Division with its own 87th Colonial Division. That the enemy was determined to hold the canal line was soon evident. The Jaeger regiments had scarcely moved into their positions along the northern bank before the whole divisional front came under heavy and prolonged bombardment from massed batteries of heavy guns. Their destructive and accurate fire was directed by observers who enjoyed a panoramic view of the battlefield from OPs located on the heights of the Chemin des Dames ridge.

Kuebler, the divisional commander, planned that his regiments would conduct an aggressive defence until he had received the order to launch them across the canal. He deployed his regiments with 99th on the left, 100th on the right and 98th covering the open right flank along the Aisne. Divisional Headquarters was set up between the village of Fresnes and the market town of Coucy-le-Château. During the week-long period that 1st Division stood defensively on the bank of the canal, the German campaign on other sectors was reaching a successful conclusion. The British Expeditionary Force had withdrawn through the port of Dunkirk and the last flickers of French resistance in Flanders were being beaten down. The Dutch and Belgian armies had long since capitulated. Now the great mass of von Bock's Army Group 'B' could unite with von Rundstedt's Army Group 'A' and move into the second phase of the campaign; the destruction of the French Army positioned south of the Somme. During the first days of June 1st Gebirgs prepared to play its part in the now imminent battle. The massive troop movements to bring both army groups into position were completed. The time for 1st Division to stand on the defensive was past. Now came the call to attack.

In outline, the OKH plan was for a succession of three massive assaults, which would strike and destroy the French host. The most important of the three blows was that which would unleash a massive armoured fist and send it crashing through the so-called 'Weygand Line', an extensive system of field fortifications but one which was neither so well sited nor so deely constructed as the trench systems of the Great War. Every Army must have faith in itself; must be of high morale. The German Army of 1940, most of whose soldiers had been trained in peacetime and who were skilled men at arms, had the unshakeable conviction that they would win the war in the west. Rudolf Flecker, certainly, had no doubts. 'The confidence we felt cannot be described. It had to be experienced to be understood. We had a glorious feeling – a certainty – that we would win. The Army of 1914–18 had never gained such a victory as we had already gained in northern France. Now we stood poised to cross the Marne, the Somme and the other great rivers of France and to gain for Germany the victory that would wipe out the memory of Versailles [the Treaty under whose conditions Germany was restricted to an Army of 100,000 men, but emasculated in that it was not permitted to have either tanks or military aircraft].

Flecker's account went on to describe the events of 5 June when the great offensive opened. 'We had been in the same trenches for almost a week and it was an unpleasant place. The ground was marshy and we suffered from mosquitoes and other flying pests. The enemy was about 20 metres away across the water [the Oisne–Aisne Canal] and smothered our every movement with a barrage of shells. Luckily for the groups in the front line, some of his heavier fire was directed upon our gun lines or truck convoys. The time came for us to move out of our trenches to the form-up positions.

'Tapes had been laid to guide us, a very necessary precaution this as it was now night time and it would have been very easy to lose one's bearings in the thick bushes. Near the Company's crossing points we found the assault boats which the pioneers had brought forward some days earlier. We carried these boats on our shoulders – six men to a boat – down to the bushes on the water's edge. Already in position and well hidden were the lads who would be the first to cross – the assault groups. So far as I recall it the surface of the canal was covered with a light mist. Everything was quiet with no artillery fire and only an occasional rifle shot. According to our divisional history the barrage went in at 5 in the morning and lasted for just half an hour. Then the firing stopped while the range was being increased in order to pound the area behind the French front line. Just before the barrage stopped to "lift" on to those new targets, the assault groups went in under the covering fire of machine-guns and mortars. The follow-up groups – I was in one of these – then moved down to the water's edge. We lifted our boats into the water and began to paddle them across. It was a trick of the mind but that little canal which could not have been more that 20 metres wide seemed to be suddenly a vast and wide river. We paddled furiously and reached the other bank. Two men stayed in the boat to ferry it back to the northern bank and then to bring a new group across. On the southern bank our officer collected the scattered groups and we set off. Here and there were dead bodies and a small group of prisoners. From that point on it was no longer an assault crossing but just a normal infantry attack.'

Post-combat reports indicate that the French counter-barrages fell more heavily upon 100th Regiment on the right flank of the advance than the left flank, 99th Regiment. One form-up point for 1st Battalion, 100th Regiment was a sugar beet factory on the northern bank, and enemy OPs on the high ground of the Chemin des Dames, detecting movement around the complex of buildings, brought down a fierce concentration of fire upon it. The positive way was to advance through the explosions, cross the canal and close with the enemy. The crossing was made and 100th Regiment, struggling through the close-packed trees of the canal's southern bank, began to move towards the first objective, the Pont St Mard. Once 99th Regiment had crossed the canal its battalions struck out to climb the slopes of a feature known as La Gloire. There comes a time in every attack when it seems to lose pace and élan. At such a time the commander's firm hand is needed to bring his units on again. Although both regiments had crossed the canal in good time, their advances had lost cohesion and power but their commanders were equal to the task and quickly regrouped the battalions, allotting to each a fresh objective. It was as well that they acted so promptly and firmly for during this regrouping phase the French commanders, sensing an uncertainty in the German advance, mounted a series of counter-attacks.

The first of these struck the already battered 100th Regiment. This had two battalions 'up' and the right-hand battalion was advancing towards Guny when the enemy artillery laid a 'curtain' barrage in front of the village barring the Jaeger advance. This furious fire ended abruptly and then out of the sudden silence a flood of Colonial troops stormed down the slopes in a bayonet charge. Although the Jaeger Companies and platoons were spread out across a wide area, the battalion's excellent discipline manifested itself. Orders were given and the Jaeger, without time to dig-in, lay on the ground of the Chemin des Dames and awaited the fire order. When at last it came the vast cloud of charging Moroccan troops broke as the massed machine-gun fire struck them. Here and there a young French officer tried vainly to lead his men on but it was a folorn hope. The surviving Colonial soldiers flooded back up the ridge and into the trenches that they had left only minutes before. The sister Jaeger battalion, on the left wing, had undergone a similar experience as it advanced towards its objective, Pont St Mard. The French charges made against it were flung back and then the battalion fought its way into the village and soon became involved in house-to-house fighting. The repeated assaults of the enemy and his furious barrages might have well destroyed the rhythm of the division's attack, but superior fire discipline and the higher morale of the Jaeger, were irresistible. Despairingly, courageously, the Moroccan battalions had rushed forward attempting to drive the Jaeger down the slopes and back across the canal. Each desperate attempt failed and with each failure the confidence of the Jaeger grew. Their own attack still moved forward and even if it did not move at the planned pace it was, nevertheless, still an advance. At some places along the divisional front the French defence hardened and threatened to halt, however temporarily, the Jaeger movement. When that happened the order was given to fix bayonets. Under fire the Jaeger formed ranks and with a three-fold cheer of 'Hurra!' stormed and took the French positions, breaking the enemy's resistance on that sector.

Behind the Jaeger, battling their way up the slopes of the ridge, the pioneers were working under fire to construct pontoon bridges strong enough to carry guns and panzers into the forward combat zone. With the support of those heavy weapons the situation was cleared up and from their maps the regimental commanders could see that both Jaeger regiments had gained their objectives. The 99th was on the line Limoval, Farm Chatillon to Crécy-au-Mont, while the heights to the south and around La Gloire had been cleared of the enemy and had been consolidated. Béthancourt alone, on the regiment's and the division's left flank, held out. In 100th Regiment's area the French hold upon Pont St Mard and the high ground to the south-west of the village was finally wrested from them at last light. The 98th Regiment, which had been in divisional reserve all day, received at last the order to move forward and as it began to advance it was struck by a long and destructive barrage. One particular blow was caused by a shell which burst in the crown of a tree killing 16 men and wounded 30 others.

The soldiers of the 1st could not know it but their day-long battle had taken them far ahead of the formations on their flanks. Their Commander was of course well aware of this and, conscious that the enemy was reaching breaking point, ordered a further advance so as not to give the French time to knit up their unravelling front. His orders were that the regiments were to reach a line between Epagny–Bagneux, a move which would take them thrusting like a lance into the collapsing Colonial Corps opposing him. As a result of the Jaeger advance the French artillery had been forced to pull back and its guns were no longer firing. But the Gebirgs artillerymen manhandled their guns forward into a close-support posture. Under their fire the regiments gained the objectives that had been set them but were given little time to rest. Patrols had to be sent out, ammunition, food and water had to be brought up to the forward Companies, the wounded evacuated from the battlefield and the dead buried. And the losses had been high. In that single day's battle the division had lost 139 men killed in action and 430 had been wounded.

The spectacular advances of 5 June brought with them the danger of French armour thrusting into the flanks of the salient which the division had created in the enemy's front. The first such attack came in during the late morning of 6 June and to meet the challenge the anti-tank Company of 98th Regiment was rushed forward. The first gun to reach the threatened area unlimbered and went into action. Then two others came up and opened fire. Their combined action knocked out all the enemy armoured fighting vehicles. The threat had been driven off. Fresh orders directed the division to advance to the Aisne and then subsequent orders sent it across the river. During the night of 6th/7th its units began to cross at a point west of Soissons. At this stage of the campaign there came a change in battlefield tactics. Now when enemy resistance was met it was to be bypassed by the first fighting echelons leaving the enemy pockets to be taken out by follow-up troops. On 10 June the enemy in front of 1st Gebirgs Division, who had been given no chance to regroup or to withdraw in an orderly fashion, showed the first signs of complete disintegration. The hopes of the French High Command to hold the Germans on the Marne were dashed and the leading elements of 1st Gebirgs Division stormed across the river during the 11th. With the fall of Paris resistance began to crumble. The OKW communiqué of 19 June announced that Germany had offered the French government terms for an armistice. The offer was accepted and an armistice was signed. Before those historic events occurred 1st Gebirgs Division was pulled out of the line and rushed by truck to Lyon. It had been given a new task; to strike into the back of the French troops who were defending the western Alps against the Italians. Mussolini had declared war on France and Great Britain on 10 June. The Franco–German armistice came into effect on the 25th, while 1st Gebirgs Division was still en route to Lyon. Its move was immediately halted and the operation was cancelled. The division enjoyed a few days' rest and then closed up to the Franco–Swiss frontier and specifically to the area of the Jura mountains. There it took up the double duty of guarding the frontier and the more pleasant one of carrying out the tasks of an Army of Occupation.

Although the war in the west had been successfully concluded there was still one major enemy – Great Britain – which remained to be subdued. If the British Isles could be invaded and Britain defeated, Germany would be the paramount power in Europe, strong enough to challenge and defeat the foe in the east, Soviet Russia. Victory over the Communist State would give Germany dominance of the European and Asian land mass. Germany could then turn against America and at the end of that confrontation would be in every respect ruler of the world. But first those troublesome islands on the other side of the North Sea had to be attacked and taken. The plan to carry out the invasion was code-named 'Sealion'.

Of the four Gebirgs divisions on establishment, only 1st and 6th were available for action. The veteran 1st was selected to form part of the invasion spearhead force and was taken by train from the Swiss Jura to Picardy. In the small market town of Arras the division set up its headquarters and located its Jaeger regiments close to the coast.

The 1st, was now part of VII Corps, a component of Sixteenth Army. When the invasion took place Sixteenth Army was to form the right wing of Army Group 'A' with Ninth Army as the left wing. It was the role of the army group to carry out the military part of the combined operations plan to invade and subdue the British Isles. An order issued by Sixteenth Army on 10 September 1940, specified the area between Rotterdam and Calais as that in which its formations would embark for the crossing. They were to debark between Folkestone and St Leonards, throw back the British forces and establish a beachhead running from Canterbury – the Great Stour – Ashford – Tenterdem – Etchingham.

VII Corps was to be one of the two in the assault wave and was to gain a line running from Sissinghurst to Burwash. It would have to hold that line for a minimum of eight days and was warned that it would be without reinforcement or replenishment of food, fuel or ammunition for the whole of that period. The spearhead units of Sixteenth Army were to include not only men of the special operations group known as Brandenburg, but also paratroops, who were to capture an airfield at Lympne on Romney Marsh, and Gebirgsjaeger who were to scale the cliffs of the South Coast. To give the Jaeger practical training, units were taken to the area of Cap Gris Nez where there was similar terrain to that found in southern and south-eastern England. Alfred Spiess, who served in 1st Division, recalled that his battalion trained to take out Hastings and the cliffs to the east of the town. 'We had been trained in alpine warfare and the task we would face when we landed in Hastings would have been very easy for us. We were to disembark, cross the shingle beach and climb the cliffs which are behind the promenade. Part of our training had included driving British Army vehicles which had been captured during the campaign in France or else taken from the Dunkirk beaches. In that way we would be able to use British vehicles once we had broken out of the bridgehead. After we had carried out the first landing on the beach at Hastings we were to move inland. A VII Corps order, also issued on 10 September, laid out that "... efforts must be made [after landing] to reach a line at least 2 kilometres [inland] from the beach ...'"

In addition to the cliff-scaling which Alfred Spies mentioned, other correspondents from 1st Gebirgs Division wrote of the exercises in embarkation and debarkation which were carried out in all sorts of weather and on all sorts of craft, usually, hastily converted, flat-bottomed barges. These vessels, which had been built for use on inland waterways, pitched and tossed in the rough seas of the English Channel. It happened on more than one occasion that barges collided and sank. Other craft had been fitted with engines of such low power that they could not make progress at the turn of the tide and usually swung broadside on to the waves. Swamping and sinking was nearly always the result. The Jaeger who were flung into the water on these training exercises would have good cause to fear for their lives when D-Day for Operation 'Sealion' was announced. To their relief it did not come and in the early autumn Hitler postponed the planned invasion.

The operation had been aborted, but a second one, not involving a sea crossing, was then planned. This was Operation 'Felix', an attack to capture Gibraltar, the only British territory on the mainland of Europe. The operation was to be launched with the passive support of General Franco, the dictator of Spain. Were 'Felix' to succeed, Britain would lose control of the Atlantic entrance to the Mediterranean and the Royal Navy, forced into the eastern half of that sea, would be unable to defend Malta. The whole balance of power in the Mediterranean would, thus, be radically altered and to Germany's advantage.

For 'Felix' only one Jaeger regiment, the 98th, was to be employed. The 99th was held in northern France, until December 1940, as part of the deception plan to cover the aborting of 'Sealion', while 100th Regiment was posted during November to Salzburg where it formed one of the two Jaeger regiments of the newly raised 5th Gebirgs Division. The 98th trained for 'Felix' in the Swiss Jura, but that operation, too, was aborted when it became clear that Franco would not co-operate either actively or passively.

The year 1940 ended with the German Army conducting no military operations on the continent of Europe, and with the Gebirgsjaeger establishment now increased to six divisions. The peace in Europe was not to last long for towards the end of the year the Army of the Italian Fascist State struck out of Albania and attacked Greece.

5th and 6th Gebirgs Divisions in Greece, 1941

THE YEAR 1941 was a fateful one for the Third Reich. It opened with Germany dominant in Europe and closed with her army reeling back in retreat through the bitter Russian winter from the gates of Moscow.

The year had begun so well. During short campaigns in 1939 and 1940, the armies of Germany's mainland enemies had been tumbled into ruin and the remaining nations of Europe were either allies or hoping to become so. The one exception; the troublesome, off-shore British, had inflicted a tactical reverse upon the Luftwaffe during the Battle of Britain in the autumn of 1940. As a consequence Operation 'Sealion', the invasion of Great Britain, had had to be postponed. Not cancelled – merely delayed. When Soviet Russia, Hitler's next intended victim, had been destroyed, the Luftwaffe would head westwards again and this time gain air superiority over England. Under that shield the German Army would cross the Channel and fall upon Britain. Victory would follow and a German Empire extending from Ireland to the Urals would be the only Power.

In the late autumn of 1940, Hitler wanted to turn his attention to planning the new war against Russia, but before he could begin to plan in earnest there were certain loose ends, political and military, that needed to be tidied away. A war, not of Germany's making, had begun in the Aegean. On 28 October Mussolini had ordered his army in Albania to invade Greece. The Fascist leader had anticipated a short campaign and a quick victory. He achieved neither. The Greeks flung back the Italians and held them fast in the mountains. On those unsheltered heights in freezing temperatures the Italian troops had suffered cruelly. Hitler's first reaction to Mussolini's aggression was annoyance that the Duce had acted unilaterally. Then he decided to hold a watching brief without becoming militarily involved. He did not wish to disrupt the movement of the units of the future Army Group South which had already begun to occupy the positions out of which they would, eventually, advance to attack Russia.

Then, as a consequence of Mussolini's adventure, an event occurred which forced Hitler's hand. British forces occupied the islands of Crete and Lemnos to bar any German expansion to the south. Hitler did not see the British move in that way. He saw Crete as a British springboard into Europe; an aircraft carrier from which the RAF could launch its squadrons to bomb the oilfields at Ploesti in Roumania, Germany's principal fuel supply. At a Fuehrer Conference convened on 4 November he directed that a great number of flak batteries be removed from urban sites in Germany and set up around Ploesti. He then issued a Directive to

OKH to plan a military campaign to destroy Greece. The High Command set to work and had soon produced Operation 'Marita'. Greece would be attacked and a threefold victory would be gained. First, it would have helped Mussolini to gain the military success that his armies could never achieve unaided. Second, it would drive the British from Crete and safeguard, thereby, the Ploesti oil. Third, the occupation of Greece would strengthen the south-eastern flank of the future Eastern Front. Then there were political problems which had to be resolved. The German Twelfth Army, which had been detailed to carry out the campaign in Greece, needed to cross the territory of neutral Bulgaria to reach its attack positions. A flurry of diplomatic activity produced a pact between Germany and Bulgaria under which List's army was granted transit facilities. A very subtle diplomatic initiative was used to woo Yugoslavia which was a predominantly Slav country, and by tradition Russia's ally in the Balkans. It was the task of the German Foreign Office to persuade a country that was instinctively anti-Teuton, into signing a non-aggression pact.

The German diplomats succeeded and a pact was signed by the Yugoslav Regent, Prince Paul. Hitler was overjoyed. Now the last of those nations that might have been Germany's enemies in a war against Russia had been neutralized. But he had not reckoned with the depth of anti-Teuton feeling that existed, particularly in Serbia. Probably encoooouraged by the landing of British troops in Greece on 7 March, there were demonstrations on the streets of Yugoslavia's cities, which led to the revocation of the newly signed treaty by the under-age King Peter. Again, Germany's southern flank was open and vulnerable. Enraged at what he considered an act of gross betrayal, Hitler, in Directive No 25, demanded from OKH a plan to crush Yugoslavia and it says much for the operational skill and logistical efficiency of the planning staffs that within ten days a plan had been drawn up and the necessary units moved into position. The attack, which was an extension of 'Marita', would be carried out by Second Army, commanded by Freiherr von Weichs. Hitler now had only to give the word and the Balkan war would begin.

Among the two German armies which stretched in a shallow arc extending from Yugoslavia to Bulgaria and which were soon to be involved in the fighting, were four Gebirgsjaeger divisions. The 1st, serving as part of XXXXIX Gebirgskorps and occupying the Lavanth valley in Austria's southernmost province, Carinthia, took part in the campaign against Yugoslavia. The 4th Gebirgs Division also fought against that country and struck into Yugoslavia out of Bulgaria as part of von Kleist's 1st Panzer Group. The principal task of 4th Gebirgs Division was to capture the high ground along the route which the panzer force would take and thus hold open the thrust-line as the panzers raced for Belgrade.

Both 5th and 6th Gebirgs Divisions, serving in XVIII Gebirgskorps, fought in Greece and both had the initial task of breaking through the Greek defensive fortifications, the Metaxas Line, opening the Rupel Pass and going on to spearhead the German Army's advance southwards towards Corinth.

Let us return in time to the weeks before D-Day for 'Operation Marita'. The 4th Gebirgs Division began its approach march to the Greek frontier and to its baptism of fire, from a concentration area inside Bulgaria. There was insufficient railway space to transport the Jaeger by train to the frontier, and not enough trucks to carry the battalions by road. Accordingly, they marched on foot to their form-up areas and one battalion covered a distance of 160 kilometres in two days. The 5th and 6th Divisions, too, marched to their attack positions in the high mountains between Bulgaria and Greece. If the Jaeger found the going hard as they marched through Bulgaria, the difficulty of scaling the mountain peaks on the Bulgarian side of the border seemed at times to be 'almost beyond our ability', in the words of Gerd Schober, an NCO in a machine-gun Company. 'On the plain it was early spring and the areas through which we marched had many trees in blossom. The first difficulties were met in the foothills. Narrow paths, steep and rocky, up which we climbed with difficulty. It was still winter in the mountains and the higher we climbed the worse became both the weather and the conditions. Rain in the foothills became sleet on the lower slopes and snow blizzards on the higher slopes. In the foul weather we made very little progress. We could scarcely see more than eight paces ahead of us in the fury of the snowstorms and it was bitterly cold. On most flat surfaces there was half a metre of snow and in some places, where it had drifted, it was nearly a metre deep.

'My Company reached its area, a sort of stony plateau on which there was absolutely no cover, and on this granite table top we settled down. We were the forward line. Below us the rest of the battalion was sheltered in the scrub woods and shielded from much of the cold and snow. We on the plateau wrapped ourselves in greatcoats and shelter halves. Thank God, we did not have long to wait for the mules to come up. They were not allowed to come as high as we had climbed and parties of us were sent down to bring up the blankets and hot food which the pack-animals had carried. We stayed for two days and one night in that snowy desert, strengthened by the hot drinks which were brought up at frequent intervals. There was no sound coming from the Greek side. We seemed to be the last survivors in a wilderness of ice, snow and high winds. It was a relief when orders came that we were to go into action. Anything, we thought, must be better than this unending waiting in an unending snowstorm.'

The mountains which the 5th and 6th Gebirgs Divisions would have to attack had peaks which, in the extreme western sector, reach to more than 2,000 metres, but which then slowly decline in height as they run eastwards to the valley of the River Struma. There is no vegetation on the highest slopes and scrub covers the lower slopes. Deep, narrow and almost impenetrable valleys score the mountains. There are almost no paths in the main range and just one inferior road crosses the mountain wall on the eastern flank. The River Struma cuts through the eastern side of the mountains and flows down into Macedonia, and a good motor road runs alongside the Struma. Once through the mountain wall and the Rupel Pass, an attacking army can descend on to the plain which leads towards Salonika.

It was in the mountain slopes on each side of the valley of the Struma that the Metaxas Line was situated. This was a modern system of defences garrisoned by local men serving in the Greek 18th Division, backed by strong artillery detachments. A system of trenches and bunkers strung across the bare slopes had been carefully laid out to provide mutual protection against an attacker. The height of the mountains in which the defences were placed and their incredible strength convinced the Greeks that the Line was impregnable, and they awaited with confidence the attack which they knew must come. A German response to the landing of a British Expeditionary Force was certain to be swift and overwhelming.

Even though in Athens the government had faith in the strength of the Metaxas Line, the garrison commanders in the bunkers set their men to the task of improving those defences with even more barbed wire, new sniper positions and machine-gun posts. On the German side the work to prepare for the coming battle was more arduous and more intense. The heaviest guns could not be taken up on the heights, not even with the help of the one road. The heavy artillery would have to fire from the valley floor. Everything else was taken forward slowly and laboriously. 'The 88s were towed behind their trucks as far forward as it was possible to take them. Artillery pieces lighter and more mobile than the 88s were towed to the higher slopes into the snow line while the mountain artillery guns were broken down into loads and brought forward by pack-animal. The same beasts carried the ammunition, food and water supplies to the guns positioned out of sight of Greek observers on the reverse slopes of cols and spurs of ground. It was back-breaking work and it went on for days. We sweated by day doing that heavy work and froze at night in our scrape holes on the slopes. It was a miserable time.

'All through the night of 5/6 April, we could hear explosions from far away down in the valley. These sounds like demolitions being carried out – bridges perhaps, being blown up to hinder our advance or else craters made at road junctions. One thing was very obvious. If the Greeks were carrying out demolitions they knew that war was coming and their troops in the block-houses would be ready for our attack.'

Careful observation and reconnaissance ensured that each Jaeger battalion knew the number of objectives it had to attack. The strength of each position had been calculated and a unit or sub-unit had been detailed to take it out. Against the very strongest targets a Company would be put in, while most of the smaller objectives were to be dealt with by a couple of Sections. The number of men in the attacking waves would be few for not every man in the rifle companies was in the line. In these mountains where every bullet and each mouthful of food had to be brought forward laboriously from Petrish, the base far below on the Strumica road, half the strength of an attacking battalion was employed in carrying stores – chiefly ammunition because of the unusually high expenditure. In addition to the supplies of small-arms ammunition, other specialist equipment had to be brought forward, notably explosive charges which would be used against the reinforced concrete bunkers. Some Company groups were accompanied by pioneer detachments whose men carried heavier types of explosive charges as well as flame-throwers, smoke flares and mines.

At first light the Jaeger had stood too, as usual, and had then had an early breakfast which seems to have varied almost from unit to unit. 'The coffee was only lukewarm and our breakfast was two thick slices of army brown bread and some pieces of salami.' Others received more substantial rations. 'One of our quartermasters was an organizing genius. How he got hot soup up to us before the attack I do not know. But we had thick pea soup with pieces of sausage in it and plenty of bread. As an old soldier he knew the psychological advantage of hot food. It not only nourishes and strengthens you for the ordeal ahead but lets you know that the rear echelons are, and will be, making every effort in support.'

The tactics to take out the objectives varied according to their type, strength and location. In some places the Jaeger crossed their start-line in a widely spread out line. At others they moved forward in single file. All were bowed under the weight of equipment and weapons. Some attacks were supported by a sudden flurry of 8.1cm mortar bombs, others by rifle grenades and the short-ranged 5cm mortars. To an artillery observer the infantry attack was 'a profoundly moving experience to see, in the bright dawn, the lines of our men moving slowly and deliberately towards the crest and to see the line break at a given point as the units moved out to attack the objectives they had been given'.

In a light and bright dawn the Gebirgsjaeger went into battle. Whatever objective they had been given and whatever the tactics employed, one factor remained constant. The resistance put up by the Greeks was everywhere hard, bitter and sometimes fanatical. One report described how even the Greeks lying wounded at the bottom of a trench fought on until they were killed. A combination of strong defensive positions set among barren peaks and defended by first-class soldiers proved what the Jaeger had half-feared, that the battle to break the Metaxas Line would be no easy one.

'Several of our light Gebirgs artillery batteries were positioned high up in the mountains and had been taken so far forward that they were close to the frontier. In such advanced positions they had to be well camouflaged with scrub branches so that they could not be detected by the Greek frontier guards, and that camouflage had to be changed each night. There was an order that there to be no movement at all in the area of the forward gun line. This meant that the crews had to lie hidden in the slit trenches all through the bitter day. They were not allowed to light fires nor to smoke. They had to be near the guns in case of a surprise

Greek assault, but had to remain hidden so as not to give him warning that our own attack would soon begin. Only at night could they emerge and move silently downhill towards TAC HQ for a hot meal.' (Hans Christoph). The infantry Companies with the same orders manned the outpost line with only a skeleton force. They were positioned that far forward to protect the guns.

During the late evening of 5 April assault groups from both regiments left the scrub in which they had been concealed and climbed upwards through the star-lit night towards the summit. Midnight passed. It was now 6 April. D-Day had come and H-Hour was close at hand.

General Ringel's plan for the battle placed 85th Regiment on the right and 100th Regiment on the left. Facing the 85th were not only the four highest peaks in the area but also four of the main bunker complexes in the Metaxas Line, Rupesco in the far west, Popotlivitsa in the centre, Sultanitsa in the east and, some distance away and to the north, Istibei. The regiment's main thrust-line was southerly and it was expected that Rupesco, which lay closest to the frontier, would be the first to be captured. It was not. The Rupesco complex held out and was, in fact, the last to surrender. The thrust-lines of both regiments were divergent, south-east for the 100th and south for the 85th. It was essential for the latter to take its objectives quickly in order to cover the right flank of the sister regiment as it thrust through the mountains and towards the River Struma bridges at Lutra.

Although the 85th had a heavy burden, that of the 100th was the heavier one. Not only did it have the greater number of enemy positions to take out, but these were echeloned in depth and positioned so as to absorb the weight of an attack. In addition, most were set so far back from the frontier that the battalions would have to complete a long approach march before they could begin an attack upon their objectives. The regiment's 1st Battalion on the right wing was to take out Trapesca and Letsitsa in succession before going on to seize Point 525, the final height that had to be taken before it could descend to Neon Patritsi and advance towards the river bridges at Lutra. The 2nd and 3rd Battalions, which made up the left wing, were also faced with a long approach march to reach their first objective, Kelkaya. Then they would swing in a shallow left-wheeling movement, take out Arpaluki and Vasano before carrying out another long cross-country march which would bring them against the backs of the Greeks defending Point 307, the corner-stone of the Metaxas Line. Once these formidable defences had been breached, both Gebirgs divisions would be free to take part in the conquest of the rest of Greece. The Jaeger attacks would be preceded by Stuka bombing raids upon specific and general targets.

So much for Ringel's plan. Let us see how the 5th performed in its first action. We know that assault detachments from both regiments had climbed through the dark night of 5/6 April, towards the frontier. Patrols from these detachments went out into the freezing dark, crawling forward to silence the guard dogs kennelled outside the Customs posts.

Well before dawn the dogs were dead. Some Jaeger, aware of the closeness of H-Hour, welcomed the opening of hostilities, believing that although it would be a dangerous time it could surely not be as hard and uncomfortable as the long cold nights and days which they had spent on the mountain slopes. They were to be cruelly disillusioned. The ordeal which faced them was to be just as cold, equally as uncomfortable and they were, in addition, to be deprived of sleep and stormed at by shot and shell.

At H-Hour the assault detachments rushed up the slopes on whose crests stood the stone huts of the Greek Customs posts. The sleeping officers were overpowered, the telephone wires were cut and the Customs men, the first prisoners of war of the new campaign, were bundled down the slope to be interrogated. There was, according to those who wrote about this action, a fairly thick mist which both obscured sight and smothered sound, adding eerie dimensions to this short-lived operation. Down in the stunted scrubby trees of the lower slopes the attacking battalions formed up, moving almost casually, and began the final stage of the climb, one which would carry them across the frontier and into the battle for the bunkers. At 05.20 the lead Section of one battalion reached the crest. The mist had now cleared and the Jaeger were visible to observers manning the enemy defence line. The Greek response was immediate. A machine-gun began to fire and an MG 34 responded. The war had begun. As yet this was still an engagement between infantrymen. It was not yet time for the artillery or the Luftwaffe to play their part. Their H-Hour was not until 05.40. The Jaeger trudged over the mountain crest and the seconds towards 05.40 ticked slowly away. Then, from far away on the plain, came the sound of muffled thuds, followed only seconds later by the screaming of shells passing just above the Jaeger pressed close to the unyielding ground. The shells burst, flinging off shrapnel and rock fragments. High overhead the squadrons of Ju 87s wheeled into position, dived and bombed the lines of pillboxes. A thick cloud of smoke from the explosions obscured the enemy bunkers. The Jaeger battle drill for taking out the enemy positions was a simple tactic which had been planned in detail and rehearsed repeatedly. Against the strongest enemy bunkers two Gebirgs light artillery pieces would open a direct fire once they had been dragged by muscle-power into position through snow drifts. The enemy was then to be bombarded by ground and air until he was, in German military parlance, 'sturm reif', that is to say, ready to be taken out by infantry assault.

At times the cannonade was halted to let the guns cool or so that the sweating gunners could drag their weapons closer to the enemy positions. Then they would open fire again, often at point-blank range and with a seemingly greater intensity. To the senior officers at Div HQ, seeing and hearing that furious cannonade and aerial bombardment, it was clear that the pounding MUST have achieved the desired result. Relying upon the experiences of past campaigns they were sure that that stage of the battle had been reached – the enemy was 'sturm reif' and that the Jaeger assaults would meet little opposition. It was a false appreciation. There were many enemy positions which had not even been attacked and others which had withstood both the high-explosive bombs from the Stukas and the armour-piercing shells of the artillery. The bunker walls were too thick to be shattered easily. Neither could the guns of the Gebirgs artillery make an impression upon them. Only heavy siege artillery could have any effect against the reinforced concrete and there was no siege artillery on these heights. The Jaeger would have to gain the victory without the heavy guns. The infantry would have to prove here that it was they indeed, who were the 'Queen of Battles'. Suddenly there was silence in the mountains. The bombers had flown away and the guns had ceased firing. The infantry battle for the peaks was about to open. It is not possible to describe the actions of the days of battle at every level and there were too many objectives for the capture of each to be described individually. A general account can, however, give a picture of what was attempted and achieved.

The opening attacks began well in most places except against Point 1224 which made no progress. Yet this was a peak that had to be captured if the artillery observers were to have first-class OPs. Along the whole divisional front fighting ebbed and flowed around the bunkers set along the upper slopes of the various peaks. Then, in a spectacular operation, 85th Regiment sent out two patrols whose common task it was to pass unseen through the Greek lines, descend into the Struma valley and capture the river bridges before these were blown. On many sectors the Jaeger attacking the pillboxes also faced the difficulty of fighting through very deep snow. As they moved off the bare rocks towards the crest they suddenly encountered snow fields, some so deep that they completely covered the enemy bunkers. Hidden under this freezing blanket were Greek positions that had not been identified by the Stuka crews and had not been bombed in the opening raids. The Jaeger toiling through waist-high snow then came under fire from machine-guns firing from slits that were almost invisible. Across the whole divisional front small unit actions were in progress to take out the bunkers.

Utilizing every fold in the rocks, every piece of dead ground and every bit of cover, the Gebirgsjaeger approached the enemy positions. Their fire, aimed at the slits in one bunker's concrete walls, was answered by streams of fire directed at them from other bunkers. Slowly the advance inched forward, not without loss, until panting with exhaustion the men of one Jaeger group crouched on a narrow goat track which ran near the vertical walls of a pillbox. Two men picked up short-handled demolition charges. An NCO flung smoke candles and waited until the screen was thick enough. Then, together with the two carriers, he covered the short distance between the track and the bunker in racing strides while machine-gunners gave covering fire. Standing breathlessly against the bunker wall, the demolition team checked the fuzes. The charges were placed side by side against the pillbox wall, the detonating cords pulled and the three men raced back to the track. There was a long pause. Nine seconds, which seemed like nine years. Then one single crashing detonation. Under the billowing cloud of smoke and dust the NCO and all his group charged back again across the grass to the pillbox wall. He fitted a new charge on to a staff, pulled the cord, waited a few seconds and then thrust the device through the firing slit. There was a crashing explosion from inside the bunker. For a few seconds there was silence. Then from another firing slit the defiant Greeks brought their machine-gun back into action again. A second and then a third charge was pushed in. Even after the second one detonated the lone machine-gun had continued to fire, but after the third explosion there was no further sound. The NCO pushed open the heavy outer door, threw in a hand-grenade and fired a burst from his Schmeisser machine pistol. The door was pushed wider open. The Greeks were all dead. They had fought to the last and yet this had only been one position, and not a very important one at that, on just one mountain peak. The NCO loaded his signal pistol and fired off a double red flare towards Company Head-quarters. No 2 Section had taken its objective.

It was one of the first successes to be reported. The strength of the enemy bunkers, the resolute defence and the weight of the enemy's curtain of defensive artillery fire together with the strain of the climb had worked together to prevent the attacks succeeding against every objective. From Division came orders to 85th Regiment to break off the attacks against Rupesco and to make the main efforts against Popotlivitsa, where two bunkers had already been taken. Pulling back under fire is neither easy nor can it be carried out without loss. Moving back from Rupesco by bounds, using the fire-and-movement tactics they had learned on training grounds in Germany, the men of 1st Battalion, 85th Regiment withdrew and regrouped out of sight of the enemy machine-gunners. The next move was to reach the Popotlivitsa sector and to reinforce the assault that was being made there.

At this point it would be appropriate to move from the 85th Regiment's sector and follow the actions of the sister regiment. Before we do so let us look at the fighting for the Metaxas Line as described by one who accompanied the 85th, not with a fire-arm but with a pencil, a note pad and a camera. The war reporter, Gert Habedanck, was attached to a Gebirgsjaeger battalion for the opening stages of the Greek campaign. He was an avid diarist and the entries he wrote covering those first days were later reproduced in a German propaganda work on the campaigns of 1941. The chapter containing Habedanck's entries in that book is headed, 'We swept the Tommies from the Continent', the title of a propaganda song of the period. His account covers the four days from 6 to 10 April and the first entry opens with the words.

'6th April. It is just after midnight. An icy wind sweeps through the loose boards in our tiny, thatched hut. Inside the hut a smoky fire is burning. Nevertheless, it is too cold to sleep. From out there in the darkness comes the sound of a sentinel pacing to and fro. The pacing stops abruptly and there is silence. Then the pacing begins again. Very carefully we ease our way out of the hut and into the darkness. Silhouetted against the clear, star-filled night sky is the white crest of the Kongur. From the Greek side of the border comes the continuous and noisy barking of guard dogs.

'There are only five hours to go before the roar of our artillery will break the deep peace of this alpine world. Then [behind that barrage] our Gebirgsjaeger will move forward into the attack . . . There is no parallel in the history of warfare, where sophisticated defences, skilfully sited and disposed, have been attacked and taken.

'We meet the dawn of the coming day with our watches in our hand. Three minutes to go !!! Two !! One ! and suddenly the gates of hell seem to open. The valley is filled with the smoke of the shells from our guns. The rocks shake, the enemy pillboxes are surrounded and obscured by massive fountains of earth, rocks and smoke. As suddenly as the gates of Hell opened, so quickly did they close again. A deathly stillness now overhangs the whole area broken only by a couple of blackbirds unconcernedly whistling their greeting to the new day. We listened intently, holding our breath. Suddenly, a new, humming noise overlaid the blackbirds' calls. It sound like a swarm of hornets . . . The humming rose to a metallic scream, to an evil-sounding roar of engines: Stukas. As the planes dived vertically upon the lines of bunkers stretched out across the mountain slopes, we begin to climb upwards along narrow paths through the snow towards TAC HQ of 1st Battalion. A series of telephone lines go out from here to the individual Companies. The first reports on the progress of the attack come in.

'No 3 Company has taken the Greek frontier post after limited resistance and is advancing towards Popotlivitsa. No 1 Company has fought its way into the trench system along the frontier and has beaten down the enemy's strong resistance. The FOO has been badly wounded. A wall of rock towers over us; the frontier between Bulgaria and Greece. From the summit of this rock wall the ground slopes away to the south. To the right, in the bright early morning sun there is the snow-covered saddle of Rupesco; to the left, seemingly close enough to touch is the peak of Popotlivitsa. The Gebirgsjaeger are climbing out of the deep valley towards the crest. Their hour has come and rifle and machine-gun fire echo in a succession of rollingthunder claps around the mountain peaks.

'Through the scissors-periscopes we can see the pillboxes on the north-western side of Popotlivitsa. The whole area is pock-marked with craters, evidence of the effect of Stuka bombs and artillery shells. The Greeks seem not to have been affected by the bombardments. Within the thick walls of the bunkers they waited until the hail of German fire had passed over then, then manned the firing slits in the pillboxes and opened a destructive fire upon the Jaeger attackers. Heavy flak and artillery guns would have soon ended that resistance but none of the weapons that were employed in Holland and in France can be used here. Only light mortars and mountain guns which the mules have brought forward along paths shovelled out for them through the close-packed snow. These mortars and mountain guns are the only support which the Jaeger have. Other'than these, they fight alone.

'We run through a hail of machine-gun fire to the first Greek frontier post and see our first dead Greek. His wide open eyes stare up at the sky. At the side of his head a few crocuses are blooming.

'Now it is evening. At battalion TAC HQ there are worried faces. The enemy is resisting desperately hard. No 1 Company reports that during the fighting in the trenches Greeks lying wounded on the ground still flailed about with knives and bayonets. The Company has taken the trenches but has suffered losses in dead and wounded. A platoon of No 3 Company has reached the first pillboxes whose concrete walls are so thick that they cannot be smashed by the explosive charges which the Jaeger carry. Similar reports come in from other sectors where the regiment is fighting.

'Deep night. The adjutant cannot put down the telephone in the headquarters. A stream of calls comes in. "No! You must do something during the night . . . Explosive charges are no good? Well, block the firing slits in the pillboxes . . . Who's there? What is your report? You've reached the north face of Sultanitsa . . . You've run out of ammunition? You are under fire from both flanks? . . . The CO orders a withdrawal to the valley. Ammunition supplies are there . . ." There is a short pause then the telephone bell rings again. Another call.

'7th April. Storm force winds drive scudding fragments of cloud. A mixture of rain and snow falling from the dark skies cuts down visibility. Now and again the flying clouds break to reveal the rain-drenched slopes of Rupesco. We are all soaked to the skin. Shaking with cold and with our teeth chattering, we lie in scrape holes in the snow. The enemy is still holding out. On Popotlivitsa the Greeks even mounted a counter-attack to take out one of our machine-gun posts. They stormed down the slopes on either side of the gun. The crew fired desperately but then had to abandon the position because the gun had jammed. A Greek soldier flung himself on to the weapon and struggled with the crew. They all fell to the ground and rolled downhill until the crew managed to overpower him.

'Up to their knees in mud and snow, the stretcher-bearers carry their human burdens down to Petrish and then climb back up again to the front line. Some collapse under the strain. A similar type of heroism is displayed by the ration parties which scale the heights under enemy fire to bring food forward to the men in the front line. It takes a runner six hours of climbing to make the journey from battalion TAC HQ to the front line platoons on Popotlivitsa. Or the mules and their handlers, who trek tirelessly between the forward Companies and the deep valley where they will load up with much-needed ammunition. They have been without sleep for two days and have found no time to eat, so urgent is the need for ammunition in the firing line.

'Towards midday there is some good news. The neighbouring battalion has taken Istiblei and captured 300 prisoners. They found that the pillboxes on that peak were connected by subterranean tunnels.

There are living-rooms dug out of the granite as well as storerooms and a hospital. No 2 Company is ordered to storm the Sultanitsa. The Gebirgsjaeger capture the peak and work their way forward toward Popotlivitsa. The defenders there are now under attack from two sides. No 3 Company is making its slow way forward trying to knock out the pillboxes with high-explosive charges or with flame-throwers.

'8th April. This was a terrible night. Heavy falls of snow gave way to rain showers and the whole time an icy wind blew. No 1 Company reported from Rupesco. The Company has several cases of frostbite brought about because the Jaeger could not change out of their saturated clothes. Lieutenant W. has been out of contact since yesterday evening. We set out with a group from the Signals. Wind swirls the clouds around us. This is fine as this deprives the enemy machine-gunners of targets at which they can aim and they just fire for effect. The closer we get to the summit of Popotlivitsa the closer fly the bullets above our heads. The path is now very very steep. We remove every stone in the path carefully and quietly in order to make no noise. The rocks glisten with rain; clouds race past us. We crawl forward on all fours. Behind us the leading man of the Signals troop carries a cable cradle on his back. It is impossible to see through the swirling clouds. Then, directly ahead of us the vertical side wall of a pillbox breaks suddenly through the mist. Only a few metres from us Greek machine-gunners fire bursts of bullets at where they think the attackers are hidden. We crawl forward, metre by metre towards the pillbox. A grim warning to us is the dead body of one of our comrades lying alongside the path. He was the last man of his group and was hit by machine-gun fire as the group tried to rush past the position. We cannot cover those three metres to bring in his body . . . We must press on.

'Just when we needed maximum cover the clouds parted. We were just crawling past an enemy pillbox. We press ourselves down as close to the ground as possible. In our minds the thought that the steel helmet shiny with rain will betray our position and act as a target for the enemy in the nearest bunker. As suddenly as they parted the clouds closed again and we race past the pillbox and link up with our comrades. They are lining a narrow goat track about 100 metres long. For more than 48 hours fifty Jaeger, surrounded and fired at from all sides, have been holding out. Those men have spent two freezing nights on those bare rocks, wrapped only in shelter halves. They have had no hot food for forty eight hours . . . just a few slices of bread and tinned meat. They are shivering with cold, lying alongside their weapons, ready to fling back any enemy thrust. Their eyes, sunk deep in their heads, show the strain of the past days.

'We are talking with the Company Commander when with a clatter a hand-grenade rolls on to the path only a pace away. Crash! and it explodes before we can take cover. "Here's one for you," the young officer shouts and flings back a German grenade in a long, looping arc. Another explosive charge is placed on the roof of the bunker. Maybe this will destroy it. The Jaeger press themselves against the rocks. The detonation shatters the rocks but it has had no effect upon the concrete of the pillbox. We must wait to see whether the pioneers can fight their way through to us bringing their much stronger explosive charges. The pioneers have been making their way from the summit of Popotlivitsa, smashing the enemy pillboxes as they move down and taking prisoners. Reconnaissance groups have passed Sultanitsa and have reached the Neon-Petrish valley without encountering resistance. During the evening the pioneer platoon coming down from the peak makes contact with Jaeger on the lower slope of Popotlivitsa. It is all up with the Greeks, now. The entrances to the pillboxes are blocked and shortly thereafter, at about 19.00 hrs, a white flag is raised. The men in the bunker emerge shaking with fear, convinced that they will be killed – victims of British hate propaganda.

'9th April. Along the battalion front only Rupesco is still holding out. Battalion TAC HQ has been moved to Vironya in the Struma valley. Here where the finest Macedonian tobacco is grown the lilac is blooming profusely. Nightingales are singing in the green bushes of the river bed and a gentle spring rain falls from the skies.

'News of the surrender of the Salonika army has spread like wildfire. An indescribable feeling of pride in our victory fills each man. The CO sends a patrol to No 1 Company. The Greek garrison on Rupesco is invited to lay down its arms with honour. Climbing alongside the mules and then continuing on foot we reach the snow line; about 2,000 metres high.

'10th April. When we bring the men of No 1 Company the news of our victory then they know why they have spent nights in rain and hail, in bitter cold fighting against a relentless enemy. Today Rupesco is shrouded in cloud again. Not until midday does the cloud lift and the enemy pillboxes in front of No 1 Company are clearly seen. A white camouflage shirt is waved to draw the enemy's attention and flares are fired, but he takes no notice. A patrol moves straight towards the Greek positions. The first man of the group carries the white flag. No shot is fired. No Greek soldier emerges from the pillbox – it is empty. The enemy pulled out during the night. His dead are still lying in their trenches. Their faces are covered with ice. The deep silence of the mountains surrounds us. From papers we have found we learnt that here as well as on Popotlivitsa the garrison was the crack Evzone Regiment.

'No 1 Company moves down into the valley. All the suffering and struggles of the past days are quite forgotten. Singing and yodelling the sons of the southernmost Gaue of the Reich move downhill. For the first time in four days they will have a warm meal and this will be followed by figs and fruit from a Greek rations stores. The hard fighting on the bare rocks is only one step in the military career. Tomorrow they will be faced with new tasks which they will meet and master using the same determination to fight and to win as they have shown in this operation.'

Concurrent with the attack by 3rd Battalion, 85th Regiment upon Istibei, 100th Regiment had begun its assault upon Kelkaya. This was, arguably, the hardest of all the divisional objectives. The approach to the summit was across a stony, open plain devoid of any cover but littered with barbed wire barricades which protected extensive trench systems and, surprisingly, a deep anti-tank ditch. Behind this lay a complex of a dozen large bunkers grouped below the crest and a great number of small pillboxes forming minor links in the chain. The Command HQ was located in a subterranean room cut out of the rock and there were underground passages running from bunker to bunker. Thus, under the heaviest barrages the garrison was protected and that knowledge encouraged the Greek commanders to call down the fire of their own artillery upon the bunkers knowing that the pillboxes and the men they sheltered were impervious to the shellfire.

The Jaeger, however, were not. Smothered by shell bursts, now pressing themselves to the ground under machine-gun fire, now racing forward through the explosions to get closer to the bunkers, the Companies of 100th Regiment worked their way forward. Whenever they halted to regroup Greek soldiers counter-attacked, storming out of the trenches in furious bayonet charges. But with the capture of one large bunker on Kelkaya a turning-point was reached for it was the corner-stone of the whole defensive system on that sector. With that vital complex taken, pillbox after pillbox was knocked out, bunker after bunker fell until 3rd Battalion could announce, early in the afternoon, that Kelkaya had been captured. The Jaeger stood, weary but triumphant on its crest. There was scant time to rest or to rejoice. The fall of Kelkaya allowed the regimental commander to swing his main effort to the centre where 2nd Battalion was embattled, and the weary men of 3rd Battalion came downhill and then climbed uphill to the new battle area. The short spring day, the first day of battle, drew to its close and the exhausted Jaeger dug shallow scrape holes and settled down in the bitterly cold night. There was little sleep; the night was too cold and patrols had to be sent out, the wounded had to be evacuated, the dead collected and all this under machine-gun and mortar fire and infantry counter-attacks. The day, which had been cloudless for the most part, changed with the onset of darkness. Low clouds swept over the peaks reducing visibility to a matter of a few metres and the rain showers of early evening degenerated into first sleet showers and then to a snowstorm which lasted for most of the night. In such conditions to dream of food or relief was masochistic. They were idle fantasies. Reality was a stony hillside in the Greek mountains wrapped in a greatcoat saturated with rain and sleet, and shaking with cold that penetrated every bone, every muscle of the body. There was the feeling that anything – a wound – even death – could not be so terrible and death would at last release the freezing Jaeger from the misery which surrounded him. But at regimental level, behind the front line held by the cold and hungry soldiers, the military machine ran smoothly. Companies were relieved from the front line and there were ration parties which did find their way to bring hot food to the men in the forward positions.

Stand to at dawn found the Jaeger hollow-eyed with exhaustion, awaiting Greek attacks. On some sectors these came in: small, dark men came storming down the slopes with fixed bayonets. On most sectors, however, the day opened with regrouping and reorganization. At 08.00 the Kelkaya Command Centre gave up the fight, but the battle continued for 100th Regiment's other objectives. During the late morning the garrison of Istibei surrendered. The breach in the Metaxas Line was being widened. But still there were positions, mountain peaks and bunkers which had not fallen and which had to be taken out one by one against an unshaken enemy. It was a bitter battle.

For four days Ringel's 5th Gebirgs Division fought its way through the mountains and into the valley. Behind the division there were on the heights still some Greek positions that would not surrender and until they did the Jaeger would have to stay surrounding the blockhouses and bunkers on those icy, lonely and desolate slopes. Rupesco was the last position to fall and with it the fighting for the Metaxas Line came to an end.

The 5th buried 160 dead in the provisional military cemetery, but what the division had achieved was unique – a strong line of permanent defences had fallen to the assaults of lightly armed Gebirgsjaeger.

In XVIII Corps the sister division of Ringel's 5th was Schoerner's 6th Gebirgs Division. The 6th, too, fought in the opening battle to break the Metaxas Line and for the operation was placed on the right flank of 5th Division. The area in which the 6th fought was the Belshanitsa mountain range which runs between Bulgaria and Yugoslavia, and the division's principal task was to thrust southwards through the mountains and gain the valley of the River Kumli.

To accomplish this the divisional assault was carried out by six battalion-sized columns marching side by side. On the extre right flank, almost touching Yugoslavia, the 2nd Battalion, 143rd Jaeger Regiment detached one Company and sent it on a long march westwards towards the Yugoslav border where it protected the division's right flank. The 3rd Battalion was placed in the centre of the regimental line and 1st Battalion, which advanced in two parallel columns, held the left wing. These two columns were to join up as they descended from the mountains into the valley and take out the final regimental objective, the village of Makriaitsa. Its capture would cut the road between Yugoslavia and the Rupel Pass and thereby prevent either a retreat by the Greek forces or their reinforcement. To strengthen the attack by 143rd Regiment its commander had under direct control a Company of Gebirgs pioneers and a battalion of mountain artillery.

The 141st Regiment – the left flank formation – mounted its assault with 2nd Battalion on the right flank, 3rd in the centre and 1st Battalion, which was on the left, touching the right-hand battalion of Ringel's 85th Regiment. Like 143rd Regiment the 141st was reinforced by a pioneer company and two battalions of artillery, one of which had been detached from 5th Division for the duration of the operation. As had been the case for 5th Gebirgs, the Corps battle plan laid emphasis on a quick penetration of the mountain barrier and directed that the artillery was to be used in direct and close-range bombardment. Once the double line of Greek defences had been captured the guns were to be brought forward to give close support to the Jaeger during the final stages of their attack.

Thanks to Schoerner's initiative and drive, as well as the fighting skills of his men, 6th Gebirgs Division battled its way through the mountains and reached the Kumli valley within a day. The defences which still held out were reduced during the second day and Schoerner's regiments then regrouped and moved to assist 5th Division which was still held up in the defensive works of the main Metaxas Line.

A special OKW communiqué dealt with the result of the first operations in Greece. These 'Sondermeldungen' (special announcements) were preceded by fanfares of trumpets and were broadcast to proclaim very special victories. The Sondermeldung on 9 April reported, 'After breaking through the bitterly defended Rupel Pass, German Gebirgsjaeger went on to capture Salonika. The Greek Army, which had been fighting east of the Vardar, realized the hopelessness of its position, offered to capitulate and has laid down its arms.'

Both Gebirgs divisions then fought side by side as Twelfth Army thrust southwards through Greece towards the Corinth Canal. Although one Greek army had capitulated, others were still in the field and these, together with the British Expeditionary Force, fought long and hard to halt the German advance. One such struggle took place at Thermopylae. The Greek–British force which held the ground was carrying out the same role as Leonidas and his Spartans at the time of the Persian Wars. They were to hold the enemy until the rest of the army had escaped. By 20 April, although the main Greek Army had capitulated, some units chose to stay with the British who were holding the Pass against the advancing XVIII Gebirgskorps. During the night of the 23/24th, 6th Division of that Corps sent in the recce battalion and found that the Allied rearguard had withdrawn to new positions. These, in the Oeta mountains, were attacked at dawn on the 25th by 141st Regiment and the Allied defenders were forced back. Athens fell on the following day and the British Expeditionary Force headed towards Corinth and the Peloponnesian ports from which it would be evacuated. The campaign in Greece was at an end.

During the time that 5th and 6th Gebirgs Divisions were fighting in Greece, 1st and 4th Divisions had been campaigning in Yugoslavia. The 1st, forming part of Kuebler's XLIX Gebirgskorps in von Weich's Second Army, attacked out of southern Austria and drove into northern Yugoslavia. The 4th, which originally had been selected to fight in Greece, found itself forming the point formation in von Kleist's 1st Panzer Group as the armour struck into Yugoslavia from the north-east; out of Bulgaria.

The part played by 1st Gebirgs, the premier mountain division on the German Army's establishment, in the new war, so impressed Hitler that during a visit which he made to the division in Kaernten, he described it as a 'Guards' formation. His laudatory words were the measure of its achievements in that short but sharp campaign.

It will be recalled that a war with Yugoslavia had not formed part of the original Operation 'Marita' and that when 'Marita' had to be extended to include that country, Second Army was given scant time to prepare a plan of campaign. To bring it up to a strength OKH took units from all round Europe. For the specialist task of breaking through the mountain barrier which separates Austria from Yugoslavia, it chose 1st Gebirgs Division which was in the Jura mountains of France as part of the army of occupation. The 1st had been posted to the Jura at the end of the war in the west and after the excitements and disappointments of the aborted operations 'Sealion' and 'Felix' the division might have expected to remain on occupation duties for the remainder of the war, but in March orders came for it to move eastwards, or more correctly, south-eastwards – into the Balkans.

The movement by rail across Europe of a division at full war establishment was a task which could not be accomplished in a single lift nor in the short time which was allotted. To avoid overstraining the railway network part of the 1st travelled from the Jura by road. The Jaeger who went by truck were not to know that they were to travel 1,200 kilometres, to Kaernten, the southernmost province of Austria. Elfriede Roesch was an 8-year-old girl living in the Steiermark and saw trains filled with Jaeger at Graz main station. 'My parents took me to the railway station which was packed with people. When I look today at the photographs which were taken at that time I can see that there were not only civilians and soldiers on the station but also Nazi Party officials, looking very important, bathing in the reflected glory of being with the troops. There were also the Party organizations, the Hitler Youth and the League of German Girls. I remember that I wished to be old enough to be in that League so that I could wear a uniform. The soldiers were leaning out of the train windows and people were handing up to them bottles of beer and all sorts of food. My father said that he carried me on his shoulders and that he worked his way through the crowd to a train window. I had a little packet of goodies, some home-made biscuits and some sweets, all neatly wrapped. I handed the packet to one of the soldiers. He asked my name and thanked me very much. Then other people pressed forward to hand over their gifts. We all stood there in the station until the train left and we all waved our little flags until it went round the curve and out of sight. The soldiers were going off to war. I knew nothing of what war meant. To me that day had been one of excitement and full of colour.'

Another young girl who saw the units of Second Army moving through the Steiermark to take part in the campaign in Yugoslavia, was Helma Oswald, née Auer. She was at that time a 13-year-old living in Gnas in the eastern part of Steiermark – the Oststeier. For days the roads leading from northern Austria down towards Yugoslavia were packed with infantry columns. One of these passed through the village of Gnas where Helma was a school-girl.

'There had been a great deal of movement for days but nothing closer to us than Feldbach. We heard rumours about some sort of trouble in Yugoslavia. There had been no fighting since the end of the French campaign [June 1940] and we all thought that the war was over. Then we heard more rumours that some sort of main headquarters had been set up in Wolfsberg and lesser headquarters in nearby towns. But so far as we were concerned all that excitement was still far away. It had not touched us.'

'We were at our lessons when the teacher told us that school was finished for the time being because soldiers were about to march through our little village. That was quite exciting. We rushed out and there passing the church was the tailend of one group. Then entering Gnas from the Feldbach side came a new column. At its head were officers riding on horses and behind them soldiers in columns of three or four abreast. They filled the village road completely. Soldiers we had all seen but never so many at any one time. Some people brought out buckets of water, milk, bottles of beer and had cut up loaves of bread. These were handed to the soldiers as they marched by and they were very grateful. We school children were kept together and were quite sad that we had nothing to give to the marching men. As the officers rode by the spot where we were standing our teacher shouted out, "These are our boys, the Gebirgsjaeger. Let's cheer our Gebirgsjaeger." and we all cheered. The column marched through and all the soldiers were laughing as if going out to war was a most enjoyable thing. The memory I have of that morning is of those laughing faces and the reply which one soldier gave to the question, "Where are you going?" I think he shouted back Crete, but I must have misheard or misunderstood his reply. It took a long time for the regiments to pass through Gnas but eventually the sound of boots clumping through the village faded away. All the people in the village square were discussing what was happening, or what was likely to happen because there had been no declaration of war. Then with school finished for the day we all went home.'

A succession of special trains and columns of heavy trucks carried the heavy equipment of the division to the concentration area in southern Austria and divisional headquarters was set up in Wolfsberg, some 20 kilometres from the frontier. Although by 8 April a number of units were in position, a certain confusion in the matter of loading schedules resulted in some reaching the area only to find that their train detachments had not yet even arrived in Vienna. The situation in the frontier area was, as can be imagined, very tense, but in order not to alarm or to warn the Yugoslavs the usual frontier guard detachments and local militia remained on duty. As each Jaeger group arrived it sent out patrols to check on roads and tracks in its area, and establish the number and load capacity of bridges. It was also given details on the strength, disposition and arms of the Yugoslav formations facing it.

The units began to close up to the frontier and small patrols of Jaeger facing the Drau slipped across to check on the permanent defences which the Yugoslavs had erected on their side of the river. Road and rail delays meant that a major part of the division was still en route and had not reached the concentration area. There was deep concern that the burden of the fighting to come would have to be borne by those units, principally the detachments of 99th Regiment, that had arrived and which were now in their jump-off positions. It was, of course, not possible to delay the opening of the campaign and upset the OKH time-table merely because 1st Gebirgs Division had not arrived and been concentrated. Kuebler, GOC of XLIX Corps, issued orders that the division was to attack on a front between Bleiburg and Lavamund, break through the Yugoslav defence line between Pollein and Unterdrauburg and then advance in a double column upon Cilli. The divisional commander created two battle groups; Kress, which was to form the right hand column and Lang, on the left.

Operations began on 8 April when local militia detachments crossed the frontier and seized some wooded heights. This short and swift raid opened the road for Battle Group Kress which took the first bunker line on both sides of Pollein, crossed the River Misbach and captured the pillboxes which dominated the open ground running down to the river's bank. Kress Group then pushed southwards to capture several areas of high ground overlooking the area through which the advance would next be taken. On the sector around Unterdrauburg the division's assault pioneers crossed the Drau during the night of 8/9 April and formed a small bridgehead on the river's southern bank. A little to the east of Unterdrauburg another Jaeger group had crossed the River Mur and an account of that crossing was supplied by Alois Redl. He recalled that an article had been written in the Corps newspaper describing how an Oberfeldwebel had carried out the assault; an exploit for which he was awarded the Knight's Cross.

'The Oberfeldwebel's plan was to take his patrol by assault boat across the Mur, entering the water some distance below the bridge. He would then take out the enemy positions [a Customs post with a large garrison of soldiers and behind it a bunker with a field of fire which dominated the bridge]. At dawn his group launched their craft and began to paddle across the Mur. Before they were halfway across an alert Yugoslav sentry saw them and opened fire . . . Half swimming and half wading the patrol reached the enemy bank and . . . shot dead a Yugoslav sentry. The Oberfeldwebel rushed past the body and flung hand-grenades in at the windows. The men inside the Customs building surrendered. By this time the soldiers in the bunker had opened fire and our battalion's engineers could not cross the bridge to remove the explosive charges. One of the battle patrol spotted the detonating cable and cut it with the blade of his entrenching tool. The sergeant fired a Very light to signal that the patrol was going into the last stage of the operation – the capture of the bunker. The patrol members gave the NCO covering fire as he charged

forward and flung explosive charges into the slits in the walls of the
bunker . . . Engineers took out the fuzes [of the charges in the bridge] and
an infantry Company stormed across to reinforce the battle patrol. The
bunker was taken. The road forward was clear for Second Army.'

Both battle group columns were now making goods progress, chiefly
because opposition had been very light. The enemy troops had withdrawn from their poorly sited outpost positions and had allowed the
Jaegers' first push – as the Germans said – to 'run into empty space'. The
situation changed as the Jaeger closed up to some wooded heights south
of the Misbach. There the defences hardened and they began to meet stiff
and determined resistance. In a sense they were victims of their own
success. The speed with which the divisional advance had been carried
forward had brought the complication that both columns were operating
in isolation without any contact between them. Nor could there be until a
line of pillboxes in the valley of the Misbach were taken. The only unit
which division could spare to carry out this task was the anti-tank
Company of 99th Regiment; the artillerymen, covered by the fire of a
single gun, raced forward, knocking out one bunker after another until
the whole line had been cleared. The two battle groups were now in
touch. There remained, however, another more urgent problem; there
were too few Jaeger in the battle line and this if not of serious concern,
certainly demanded a quick solution. So rather than rest the Jaeger
Companies as they arrived by road and rail into the concentration area,
they were rushed at top speed to strengthen the divisional assault.

The first day of the new war came to an end and the Jaeger,
exhausted by the double strain of marching and fighting, sank wearily to
the ground. Many slept where they fell and woke to find themselves
soaked from the rain which had begun to fall soon after last light. During
the second day of the campaign Kress's column passed along a valley to
reach Crna and then climbed out of that to cross the St Vid Pass. Spring
had come late to the mountains and the road through the pass was coated
with thick ice over which the battle group passed only slowly and with
great difficulty. The valley beyond the pass and which the battle group
now entered was a natural killing ground; narrow and dominated by
wooded heights in which a whole division might have hidden. The day's
march had wearied the Jaeger and rather than risk a night assault with
tired troops, Kress halted the attack, intending to resume it on the
morrow when fresh supplies had come forward, and when, as he hoped,
reinforcements might also have reached him. Another advantage was
that his men would have had a good night's rest.

It was as well that he had halted to consolidate for, during the night
of 10/11 April, a motor-cycle platoon, acting as point unit, was attacked
and sustained heavy losses. At daybreak the Yugoslavs withdrew into the
thick woods on each side of the pass and offered no opposition to Kress
Group as it pushed on towards Cilli. During that day it reached the town
and gained touch with Lang's column which had thrust swiftly southwards from Unterdrauburg against medium to heavy opposition and had

been the first to reach the divisional objective. The 1st Division should then have halted in Cilli, so that the rear echelons could come forward and the Division could be, at last, firmly grouped. A rest period was out of the question for Lang's battle group which was ordered out on a new mission. Lang created a smaller column, a fully motorized group, and sent this out to undertake a swift drive to capture Agram [Zagreb]. By this time the Yugoslav Army seemed to be in a state of dissolution and such units of it as were met on the road consisted of men without weapons and all of them heading for their homes. It seemed to many Jaeger that the end of the campaign could not be far off, but this was not a true assessment of the situation. At Second Army level it was believed that the Yugoslav High Command was pulling its main strength back into the mountains of Bosnia and intended, perhaps, to hold that trackless and arid area.

En route to Agram the battle group received new orders. It was to retrace its steps and drive with best possible speed to Rudolfswerth on the River Gurk. There it was to carry out an assault crossing of the Gurk and to establish a bridghead on its southern bank. Second Army had begun to plan for the pursuit of the Yugoslav forces into Bosnia and needed a bridghead out of which its divisions could erupt to drive upon the town of Bihac before going on to gain Sarajevo, the capital city of Bosnia. On the 13th Bihac was taken without a struggle and as Lang's small group was preparing to resume the pursuit during the afternoon of the 14th, an order from Corps halted it. New orders took the division back into southern Austria where it spent a few weeks resting and refitting before heading by road and rail into Czechoslovakia. The twelve-day war against Yugoslavia was at an end. Would that victory now bring peace to Europe was the question many Jaeger asked themselves?

1st and 4th Gebirgs Divisions in Yugoslavia, 1941

I T HAD BEEN OKH's original intention to use three Gebirgs Divisions, 4th, 5th and 6th, to smash the Metaxas Line and then for them to advance into mainland Greece. The volte-face of the new and anti-German government in Belgrade meant, as we have seen, a change to Operation 'Marita'. This meant for 4th Gebirgs Division that it was to take part in the campaign against Yugoslavia. Thereby, its axis of advance changed from south towards Greece to almost due west. This redeployment involved the regiments in a march from their original concentration areas to new ones on the Yugoslav–Bulgarian border. It will be readily understood that half a century ago the rural areas of the Balkans were unsuited to the passage of modern armies. The roads were few in number and poor in quality. There was only one all-weather highway in 4th Division's new theatre of operations and that ran between Sofia and Belgrade, the Bulgarian and Yugoslav capital cities. The first task of von Kleist's Panzer Group 1, in which 4th Gebirgs Division was serving, was to reach and hold that part of the highway which wound through the mountains from the Bulgarian frontier as far as Nisch in Yugoslavia. There part of Kleist's Panzer Group would cross the River Morava. With only a brief pause to regroup it would then drive north-westwards towards Belgrade, a city which would by that time be under attack from Second Army coming down from Austria, as well as by a third blow being made out of Roumania.

The re-alignment of 4th Division to face Yugoslavia was no easy task and although movement on the Bulgarian plains, where it was already spring, was comparatively trouble free, this was not the case as the units entered the mountains where winter conditions still obtained. Deep snow and ice, with their inhibiting effect upon movement, were met with at only modest altitudes. Aware of the difficulties which the 4th would encounter in moving its heavy guns through the Petrohan Pass, a Bulgarian divisional commander lent the division 600 oxen, but even with that additional help the 4th's passage through the mountains required two whole days. The redeployment ended during the morning of 7 April, and XLIX Corps promptly issued orders that operations were to open on the following day. The task of the 4th Division's Jaeger regiments was to occupy and advance through the high ground on both sides of the Sofia–Nisch highway, an action which would prevent Yugoslav units from striking into the flanks and halting the advance of 11th Panzer Division as it thrust up the highway.

It is interesting to note from orders issued by 2nd Battalion, 13th Gebirgsjaeger Regiment that haversack rations for three days were to be carried. It was clear that during the seventy-two hours fighting of the opening assault the Companies could expect no issue of hot food. The battalion orders also directed that the Companies start their march to the form-up point at midnight on the 7th so as to be in position in time to cross the start-line at 05.30 on the 8th. During the evening of the 7th, rain fell and the temperature began to drop so that by midnight it was well below freezing point. In that bitter cold the Jaeger of the assault Companies began their climb and were soon sweating with the effort. They were aware that once they stopped climbing and settled down to wait for H-Hour, they would be bitterly cold. They ascended as silently as possible, given that there were more than 1,100 men scrambling across loose shale. Division had directed that there be no clattering of equipment and had stressed that no lights were to be shown. This meant no smoking, and the Jaeger, now waiting for the dawn, sat cold, tired and without the comfort of tobacco on the windswept, snowy mountain slopes.

Division had planned that its main effort would be on the right, or northern side of the road and that 13th Regiment would carry that burden, so it is 13th's part in the battle that is related here. Two battalions of the regiment were placed on the right flank, together with the divisional recce battalion and the heavy weapons groups. On the southern side of the road was 2nd Battalion which, initially, had been detached from 4th Division to strengthen 6th Gebirgs Division's assault on the Metaxas Line. When its employment in that role was seen to be no longer necessary, 2nd Battalion was ordered to return to its parent formation and it moved at top speed across country so as to take part in the division's opening assault. Arriving as it did at the last moment, it could not be inserted into the battle line between 1st and 3rd Battalions on the northern side of the road, and accordingly fought in isolation on the southern side. Punctually at 05.30, the heavy howitzer batteries of 844 Artillery Battalion, supported by the 10cm batteries of 2nd Battalion, 60th Artillery Regiment, opened fire and as the shells crashed down on the Yugoslav Customs post and the heights around it the Jaeger assault groups moved off. The 4th was going into battle for the first time. The fury of the barrage at first paralysed the Yugoslavs but they soon recovered and opened a withering fire with rifles and machine-guns on the long files of Jaeger toiling up the slope. Forward observation officers with the leading Jaeger files switched the fire of their guns from target to target, smothering each enemy position with a storm of high-explosives which forced the Yugoslav troops to pull back from their exposed positions on the mountain crest and into the comparative protection of the reverse slope. Although shellfire had driven the enemy infantry from their positions, they were by no means shattered and defended with rare tenacity the isolated and scattered villages which had been fortified and converted to strongpoints.

The Yugoslav units holding the area were not only skilled infantry-men but were themselves mountain men who knew every good defensive position and exploited to the full the advantages of their local knowledge. Whenever the Jaeger had to cross open ground, snipers and machine-gunners struck, inflicting casualties and in some places forcing the Companies to go to ground. Radio messages to the heavy weapons Companies soon brought teams rushing into action, man-handling the infantry guns or dragging the heavy mortars into positions from which they could deal with the stubborn defenders. By late in the morning it was clear to the regimental commander that more than five hours of wearisome and costly battle had blunted the edge of his attack. A halt was ordered so that the Jaeger could rest and regroup, but the artillery was to continue firing upon known or suspected strongpoints. The infantry attack was to resume at 13.15. The guns, whose operations had been reduced to 'harassing' fire, stepped up the pace of their bombardment as the time came for the Jaeger to swing back into the assault, a battle which was to continue until last light. Then, when the fighting died away, it was a matter of tired men whose stomachs rumbled with hunger, standing guard in shallow scrape holes throughout the long night. It was too cold to sleep and the day's haversack rations had long since been eaten. Rain and low clouds cut down visibility and nerves were strained as the Jaeger listened for evidence of an enemy attack. It was recorded that, generally, the night passed peacefully with only weak enemy assaults and these made on just a few isolated sectors.

This was the pattern of the fighting for the rest of the short offensive. Strong enemy resistance in the morning of each day which diminished as the day wore on. Much of this early morning resistance was from snipers and *francs-tireurs* who opened fire upon runners and signallers making their lonely way from Company to Battalion Headquarters. The snipers were an accepted risk, but the guerrilla was a vicious enemy who was hunted ruthlessly. During the second week of April the weather worsened with driving snowstorms and sub-zero temperatures. Day after day the Jaeger fought their way up into the mountains or descended into the valleys, climbing along goat tracks or across trackless terrain to reach the crests of the mountains that were their objectives. Pirot, an intermediate objective on the road to Nisch, would soon be within striking distance and then the terrain would no longer be high and glacial mountains, but gentle foothills. When that time came Division would have carried out its orders to penetrate the mountain barrier. In its advance 4th Gebirgs had fought a tough and uncompromising enemy and had struck him hard. A contemporary report on the fighting spoke of the completeness of the defeat of the enemy's Krajinska Division. In the valley of the River Morava, there were guns and ox-drawn ammunition trains abandoned by the Yugoslav division as it fled.

Yugoslavia's capitulation on 17 April brought the twelve-day campaign to an end and 4th Gebirgs Division spent a few months in the army of occupation before entraining – not for Germany as many had believed and all had hoped – but to eastern Hungary. From there the regiments set out on long foot marches through Poland. The German Army was heading eastwards and in the east the only enemy powers were the Soviet Union and the British Empire in India. The latter was an exciting prospect, and belief that the Jaeger were to invade the sub-continent was fuelled by every type of wild rumour, but the truth was soon to become known; the next enemy would be the Red Army.

5th Gebirgs Division in Crete, 1941

ORIGINALLY, the High Command had not planned that a Gebirgsjaeger division would take part in the battle for Crete. The operation was to have featured only Luftwaffe forces. Paratroops and glider-borne detachments were to seize the airfields on to which aircraft carrying the 22nd Air Landing Division would land. The airborne forces would then go on to enlarge the original bridgeheads and capture the island. The OKW warning that 22nd Division was not available for the operation meant that a replacement formation had to be found. This had to be one that was already in the Balkan theatre and which was experienced in combat in mountainous terrain. From the Gebirgs divisions available in Greece OKW selected Ringel's 5th. An operational order, dated 3 May, detailed the role that his division was to play in a campaign which was to open in less than three weeks. With his accustomed energy Ringel set to work planning and preparing for the new operation.

The battlefield on which 5th Division was to fight was a mountainous island about 260 kilometres in length and between 20 and 50 kilometres in width. Crete lies in the eastern Mediterranean, some 100 kilometres from the southernmost point of the Greek mainland, and is divided by four mountain ranges. The two relevant to this account are the White Mountains in the west of the island and these lead into a central massif, the Ida range. It was across these ranges that the Gebirgsjaeger were to fight. This treeless and barren region was, in 1941, almost unexplored. The civilian population did not, generally, go into the mountains. There was nothing there to find or to do. As a consequence, the area had few roads or paths and much of it was said to be impassable.

The operational orders laid down that no mules or pack-animals were to be brought to the island. This meant that everything would have to be man-carried. Each mouthful of food, every round of ammunition and each bottle of water would have to be carried. The last named was very important because there were no natural sources of water in either the White or Ida ranges. The need to form carrying-detachments would, of course, reduce the number of Jaeger in the fighting echelons. The heavy equipment, chiefly the mountain artillery, mortars and machine-guns, would have to be broken down into man-sized loads and carried by Ringel's soldiers through an arid, almost trackless wilderness.

The operational order was issued on 3 May and D-Day for 'Mercury', as the new campaign was code-named, was set for 20 May. Time was short and the staff officers at 5th Divisional HQ had a great number of difficulties to overcome. The first was transport. The Luftwaffe had too few transport aircraft to lift both the assault detachments – the Fallschirmjaeger and the air landing component, 5th Gebirgs Division. There were, in fact, too few aircraft to fly all the Fallschirmjaeger in one lift. There would have to be two para drops; one in the early morning of D-Day and the second during the afternoon. The task of the airborne troops was to capture the airfields at Heraklion, Canea and Maleme, all of which were on the northern side of the island. Canea and Heraklion were intended to be the principal objectives, but Maleme, where the first firm perimeter was formed, became the airfield towards which the German main effort swung and where it was then concentrated.

At this stage of the war, not only did the Luftwaffe have insufficient transport aircraft but those they had were not capable of carrying heavy and bulky loads, so all the heavy equipment of both 7th Para and 5th Gebirgs Division was to be taken by ship from ports in southern Greece. The movement of the 5th to Crete would have to be made by air and by sea. The airborne wave was to be landed on the short and primitive runways of Maleme. The second wave would accompany the heavy weapons and would be carried in ships.

Ringel had been given a free hand in the matter of procurement of vessels to carry his regiments, and although he received little help from the Kriegsmarine and despite the fact that a great many Greek seamen deserted their ships before sailing, did manage to commandeer and man 63 vessels. Twenty-five of these were caiques, Greek fishing boats whose sails were augmented by a low-powered auxiliary engine. Each caique was expected to carry a Company of Jaeger, about 90 men, and the other 38 commandeered vessels were to transport 4,000 men and most of the heavy equipment. The destination of the first, or caique, convoy was Maleme. The second convoy was to head for Heraklion, on the north coast, in the central part of the island.

It was planned that because of their slowness and mechanical unreliability the caique convoy would have to depart from the ports of southern Greece well before D-Day, so as to debark their troops shortly after the first airborne landings had gone in. The Heraklion convoy was scheduled to leave at dawn on D-Day and was expected to arrive in the late evening of that day. Certain factors affected the smooth running of 'Mercury'. The first was that the airborne operation did not gain the airfields on the island's north coast as quickly as had been expected. The only major foothold was at Maleme and with their usual speed of decision the High Command officers changed the destination of the second convoy. Both convoys were then directed to sail to Maleme. The second factor, and one affecting the Jaeger role in 'Mercury', was that the convoys were intercepted by the Royal Navy and shot to pieces.

The caique flotilla was transporting 3rd Battalion, 100th Gebirgs-jaeger Regiment, and it set out from Piraeus during the evening of 19 May. The speed of any convoy is determined by that of its slowest vessel, and the fastest rate that the caiques could achieve was 7 knots. The reports received in Greece about the fighting on Crete were confused. As

a consequence of this uncertainty, High Command then delayed the
sailing of both convoys. Eventually, with the situation on Crete finally
resolved, the order to sail was given and the convoys set out but were
caught during the night of 21/22 May by the warships of Admiral
Cunningham's Mediterranean Fleet. It has been mentioned earlier, in the
chapter on the Narvik operation, that the sea was an element unfamiliar
to the men of the mountains. Consider then their feelings as in the dark of
the night the ships in which they were sailing came under attack by three
Royal Navy cruisers and four destroyers. At about 2300, some five
nautical miles north of Cape Spatha, the British ships opened fire. For
hours they hunted the wooden hulled Greek fishing boats but were
forced to break off the engagement and sail away from the area at first
light. By night the seas belonged to the Royal Navy, but the Luftwaffe
ruled the skies by day. Meanwhile another group of British ships, under
orders to enter the Aegean, was sailing northwards in broad daylight
when shortly before 0830 its radar sets picked up the vessels of the second
flotilla, twenty nautical miles from Milos. Action stations was piped and
the British ships opened fire. Some time later the Luftwaffe appeared
overhead, causing the warships to run for home, leaving behind them the
shattered wrecks of the second convoy. Accounts by the survivors of the
British naval attacks have been summarized to prevent repetition of the
salient points.

'We were aware of the sinister significance of those low, narrow,
grey-painted ships that moved towards us and knew that our slow-
moving tubs could not outrun them. We were all crammed together on
the deck and the order came for us to put on our life-jackets. We hauled
down the rusty red sail of the caique and stopped the engine. Our officer
had told us that if it came to it and we had to abandon ship, at least we
would be jumping into the hostile sea from a stable and halted platform
and not from a moving one whose stern screw might cut us to pieces. I
heard later that one Company commander ordered all the non-swimmers
on his ship to get into the life-rafts which were then launched. Certainly
there were rafts filled with men floating about . . . Our Lieutenant gave
orders for us to stand fast but to be prepared to jump overboard if he
ordered it. We stood on deck facing outwards and our boat rocked
violently as the whole sea was a turmoil. Destroyers raced about creating
huge waves which threw our boats about while above them our Stukas
dived down dropping bombs whose explosions raised geysers of water
and all the time our caique wallowed about trying to avoid the gunfire
and hoping to hide itself in the smokescreen which the Italian ship [the
escort destroyer *Lupo*] was trying to lay . . .

'A few caiques were sinking and ours suddenly turned over. She had
been hit by shells but these had hit high and had exploded in the rigging
and masts. None, so far as I knew, had hit the actual vessel. But suddenly
she went over and we were all flung into the sea. Now that was really
frightening, especially when the British ships came steaming towards us.
Some of our casualties were caused when Jaeger were run down by the

ships. One body I saw had shocking damage caused to it. I cannot remember much noise, although there must have been a considerable amount of it. I do remember the concussion of exploding bombs, even far away ones, for they seemed to burst my whole body. I hauled myself on to some wreckage and found I still had on my waist-belt, water-bottle and bayonet. I drank some water and felt a lot better for it. Some time later, an hour or two perhaps, a Ju 52 flew over the scene. It seemed to me as if I were the only living person in the whole area. The British had gone, some caiques were burning, there was lots of rubbish in the water and lots of German soldiers, chiefly Gebirgsjaeger, all of whom seemed to be dead. Then another aircraft came along – a seaplane – and began slowly cruising about. When it came over to me I stepped from my wood pile on the float and was helped into the body of the machine where a couple of Jaeger were already lying. So I hadn't been the only living thing. The aeroplane flew us back to Greece and to a divisional rest camp. I never actually set foot on Crete.'

Many of the Jaeger in the caique convoy who were now swimming for their lives organized themselves into detachments and towed life-rafts, filled with their badly wounded comrades, towards the north shore of Crete. Confronted by sheer cliffs which they could not scale, the exhausted men headed out to sea again and were among the 178 rescued by aircraft of the air-sea rescue service. A further 64 Jaeger were picked up by launches. The War Diary of 5th Gebirgs Division recorded with pride that one group of Jaeger which reached divisional headquarters almost naked and suffering from exposure were still carrying their weapons. Losses among the sea-borne component had been heavy and one battalion which had suffered 300 dead was temporarily destroyed as a fighting formation and could take no part in the land fighting. Of the two battalions of men who had embarked to sail to Crete, only 52 saw action; a single platoon in strength out of the regiment which had set sail with such high hopes.

Meanwhile, on the island, the paratroops were fighting, out-numbered but buoyed-up in the belief that reinforcement was coming by sea. The destruction of the convoys presented the High Command with the problem of how to reinforce the Fallschirmjaeger. Although the airfield at Maleme was still under artillery and machine-gun fire, it was the only one that could be used. Neither the airstrip at Heraklion nor that at Canea had yet been captured. The main effort at reinforcement must, therefore be made at Maleme, irrespective of losses, and it was upon that airfield's short and dusty runway that the Junkers carrying the Jaeger reinforcements were ordered to land. Touchdown under fire was an extremely hazardous enterprise and at Maleme it was made even more dangerous because the runway was littered with the wrecks of aircraft smashed as they had attempted to land. The Luftwaffe pilots bringing in the transports had to avoid these wrecks and taxi along the short and crowded strip. The Jaeger then deplaned, usually running crouched and with their heads bowed as if to avoid the intense fire which was being poured down upon them by the New Zealander defenders. They raced across the bullet-strewn ground to fling themselves into the slit trenches which marked the Para perimeter. With their Jaeger passengers now safely deplaned the pilots then had to swing the huge metal aircraft, give full power to the engines and take-off, still under fire. Overhead other Jus waited to make their own run-in, noting the billowing, obscuring clouds of dust which overhung the airfield and which destroyed visibility. A single statistic shows the difficulty of the build-up operation. The quickest turn-round time from landing to take-off was ten minutes and each aircraft could carry only a dozen men. Thus to airlift a single battalion took more than four hours.

The huge, slow-flying transports came under attack from AA artillery and some were intercepted and shot down by one of the few Hurricanes which made fast sorties over the island. Given the ground fire and RAF aircraft deployed, it goes without saying that there were some remarkable escapes when the Junkers made forced landings. The Jaeger in one Ju 52 which had been hit and was on fire, sat calmly in their seats until the pilot had pancaked the aircraft on the sea just off shore. They then climbed out of the fuselage and waded from the sinking aircraft to the beach.

The airlift progressed; more Jaeger were brought in and slowly the small perimeter was expanded. By midday on 22 May a battalion of Jaeger had been airlanded at Maleme to reinforce the Para perimeter. Ringel then assumed command over all the forces on Crete. His immediate task was to establish contact with the Para units isolated in the central sector of the island before capturing Canea and Suda Bay and then going on to clear the British forces from the remainder of the island. The 2nd Battalion, 100th Regiment and 1st Battalion, 85th Regiment were both airlanded as was 95th Pioneer Battalion. With these reinforcements Ringel could now take the initiative and expand both eastwards and southwards out of the perimeter. Before doing this he sent detachments to clear his back by destroying the enemy forces in the area to the west of Maleme. That done, he could thrust into the main part of the island.

From battlefield conferences with para officers and from his own assessment of the situation, Ringel appreciated that Freyberg, commanding the British and Imperial forces, had disposed his units along the northern coastal strip, in anticipation of an assault landing from the sea. The remnant of 5 Brigade of 2nd New Zealand Division garrisoned the west of the island and had the task of defending Maleme airfield. An Australian brigade defended the town and the area around Retimo, while a brigade from the British Army held the area around Heraklion and the town itself. The Imperial forces were, therefore, spread out along the length of the island in small groups with little liaison between them. These Imperial groups mounted counter-attacks and had great success in containing the initial para and glider-borne landings. Ringel realized that the defenders were under pressure from the aggressive Fallschirmjaeger and that each group was concerned about the defence of its own sector with little or no central direction. The enemy would not be expecting an assault from the mountains and Ringel's obvious move was to create battle groups one of which would move swiftly through the mountains and strike into the enemy's left flank.

Three battle groups were formed. The first of these, made up of the Gebirgs pioneer battalion and some heavy weapons, was to defend the town of Maleme and also fight its way into the western part of the island and destroy any enemy encountered there. They would, thus, be fighting a two-front battle. The second group was a para formation commanded by Colonel Ramcke whose task it was to seal off Maleme to the east against any probe which the New Zealand battalions might make. With these first two battle groups formed and fighting, Ringel knew that Maleme and the vital airfield outside the town were secure both to the east and to the west. The third battle group, commanded by Colonel Utz, a composite group made up of battalions from 85th and 100th Regiments, was to thrust through the White Mountains. The advance of 1st Battalion, 85th Regiment was pushed towards Platanias until its leading elements reached a point near Modion. Up to that time the march, though arduous, had been uncontested. But Modion was held by a New Zealand group whose accurate and rapid rifle fire stopped the Jaeger advance completely. Immediately behind 1st/85th, the second battalion of the battle group, 1st/100th Regiment, seeing the advance of the sister battalion halted in front of the village, swung wide and came in upon the village from the flank. Modion fell but this was not the end of the affair. The local Kiwi commander then put in a series of counter-attacks to recapture the village, but these were too weak to throw back the Jaeger and, indeed, 1/85th carried out further attacks which began to force the defenders back towards the coast. The 5 Brigade's battle line pivoted on a dominant hill, Point 259, which the defenders were determined to hold and the Jaeger to capture.

The New Zealanders were armed with rifles and Bren guns backed by a few mortars and EY rifles, which projected a hand-grenade over a distance of about 100 metres. The Gebirgsjaeger were only a little better armed. Their machine-guns could be tripod-mounted to give them extra range and they had a greater number of mortars. That was all. What then developed around Point 259 was a true soldiers' battle; one in which combat skill, use of ground and determination were displayed by both sides. It was not a *matériel* battle featuring masses of artillery, armour or aircraft – just men. The Jaeger had the advantage of numbers, but the New Zealanders had the advantage of the higher ground. In the heat of the afternoon the leading Companies of 1st/100th opened their attack and moved towards the crest of Point 259, covered and supported by flank fire from 1st/85th's machine-gunners. The assaulting Jaeger of 100th Regiment used the ground well, advancing by bounds against enemy positions which they could not yet identify. The Kiwi troops had sited their trenches well and had camouflaged them expertly. The stifling heat of a late spring afternoon enfolded the Jaeger as they trudged uphill. Where the ground did not favour them and they came into view of the defenders the full force of the enemy's accurate fire was poured down upon them and they took casualties. When the advance faltered, as it occasionally did in that hail of bullets, the New Zealanders, quick to exploit the hesitation, rose out of their slit trenches and sangars and took the bayonet to the Jaeger. But the defence by a single battalion, however gallant and well conducted, could not prevail against the co-ordinated action of two Jaeger battalions, and by nightfall on the 23rd, the crest was in the hands of 1st/100th. Both Gebirgsjaeger battalions were now poised on the left or landward flank of 5 Brigade, but the New Zealander brigadier's resolve was not weakened until 2nd/100th reached the Modion area. Against such a concentration of enemy strength the commander realized that he could no longer hold the ground. To avoid his battalions being cut off he ordered a withdrawal eastwards. In the darkness of the night 5 Brigade began to pull back towards Canea. The chief consequence of this was that British guns no longer dominated Maleme airfield. An uninterrupted flow of reinforcements soon began to flow in.

The Luftwaffe's speed of operations was impressive and soon one aircraft was being turned round every three minutes. These transport aircraft brought in not only men but light artillery, anti-tank guns and mortars. With that accretion in strength the battle began to swing in favour of the German forces and when the motor-cycle battalion of the 5th landed on Crete, the division gained the mobility it had so far lacked. Ringel ordered the main body of the motor-cycle battalion to drive southwards through the mountains, to reach the coast on the south side of the island and capture the ports from which a British evacuation would have to be made. Then he regrouped his regiments and prepared the next phase of the campaign, the drive into the heart of the island. The opening move of his new offensive would be an advance up the Aliakanu–Canea road to take Galatas and relieve Heydrich's paratroops who were still holding out there. Touch with the Fallschirmjaeger was gained during 24/25 May, but the New Zealanders held Galatas too strongly for it to be taken by the few troops which Ringel had to hand. Either that objective must wait for reinforcements to come up or else the British must be forced to abandon it. Ringel decided to commit a battle group to a frontal attack against Galatas as soon as a second battle group, under Colonel Krakau, had completed a fast outflanking march of 80 kilometres through the mountains. The outflanking force would have to move quickly. Until it reached a position behind the New Zealanders' front and cut the Canea–Retimo road to the east of Suda bay, the assault on Galatas could not be launched. The success of these two operations would force Freyberg, the British commander, to withdraw his forces into the east of the island. In this two-part operation let us first follow the Galatas group and then go on to Colonel Krakau's report on the outflanking operation carried out by 85th Regiment.

The battle group committed to the Galatas operation was made up of two Fallschirmjaeger detachments and two battalions of 100th Regiment.

The main burden of the attack would be carried by the Gebirgsjaeger supported by Stuka dive-bombers and Messerschmitt fighters. Galatas was a naturally strong defensive position set on high ground and having observation over the roads Agia Marina–Canea and Alikianu–Canea. Galatas, the last natural defence line west of Suda, was the key to Canea just as Canea was the key to Suda, the British naval base on Crete. If Suda fell the Royal Navy would have no base on the island and the British would have to evacuate Crete. The 1st/100th on the right flank was to take the high ground to the north of Galatas, and 2nd/100th on the left was ordered to capture the town. It will be recalled that the Regiment's 3rd Battalion had been lost at sea when the caique flotilla was sunk. The 1st and 2nd Battalions moved over their form-up lines shortly after midday and opened the attack at 1700. The 1st/100th went in, covered by the indirect fire of Fallschirmjaeger machine-gunners, with three Companies in line abreast moving uphill towards the objective. The situation which had obtained around Modion some days earlier was repeated. The assault faltered under heavy New Zealander fire and when it did the unshaken Kiwis launched spirited bayonet charges. But the Jaeger advance could not be resisted for long and within two and a half hours the first patrols had penetrated Galatas, but at a cost of sixteen of their number who lay dead on the slopes of the hill. It was a confused and bitter battle with the Kiwis contesting the Jaeger advance. To hold the advance of 100th Regiment, the New Zealanders attacked with what the German battle diary called tanks, but which must have been Bren gun carriers. These were knocked out by anti-tank rifles, but then the gunners were themselves attacked by their bayonet-wielding opponents. Dusk brought no end to the battle and it continued throughout the night. The Kiwis put in a swift thrust at dawn and this drove 1st Battalion from Galatas but the Companies rallied and went into a counter-attack. Meanwhile 2nd Battalion had moved off with two Companies 'up': No 6 on the left and No 7 on the right, with No 8 in reserve. The advance by the two battalions began to lose pace, so to strengthen the regimental effort the colonel of the 100th concentrated into one group all his machine-guns and saturated the New Zealand positions on the high ground with fire. The arrival in the area of the PAK (anti-tank) Company and mountain artillery batteries decided the outcome of the battle. During the night 5 Brigade pulled out, leaving Galatas a charnel-house with Germans and New Zealanders linked in a comradeship of death. The road to Canea and to Suda was open, forcing Freyberg, the British commander on Crete, to accept the inevitable. He would have to withdraw his forces from the island. We have seen how 100th Regiment's frontal attack captured Galatas. Let us now concentrate upon the outflanking operation conducted by 85th Regiment.

Post-battle reports in the German forces were written by the officer commanding the unit that had carried out the mission. These men used sober, moderate language, setting out the intention behind the operation, the salient details and the end result. There was no hyperbole or lurid description. The post-battle account was expected to be an objective report on the operation – nothing more. Consequently the writers of these accounts saw it was no part of their authorship to elaborate upon the hardships and sufferings which accompanied the battle. For the unemotional details of Jaeger operations in Crete I have drawn upon two reports, the first of which was written by Colonel Krakau and deals with the actions of his group from the landing of the first contingents in Crete until 29 May. His report is followed by that of Lieutenant-Colonel Wittmann, who commanded the point unit which spearheaded the advance of 5th Gebirgs into the eastern part of the island.

'Combat report on the outflanking attack south of Canea, against the British routes of retreat at Stylos carried out by Gebirgsjaeger Regiment 85:

'The 1st battalion of Gebirgsjaeger Regiment 85, the first unit of the regiment to be emplaned, landed under heavy artillery fire on the airfield at Maleme. Placed under command of Gebirgsjaeger Regiment 100, it was ordered to take out the enemy artillery which was positioned near Ag. Marina and to gain touch with the hard-pressed paratroops. This would be accomplished by an outflanking to the south but battalion was given no details of the enemy situation. The advance would have to be carried out across steep and trackless terrain.

'The battalion drove into the flank and rear of the enemy south-west of Ag. Marina . . . [and an enemy] in superior strength . . . was forced to withdraw. The battalion had . . . seized the high ground around Ag. Marina, which the enemy needed to conduct defensive operations west of Canea. It also gained contact with the paratroops.

'Battalion renewed its advance to cover the right flank of the Gebirgsjaeger and the paratroops fighting their way along the coast road . . . and having concluded a number of separate and successful battles reached and consolidated its allotted positions in the Alikianu sector.

On 24th May, regimental headquarters and 3rd battalion/85th were landed and were followed on 25th May, by elements of 2nd battalion/ 85th and No 16 Company. The several groups then concentrated in an area south of Platanias. On the evening of 25th May, orders were received. These read that regiment was "To attack eastwards across the mountains south of Canea, to drive on Retimo and to gain touch with the paratroops there." The three battalions were without anti-tank guns or artillery pieces and No 16 Company [which had brought six guns] could only follow along the road . . . leading to Stylos, once this had been cleared of the enemy. The 3rd battalion, moving via Alikianu, seized the heights south-west of Varypetron . . . The regimental commander's original plan, to begin the operation once 3rd battalion had gained the high ground east of Alikianu was amended so as to get behind the dogged English defence around and to the south of Canea. The regimental orders were that "1st/85th will head the regiment's advance towards Malara. The 2nd battalion . . . will follow . . ." Air attacks by our own aircraft unfortunately delayed the opening of 1st battalion's attack for two hours, but it began and after beating down determined enemy resistance, the height immediately south-east of Pirgos was taken during the evening of 25th May. One Company of 1st battalion carried out a most difficult climb and followed this with a bitter battle to break the enemy's resistance on Point 542. The 2nd battalion followed closely while 3rd battalion protected the right flank of the attack.

'In suffocating heat and across steep, broken and trackless mountain terrain 2nd battalion (on the right) reached Point 507.50 at 12.15 hrs. The 1st battalion reached the road across the pass 4kms to the south of Canea at about 11.15 hrs having overcome enemy resistance . . . The regiment reached Points 610.40; 284 and 444, which were vital to a resumption of the advance on 28th May. Enemy resistance was smashed everywhere. Thus, by the evening of 27th May, 1941, the regiment was deep in the flank of the English around and south of Canea . . . Led from the front by commanders who brought out the best in the regiment the encirclement of the hard-fighting British around Canea was successfully completed.

'At dawn on 28th May, the regiment's eastward attack was continued. No 3 Company, did not halt on its given objectives but, acting on its own initiative, took Point 231.73, as well as reaching the bridge 2kms south of Kalami. The explosive charges . . . were removed and a bridge which we needed to pursue the enemy was taken intact. The main body of 1st battalion then reached the road south of Point 194 and east of Point 284. The 2nd battalion, fighting on the right flank, advanced as far as Stylos and took Point 76.1, north of the town against strong enemy resistance. The enemy, who was grouped in force around Stylos, reacted strongly to our attacks upon roads down which he would have to retreat and exceptionally heavy fighting then developed. Much of this consisted of bloody hand-to-hand combat but 2nd battalion finally succeded in gaining and holding the roads which the enemy needed together with the commanding heights immediately to the west of Stylos. Unfortunately, the regiment had no artillery with which it could have taken under effective fire the enemy groups seen retreating in the direction of Neon Chorion.

'The 2nd battalion destroyed . . . two modern British medium tanks. The enemy suffered heavy losses and the booty included a number of lorries and a large ration dump . . . As a result of the regiment's outflanking manoeuvre through difficult and steep mountain country south of Canea, by its determined breaking of enemy resistance and by the drive into the rear of . . . the British roads of retreat, the strong enemy position in Suda Bay was finally smashed. The advance guard which the Division sent out to pursue the beaten enemy was able to move forward along those roads. The regiment had taken a decisive part in smashing the enemy's strong positions in the Suda Bay area . . . On 29th May, the advance guard took up the pursuit of the enemy towards Retimo.

During the fighting the regiment took over 500 prisoners, English and Greek. Our own losses were 1 Officer killed, 3 officers wounded, 30 non-commissioned officers and men killed in action or wounded (not including the losses suffered in the ship flotilla).'

Pride in the victory gained is not stated in Colonel Krakau's post-operation report but is, nevertheless, evident. Ringel and his subordinates were also very confident. But one man who endured that trek through the mountains of Crete was quite emphatic that his memories of the battle group's march were bitter ones. He wrote:

'I have never in my life been so depressed as on that terrible march. Mountains are empty places but even on the tallest peaks at home there is sometimes a patch of grass, a clump of flowers, something homely. In Crete the mountains were forbidding and dreadful. Never had I seen such a hostile terrain. There were no paths, not even animal tracks along which we could have moved. There was nothing. The point unit had to cut a trail for the rest of us to follow and that path led uphill and downhill.

'As part of the machine-gun group I had, at times, to carry the tripod of the gun. Even without it my knees were trembling with the strain of the climb within only a few hours and when we halted at midday for a three-hour rest, I was almost unconscious. My comrades were all the same; we were exhausted. The column stopped and we flung ourselves down where we were. I slept immediately for more than half an hour and woke up with my face burning. I tried to find a shadow to keep my face out of the sun and lay with my head behind my rucksack. It was a cloudless afternoon, not one little shadow to hide that burning golden disc. The area was a desert of mountains peaks and on the very few occasions when we stopped the air was as hot as in a greenhouse. It was as hot as the desert and about as lifeless and as inhospitable. There were no wells from which we could top up our water-bottles. My battalion's march discipline was very strict and we had not drunk more than a couple of mouthfuls of tepid water from our bottles since dawn. The afternoon march was worse. Our rucksacks dragged on our backs and the ammunition cases seemed like lead. Each of us carried 30kilos of weight on his back. The tent half was appreciated when we stopped for the night but we cursed it by day and for its weight. I cannot tell you how much we longed to throw everything away and to march unencumbered by rucksack, ammunition cases and all the heavy bulky and bruising equipment. The only good thing about the afternoon march was that the sun was behind us and did not shine into our eyes. Also it shone on to our rucksacks and not on to our backs. Many fell out with a sort of heat stroke or exhaustion and lay there almost paralysed. The stretcher-bearers moved them into whatever cover there was and left them to rest until the cool of the evening made their march easier. For myself I had a terrible headache, my vision began to go and I stumbled repeatedly. I cursed everything and everybody, including the inhabitants of this miserable island. We were lucky that the English were not mountain men for just to cross the White Mountains was terrible enough. To have had to fight across them would have been impossible. In the mountains the defender has the advantage and a handful of determined English and a few machine-guns would have held us off for days. As it was we saw nobody and nothing, except for a few birds.

'When we did meet the Tommies they fought very hard to hold us and several times attacked us with rifle and bayonets. I think they were desperate men knowing that if we won it was a prisoner-of-war camp for them. Their attacks cost them a lot of men and I remember Crete as the place of black corpses. Formerly [in earlier campaigns] we had advanced so quickly that the dead were often only a day or two old and had not begun to decompose. But the bodies on Crete, left lying for days in the hot sun, had all turned black and had swollen. Most of them were covered with greenbottles and the stink of decay was everywhere. Night was bitterly cold and we lay shivering in our tents which we weighted down with stones because we could not bang tent pegs into the almost solid, rocky ground. We had no hot food because the Field Kitchen had not come up with us. Nothing on wheels could have kept pace with us even though our slowest speed was only one kilometre an hour and our fastest only four. When we started out that first morning we had been in good spirits and looking along the trail both backwards and forwards I could see the long grey column as it wound its way up and down the slopes. By evening we didn't care who was in front and who behind. The big question was how soon could we rest. About an hour before last light we stopped and bivouacked. Everything had to be done quickly for once the sun went down it was soon totally dark and no lights were allowed. A low sort of gargling with a mouthful of water, swilling it round and round the mouth. Allow a little trickle down the back of the throat and then swill the rest of the water around again to cleanse the inside of the mouth. I didn't feel hungry and certainly did not want to eat the dry ration bread . . . We were up at dawn. There was no breakfast and no spare water to wash. Then we marched, going on and on and on sliding off the narrow paths with tiredness and almost crying with exhaustion. I hated Crete and I've never been back. The memory of that three-day march has never left me.'

Luftwaffe reconnaissance indicated that the British forces were boarding ships in the small harbours on the southern side of the island. It was clear that the British Command had conceded victory to the Germans and were evacuating their troops. Ringel was determined not to let the British escape but to pursue and destroy them. He created a battle group to carry out these tasks and placed it under the command of Lieutenant-Colonel Wittmann. The General's orders were simple and direct. Wittmann was to open the way to Suda Bay, advance to Retimo and gain touch with the Fallschirmjaeger units which were encircled there. He was then to gain touch with Colonel Krakau's battle group and then lead the advance towards Vrases and Vramos.

Wittmann's edited and abridged report, states that during the afternoon of 27 May, Division issued orders for the battle group to leave the Platanias area at 03.00 on the 28th. This departure time had to be postponed for 50 minutes because some elements of the battle group were not able to reach the start-line on time. The march to Suda was made without incident but the road some 5 kilometres west of Suda had been rendered impassable and could not be repaired until 09.00. While the road was being repaired the motor-cycle battalion and a platoon of anti-tank guns joined the column. When the advance was resumed the battle group struck enemy resistance on the heights running parallel to the road and found that demolitions had made the road impassable.

A motor-cycle squadron carried out a right-flank attack to seize the passes to the southern heights near Mega Chorafiam, covered by the fire of a heavy battery of mountain guns. Under this fire the lead motor-cycle Company broke through the southern passes at about 12.00, meeting only the light resistance of a rearguard detachment. Despite meeting only minimal opposition, losses to the group were quite high.

The column advanced and gained touch in Stylos with the leading detachments of 2nd Battalion, 85th Regiment. Against light opposition the thrust continued via Neon Chorion towards the road crossing south-west of Kaina. There the advanced guard's leading groups caught up with the enemy on a ridge 11 kilometres north-west of the crossroads. The first Jaeger attack failed and it was soon clear that the enemy intended to hold this position for as long as possible and that his forces in the area included an armoured fighting vehicle. The British not only held their ground but launched counter-attacks some of which resulted in close-quarter fighting. For lack of heavy weapons support the Jaeger attack was not resumed and then the encirclement operation by Krakau Group began to take effect. At last light the left-hand Company of the battalion captured a commanding height from which it poured enfilading fire upon the enemy, while on the right flank another Company reached to within 1 kilometre of the crossroads. Shortly thereafter the enemy withdrew. The battle group had lost three officers and 27 other ranks in the course of the day's fighting.

At first light on the 29th the pursuit was resumed, encountering only roadblocks and minefields. Many of the latter were found to be dummy fields. Delay was caused by the damaged bridge at Episkopi, but by 11.00 the motor-cycle group had crossed it and was advancing on Retimo against light resistance. Tactically important areas of high ground were taken and then the advance continued to gain touch with the paratroops holding a crossroads 3 kilometres east of the town. From reports received it was clear that to the east of Retimo the British had at least three guns and a great number of machine-guns in position and fire from these fell continuously in the paratroop area. Because the battle group had neither artillery nor heavy weapons, any assault which it launched was not likely to succeed. Orders from Division and Corps ordered an attack for the following day, by which time two armoured fighting vehicles and two heavy infantry guns would have been brought forward. The rest of 29 May was spent in consolidating the hold upon Retimo and carrying out reconnaissance patrols.

The attack on 30 May brought a number of successes. The barrage fired by the divisional artillery had the effect of forcing the surrender of the Imperial troops holding the hills and the advance was then pushed forward to gain touch with another group of Fallschirmjaeger near Retimo. By 11.45, shortly after crossing the pass 10 kilometres to the west of Heraklion, touch was gained with a reconnaissance patrol from Colonel Brauer's paras. Another group leap-frogged through the point unit and carried the advance forward to Iarapetra, the objective for the day. This marked the end of the fighting for Crete. As Wittmann wrote in his report, 'The battles themselves were purely ones of pursuit . . . In the interest of maintaining a fast pace it was not always possible to consider the safety factor and the risk that there might be a sudden and surprise attack upon the advance guard had to be accepted.'

While Wittmann Group was advancing eastwards, other units of 5th Gebirgs Division were striking southwards towards the British debarkation ports. Mention was made at the opening of this chapter that the need to provide carrying parties reduced the numbers of men in the firing line. This situation developed during the southwards march when some battalions of both 85th and 100th Regiments were taken from the battle line and put into service as supply columns in order to carry ammunition forward to 1st Battalion, 100th Regiment, which was fighting the battle. British resistance was now mainly that of rearguards holding good positions, but however strong these positions might be, the resistance put up by a rearguard could only be of short duration. There were some short, sharp fights in the Lutra–Sfakia area, around the positions which the British had set up to defend the embarkation points. These last flickers of resistance had been extinguished by the afternoon of 31 May. The war diary of 5th Gebirgs Division states that at 16.00 the last English resistance was silenced in the mountains north of Sfakia and later records that 20 officers and 305 other ranks had been killed in action. There had been thirteen officers and 274 other ranks wounded. Among those recorded as 'missing in action' were eighteen officers and 488 other ranks who were drowned when the caique convoy was attacked and sunk.

1st and 4th Gebirgs Divisions on the Eastern Front, 1941

B Y THE END OF MAY 1941, the fighting for Crete had ended but the peace which then settled over Europe was a false one – merely the lull before a violent conflict; the war between Germany and Russia.

Studies had been prepared by general officers, conclusions drawn and decisions taken, the consequence being the battle plan code-named Operation 'Barbarossa', which foresaw an invasion of Soviet Russia by three German Army Groups supported by contingents from Germany's allies. Army Group North, commanded by Field Marshal von Leeb, was made up of two infantry armies; Sixteenth and Eighteenth supported by 4th Panzer Group. Collaborating with the Germans but independent of their control, was the small but highly professional army of the Republic of Finland. It was the task of Army Group North to strike out of East Prussia and destroy the Soviet forces holding the three Baltic republics, before going on to invest the city of Leningrad. The Finns would co-operate in that investment.

Field Marshal von Bock's Army Group Centre was the largest of the three with Second, Fourth and Ninth infantry Armies as well as 2nd and 3rd Panzer Groups. The task of von Bock's forces was to destroy the Soviet armies in Belo-Russia and then collaborate with Army Group North in its operations against Leningrad. The commander of Army Group South was Field Marshal von Rundstedt who directed the movements of Sixth, Eleventh and Seventeenth infantry Armies as well as 1st Panzer Group. He also had under his command 3rd and 4th Roumanian Armies. Army Group South had two major tasks. It had to protect the German Army's right flank and advance into the Ukraine using Sixth and Seventeenth Armies whose infantry would follow-up the rapid advance of the panzer group. In the course of its advance Army Group was to cut off and surround the Red armies facing it and destroy them along the line of the River Dnieper. I do not propose to analyse Hitler's strategy for his war against the Soviet Union except to remark that not one of the three army groups had the capital city of Moscow as an initial objective. His Directive No 21, dated 18 December 1940, had laid out the idea behind 'Barbarossa': 'The German Armed Forces must be prepared, even before the conclusion of the war against England, to overthrow Soviet Russia in a quick campaign . . .' A quick campaign was envisaged and planned for. Whatever reservations the military commanders may have had about the wisdom of starting a new war, Hitler had none and yet their reservations would have been justified. The German Army, three million strong and fielding only 145 divisions, was expected to attack and destroy quickly an enemy army which Intelligence sources reported to be no less than four and a half million men strong. Why it was believed that the Red Army would be so accommodating to the German battle plan as to stand and fight and allow itself to be destroyed west of the Dnieper can be traced back to the study produced by General Marcks. He declared that a modern military force, such as the Red Army, could not simply abandon its supply centres but MUST fight to hold them. Neither Marcks, nor anyone in OKW or OKH knew that other Russian centres of production lay not in the west of Russia but east of the Urals. The coal and iron reserves in the Urals could easily cover the loss of those facilities in the West. It was, therefore, a false premise on which Marcks based his plan. It was not the only false assumption made in the planning of the new war but it was the most serious one for upon it was based the whole German war-plan.

False assumptions were not restricted to the German side alone. The Russians believed that Bolshevik élan MUST prevail, and this mistaken notion dominated the military thinking of Stavka, the Red Army's Supreme High Command. Then, too, Stalin had refused to accept that the Germans were building-up to start a war. Another disastrous factor was the rigidity of the Red Army's tactics and strategy. All these compounded to produce the disasters of the first months of the war which will shortly be recounted. Four million dead soldiers and more than three million taken prisoner was the penalty which the Red Army paid for the blunders of commanders whose military experience had been gained in the Civil War and whose knowledge was fixed immovably in the past.

Four of the six Gebirgs divisions on establishment in June 1941 were involved in the mass movement of men and equipment to the concentration areas in Poland, Roumania, Slovakia and Lappland. The 1st and 4th Divisions, as part of XLIX Gebirgskorps in Seventeenth Army, fought with Army Group South. The 2nd and 3rd Divisions were in the northern sector, the 2nd in Lappland and the 3rd in Norway. The 5th was still in Crete and 6th Gebirgs Division was on occupation duties in Greece.

The story of the Gebirgsjaeger on the Eastern Front at the start of Operation 'Barbarossa' begins with the advance of 1st and 4th Divisions to Cracow and their successful smashing of the Stalin Line. The divisions then went on to take part in the Battle of Podvyssoya, which is better known as the encirclement battle of Uman. We shall then turn from the fighting in the Ukraine to describe the events in Lappland, where 2nd Gebirgs Division, part of 'Norway Corps' fought its way eastwards towards the Russian port of Murmansk. It was at this time and in that area that a battle group which was to develop into 6th SS Gebirgs Division 'Nord' first saw action. It was, in fact, in Lappland that 2nd, 3rd, 6th and 7th Gebirgs Divisions of the Army as well as 6th SS Gebirgs Division were to spend the greatest part of their military life. But let us, to begin with, concentrate on the southern wing of the German Army, on XLIX Gebirgskorps and to the battles in which its men were soon to be involved. D-Day for 'Barbarossa' was 22 June, and shortly before H-Hour

– 03.15 – groups of Jaeger and pioneers slipped out of the forward edge of the woods in which the battalions lay concealed and crossed No Man's Land to cut gaps in the enemy wire.

The XLIX Gebirgskops lay in its positions ready to begin the opening attack of the Russian war and for this first operation General Kuebler, the Corps Commander, placed 4th Division on the right flank and 1st Division on the left. It is the 1st Gebirgs Division that we are to follow in this first offensive which concluded with the smashing of the Stalin Line and it is specifically upon Colonel Kress's 99th Regiment of that division, that our concentration will be fixed.

When Corps moved into its concentration area, several weeks before the opening of hostilities, Kuebler issued strict orders that his units were not to betray their presence by unnecessary noise or road traffic. Great emphasis was laid on camouflage, and a strip of territory on the eastern edge of the woods marked the point beyond which no one was allowed to go for fear of being seen. Although it was obvious that the major troop movements that had been in operation for many months past could not all be hidden from Soviet observers, it was Kuebler's intention to present a picture of day to day normality on his Corps' sector.

The last night of peace on the Eastern Front was a warm one and the Jaeger were wakened just after 01.00. Quietly and unhurriedly the men of the assault companies prepared themselves for battle. At 02.00, after the Fuehrer's Order of the Day had been read out to them, their silent columns marched eastwards to the edge of the woods, close to the demarcation zone which separated the territories of the Third Reich and Soviet Russia. This zone, an area of open ground between the edge of the forest and the Russian barbed wire fence, was still covered with a light mist which had hidden the wire-cutting groups who had gone out a little earlier. At 03.15 the German artillery opened up – the war against the Soviet Union had begun. That first day of battle was described in the War Diary as the bloodiest in the experience of 1st Gebirgs Division. The fighting lasted for sixteen hours and although both regiments of the division fought their way to the first objective, the River Lubaczovka some 16 kilometres from the start-lines, losses had been severe.

At this point it is apposite to record the feelings of the Jaeger as they went into the war with Russia and their first impressions of that country. To avoid repetition I have taken the salient points from the accounts which were received and have formed these into a single narrative. The first impression was the sheer size of the country, or rather the size of the fields across which the regiments advanced. These were not the pocket-handkerchief sized fields of their alpine homeland but were instead vast stretches of land extending for kilometre after kilometre, usually sown with a single crop; either maize or sunflowers. One man wrote of 'fields which extended from horizon to horizon in all directions . . . Sunflowers which in the early morning dipped their heads so that the colour of the field was a monotonous shade of brown, but when the flower heads stood upright as they did at midday, they pointed to the sun and changed the colour of the field to a bright yellow . . . An unforgettable picture of fruitfulness . . .' The second impression was of the astonishingly primitive standards of living, standards which became worse the farther east that one went. The third most quoted impression concerned the weather – remember, what are being recounted here are the impressions of the days and nights of high summer. The horror of the first winter was yet to come.

'I shall never forget the first months of the fighting. Before the war began we had concentrated in eastern Poland and the conditions we encountered were abysmal. The houses in the villages, one should not really dignify the miscellaneous collection of hovels as villages, were wooden, in a ruinous state and verminous. There was no sanitation, no electric light and the so-called roads were rutted tracks in the sandy soil. The great mass of the battalion was quartered in tents in the forest, in properly laid out areas with dug latrines. Fresh drinking-water was brought in three times daily. We fed from the old familiar "Gulasch Cannon" [the field cooker heated by solid fuel] and ate very well indeed. Although it was strictly forbidden we all fed the Polish children who hung around our camp site.

'On the day war broke out – it was early morning, really, as we were getting ready we were called together. Our platoon officer read out the Fuehrer's proclamation but I can't recall it being discussed or whether anyone was excited by it. That day, we fought, it seemed, from dawn to dusk and then fell exhausted into our shallow slit trenches. That first night the NCOs and officers kept watch while we slept. We were awakened just after 3 in the morning, had a quick wash, a hasty breakfast and were on the march by dawn. The regimental commander had been ordered not to lose touch with the retreating enemy. We must keep on their tails. We marched and marched, kilometre after kilometre. The roads, such as they were, were so bad and so congested with lorries and other vehicles that we preferred to march across country. The weather I recall as being blinding hot. When we marched on the roads we were shrouded in a cloud of dust; the sandy roads were ankle deep in a fine yellow dust which clung to our sweating faces.

'The enemy seemed to have vanished; except that is when a little group of them formed a rearguard and opened fire. That really was a suicide mission. For the first few days we deployed as we had been taught to do, but were soon ordered to stop such time-wasting tactics. Instead a small group, usually a Section of the leading Company, would move forward to where it was thought the fire was coming and once the location of the enemy had been established the infantry guns would be brought into action. Four or five rounds were usually sufficient and then the Ivans would come stumbling forward with their arms raised. It was not always that easy. Sometimes the enemy backed his defence with tanks or artillery. Sometimes his infantry fought to the last man. I have read since the war reports which said that if an Ivan was knocked unconscious by shell blast or something else, his first action on regaining consciousness was to reach out for his rifle.

'Once the opposition was overcome the march resumed and there were times when we carried on marching well into the night. At the end of each day's march it was a matter of digging in and standing guard until the march started again. We soon became accustomed to the weather pattern. By day blazing hot and then, in the evening, at about 8 or 9, torrential rain which persisted for hours and which kept us soaked to the skin all night. We dried out during the next day's march and were soaked again the following night. The days passed without our knowing whether it was Monday or Friday. We were just a column of men, trudging apparently aimlessly in a void. We could have been any one of the armies which had invaded Russia in the past. We had horses, as those other armies had, and the only sign that we were in the 20th century were the Stuka squadrons which flew overhead almost constantly and the occasional dispatch rider who would come racing up in a cloud of dust to deliver a message to the battalion commander. We got to hate the sound of the DR's motor cycle. It always seemed to coincide with orders that we were to march until nearly midnight. How the ration parties ever found us was a mystery, but usually within an hour or two of arriving at some map reference the ration parties would arrive with hot food, fresh water, mail and sometimes, even canteen goods. We went without alcohol. There was none, anyway. The only time we had spirits was once when we were given a day's rest and this spirit ration came with the announcement that we had a difficult task to achieve. On the old Polish border the Reds had put up a line of fortifications. It was our Corps task to smash through a set of permanent defences which were known as the Stalin Line.'

Orders from Seventeenth Army that Corps was to undertake that operation were issued on 12 July. The Stalin Line was a series of defences which, although sited to a depth of between 3 and 5 kilometres, could not be compared in strength to the Maginot Line which the 1st Division had seen in France nor with the Metaxas Line which 5th Division had captured in Greece. Nevertheless, the blockhouses of the Stalin Line were numerous, well constructed and protected by trenches fronted by barbed-wire entanglements. A very deep and wide anti-tank ditch ran its entire length. The Line's first defensive zone was set on rising ground and suffered from a serious tactical defect on the sector that 1st Division was to attack; there were areas over which the defenders had only limited observation, and others where the attacking force could advance using concealed lines of approach. The Gebirgsjaeger were able to exploit every piece of this cover.

For the assault Kuebler placed the 4th Division on the left and 1st on the right flank. Corps' maximum effort would be in the centre and would be made by the units forming its inner flank, that is to say, by the right wing of 4th Division and the left wing of 1st Division. Between these two wings ran a railway line from the villages of Deraznia and Volkovinche. In the rural areas of the Soviet Union a railway line, even a rural one, constituted an objective of considerable military value and Seventeenth Army ordered Kuebler to press the advance relentlessly to capture the line. But before Corps could thrust up the railway line it would first have to capture the north–south road from Deraznia to Bar which ran along the front of the Stalin Line. When that had been taken Army could use it to switch units from one sensitive spot to another during the attack. The road was such an important feature that the Soviets would be certain to defend it to the last, and anticipating that resistance Corps had committed both its Gebirgs divisions to the operation leaving no reserve to exploit a gain or reinforce a failing attack. Kuebler had been told that the Stalin Line must be broken quickly and used his whole Command to accomplish this urgent task. He warned his divisions that the artillery support would be neither strong nor prolonged because supplies of shells were not coming forward. That the Russians suffered no such shortage was well known and, indeed, their superiority in gun numbers might well inflict heavy casualties upon the attacking regiments if the assaults were to be bogged down. Seventeenth Army and Corps stressed that this must not be allowed to happen. Speed and movement would help to keep casualties down.

It is interesting to see the way in which the divisional commanders deployed their regiments for the operation. The commander of 4th Division planned for an advance on a broad front behind a conventional barrage whereas the 1st Division commander decided to concentrate the artillery forces available to him and to smash a narrow corridor through which a single Jaeger battalion would thrust like a lance. The unit selected was 3rd Battalion, 99th Regiment.

D-Day for the operation was 15 July and H-Hour was 07.00. At that time the batteries supporting 1st Division opened up and continued to fire for a further 45 minutes on pre-selected targets. Once that first, furious fire storm had subsided, the artillery role was restricted to targets selected by the FOOs who were up with the leading Companies. The 3rd Battalion made its approach march almost without opposition and less than three hours after leaving the concentration area had taken its first objectives and reached its start-line for the final assault; the small stream which formed the outlying part of the Stalin Line. Above the Jaeger lay the heights upon whose crests were the bunkers and trenches which they had to assault and capture. Now there could be no pause. The pace of the advance must be swift and decisive. Artillery fire was directed upon bunkers from which the FOOs had detected opposition and 'leaning' on that fire the Jaeger stormed the first enemy positions. The opposition was not as fierce as they had been led to expect or which they had, perhaps, feared.

The Soviet troops had been shattered not only by the weight and accuracy of the German shellfire but also by the sudden appearance of the Jaeger storm troops. Satchel charges placed against the pillboxes shattered the bunker walls. Other charges pushed through firing slits exploded inside the bunkers with devastating effect and where the defence was particularly stubborn flame-throwers soon brought an end to resistance. Through the lines of bunkers, into, through and out of the small woods which covered the area, across trenches and barbed wire entanglements, the men of 3rd Battalion swept in an almost irresistible wave. The first part of the bunker line phase of the assault had gone well. By 11.30 all the positions on the first hill had been taken and Jaeger groups had penetrated into the southern edge of the tactically important village of Hautuzinche. The mass of 3rd Battalion charged behind the spearhead of storm troop detachments and with them came the PAK and flak guns of the heavy weapons Company to 'beef up' a faltering attack or destroy any last flickers of resistance. At Hautuzinche the heavy weapons detachments were halted and deployed facing north to protect the flank of the Jaeger companies as they continued their storming eastwards drive. No 11 Company, 3rd Battalion was ordered to capture the village.

Soon the battalion had created a narrow but firm salient into which the general intended to cram the other units of his division. These would then burst out of the salient and advance upon Komarovcze from where they could strike and penetrate the last defences of the Stalin Line. But before the divisional commander could order this movement to begin he had first to deal with a crisis which threatened his left flank. The Corps advance had been pushed forward with such energy that one of the units on Division's left flank, 97th Infantry Regiment, had not kept level. A small gap opened as the Gebirgsjaeger continued to push ahead and soon it had widened to become a dangerous breach. This was a situation which the Red Army commander was determined to exploit. His plan was simple and obvious. He would concentrate units and open a strong counter-attack with a choice of either cutting 3rd Battalion's salient and destroying it, or, if the salient proved too strong, deflecting the line of his thrust and rolling up 97th Division. The main point of the Red Army's counter-attack was the village of Hautuzinche which No 11 Company was still fighting desperately hard to capture.

The Soviet troops fighting in the streets of the village suddenly found themselves reinforced as waves of Red Army men swung into the counter-attack. Under this overwhelming pressure No 11 Company seemed certain to be destroyed, but then the battalion's pioneer Company entered the battle driving into the village from the east. With them came a platoon of SP guns under whose fire the Russian advance began to waver. Fresh Soviet formations which entered the fighting turned the balance against the Jaeger who were, by this time, fighting hand-to-hand, man against man in a struggle in which there was no quarter asked nor quarter given. Slowly the handfuls of Jaeger and pioneers began to gain the upper hand using flame-throwers to sweep back the Soviet assault. Those Russian soldiers who continued to hold out in houses or in strongpoints were killed by machine-gun fire or hand-grenades. A Jaeger storm troop thrust through the village and captured a height to its west from which they had observation over the whole area. Russian resistance continued in and around Hautzinche so that it was not until the morning of 16 July that No 11 Company could report to battalion that the ruined village was completely and firmly in German hands. An illustration of the savagery of the fighting for that little place can be gauged from the divisional post-battle report which listed more than a thousand dead Red Army men in and around the village. On the German side 1st Gebirgs Division had lost five officers and 26 other ranks killed in action during the two days of battle. But theirs had not been a vain sacrifice. XLIX Corps had broken through the Stalin Line on a front more than 20 kilometres wide and had destroyed that defensive system.

But XLIX Corps' successful penetration had brought with it a serious consequence. It had created a wide salient in the Soviet front against which the Red Army flung a rapid succession of tank and infantry assaults. Under these smashing blows the components of Gebirgskorps, already separated, were forced farther and farther apart. Each division fought its own battle and often each regiment of a division fought isolated from the other detachments of its parent unit. In one sense Stavka was not primarily concerned with forcing back XLIX Corps. The Russian High Command accepted that in time it and the rest of Seventeenth Army would race forward again. Stavka's immediate priority was to delay the German advance and the Soviet commanders' method of achieving this was by launching waves of counter-attacks against the salient walls. The reason behind the senseless sacrifice of so many Russian soldiers, which marked those July days, was that to the east of Gebirgskorps' front line, if one can talk of a front line in such a fluid situation, lay the River Bug and the town of Vinnitsa with its several bridges, towards which the shattered remnant of a great mass of Red Army divisions was retreating. Their withdrawal was jeopardized by the Gebirgsjaeger whose salient lay athwart the main Russian line of retreat. Stavka ordered that the Jaeger advance be delayed so that the great mass of Red Army units could escape and to achieve this directed that the counter-attacks be continued irrespective of losses. These attacks were, therefore, almost suicidal in their intensity and number.

'It would be true to say that the Russian soldiers attacked across a carpet of their own dead comrades – and not just once but repeatedly. The failure of earlier attacks and the losses which they had incurred seemed not to deter them. They came forward in long lines and persisted in making frontal charges against machine-gun fire until only a few were left standing. Only when those few survivors realized their own isolation did they waver and begin to retreat, sometimes not even running away but walking. It was as if they no longer cared about being killed or thought, perhaps, that we would not shoot at retreating soldiers.' Reeling under the fury of the Soviet attacks the dispersed divisions of XLIX Corps struggled to maintain contact with one another. Kuebler, the Corps Commander, realized that only when his formations gained touch and created a unified force would he be able to reach the Bug and thereby prevent the broken Red Army from escaping into the wide and open steppe land.

His orders were for the divisions to close up to one another, but this was a directive which they could not all carry out. Some, certainly, managed to comply with the order but others, particularly 1st Gebirgs Division, reported to Kuebler that his men were at the point of total exhaustion and that his division, extended along a 45-kilometre battle line, was being attacked from all sides. Unless help came within a matter of hours 1st Gebirgs Division would not be able to prevent the Red forces from escaping to fight another day. The help for which Lanz asked and which Kuebler promised did not arrive and the Russian host, made up principally of formations from 6th and 12th Red Armies, crossed the Bug, heading eastwards and reaching, as they thought, safety on its eastern bank. Their euphoria in having evaded captivity was to be brief, as we shall shortly see.

1st and 4th Gebirgs Divisions in the Encirclement Battles around Uman

A MONG THE GERMAN MILITARY VICTORIES which marked the fighting of the autumn of 1941, the most spectacular were those which surrounded whole Russian armies and tumbled them into ruin. Included in the most successful encirclement battles of the first months of Operation 'Barbarossa' were those at Minsk, in which 324,000 Red Army men were taken prisoner; Kiev, in which more than half a million were captured; and Uman, in which 103,000 Red Army men surrendered.

It is known from diaries and other sources that, as early as July 1941, the victories that had already been gained after only six weeks of campaigning encouraged Halder and the other officers at OKW to believe that the Fuehrer's strategy had been proved correct. He had said that the corrupt Bolshevik system would collapse after a few good kicks at the rotten front door. And it looked as if it had, indeed, collapsed. He had planned for the destruction of the Red Army east of the Dnieper and the proof of the Fuehrer's unfolding strategy and immaculate planning could be seen in the Russian dead which carpeted the steppes and in the long columns of prisoners marching from the battlefields of the Eastern Front to labour in factories, farms and mines in Germany. A summary of Intelligence reports produced in July 1941 concluded that no fewer than eighty-nine Red Army Divisions had been destroyed and since the enemy had entered the War with about 180 divisions, according to the estimate of the Intelligence Officers of Foreign Armies (East), the Soviets had already lost nearly 50 per cent of their Field Army. Even the vast population resources of the Soviet Union could not take losses on such a vast scale.

At the end of July senior military commanders had already forecast imminent victory. How much more confident must they have been when, during August and September, a number of encirclement battles were fought and won. The High Command's planning and directing of these operations had been both flexible and dynamic, but the honour was not theirs alone. It was the ordinary soldier, particularly the infantrymen, who won for the generals the victories they had planned. The military successes achieved by the German soldiers did not come about by their being more brave than the Red Army's warriors, because the Russian Ivan was equally as brave as the Landser. Nor was it to be found solely in superior German tactics. Nor even in a higher morale. The answer lay in all these as well as in many other things, but more especially in the German Army's remarkable marching ability. And in the Soviet Union the German infantrymen had tremendous distances to cover. So far as he was concerned road and rail communications stopped at the old Polish/Russian border. In Russia proper there were few railways and those which were still operational were needed, so the Landser was told, for the transport of *matériel* to the Front. There were even fewer all-weather roads and this handful of highways connected only the principal cities. These 'rollbahn', as the High Command named them, like the railways, were reserved exclusively for the movement of supplies. Thus, there was neither road nor rail transport to 'lift' standard infantry units. Panzer divisions, of course, had troop-carrying trucks and half-trucks as an integral part of their establishments so that the Panzergrenadiers could accompany the armoured spearheads. But the infantry and Jaeger divisions marched across Russia as the armies of Napoleon had done. And the distances they covered were truly prodigious. Fifty kilometres per day was standard and this rate was maintained day after day and for week after weary week. In the blazing heat of autumn days or in the torrential rain of autumn nights' the infantry, who responded unfailingly to the repeated calls for more and greater efforts, were often committed immediately to battle at the end of a long march.

The 1st and 4th Gebirgs Divisions took a prominent part in the encirclement Battle of Uman and in that vast operation, von Stulpnagel, the Army Commander, depended for much of his victory upon the endurance of the men of XLIX Gebirgskorps. Without their marching prowess the victory would have been less complete. The Battle at Uman led into, but was overshadowed by, the greater success at Kiev. The fanfares which proclaimed the end of the Kiev encirclement and capture of the Ukrainian capital drowned out those which were sounding for Uman, so that the vital role of XLIX Corps in producing that victory has gone generally unrecognized and unremarked.

It will be recalled that the composition of XLIX Gebirgskorps was 1st and 4th Gebirgs Divisions. At certain times during the Uman operation, 97th (Light), 100th (Light), 125th and 295th Infantry Divisions and a Slovak motorized brigade all formed part of Corps strength. The reason for this lay, as was explained in the foreword chapter, in the fact that Gebirgs Divisions 'fielded' only two regiments of infantry instead of the three with standard infantry divisions. In alpine operations, a two-regiment structure was the most efficient tactical arrangement, but in non-mountainous campaigns the lack of a whole infantry regiment placed each Gebirgs division at a disadvantage. A Gebirgs corps with two infantry regiments fewer than a standard corps, could neither meet the same operational demands nor cover the length of front which such a standard corps was given to hold. To cover the shortage of infantry, certain divisions were attached temporarily to Corps and by that attachment helped to overcome the other organizational defect of a Gebirgs Division – the shortage of motorized transport.

During the second week of July, XLIX Gebirgskorps, its morale high as a result of the decisive part it had played in smashing the Stalin Line, had crossed the River Bug at Vinnitsa and was conducting a vigorous

Above: New recruits taking the oath on the Regimental Colour, Bavaria, April 1938. The six soldiers in this photograph represent their comrades who are standing in hollow square around them.

Below: Men of a Gebirgsjaeger Company, in a form-up position, ready to carry out an attack, Poland, 1939.

Above: The Polish plenipotentiary comes in under a white flag to offer the surrender of the city of Lemberg (Lvov) on 21 September 1939. The Polish garrison commander insisted that the city would only be surrendered to the men of 1st Gebirgs Division who had fought so hard to capture it. The Polish plenipotentiary offering the surrender of Lemberg to Major Schrank, a staff officer in 1st Gebirgs Division.

Below: Gebirgsjaeger disembarking at a Norwegian port during the operations in Scandinavia, 1940.

Above: Gebirgsjaeger prepare for the coming battle, in the Norwegian campaign, 1940.

Right: General Eduard Dietl who commanded 3rd Gebirgs Division. For his defence of the mining town he was known as 'The Hero of Narvik'.

Above: Gebirgsjaeger in a sangar, during the campaign in Norway, 1940. Note the scissors-periscope through which the commander is peering.

Below: Jaeger of an anti-tank Company man-handling their 3.7cm PAK in northern Norway. Operation 'Bueffel', April 1940.

Above: Jaeger on their start-line ready to carry out an assault river crossing, France, 1940.

Below: Many of the Jaeger who were training to invade England had never seen the sea and training in boats in the English Channel was very unpopular.

Above: The proposed invasion of England was seen by the German High Command as little more than a river crossing. Lacking properly constructed invasion barges, the German Army relied upon flat-bottomed vessels taken from inland waterways and hastily converted to carry troops. This picture shows one such vessel.

Below: Gebirgsjaeger of 1st Division on one of the embarkation and disembarkation

exercises connected with Operation 'Sea Lion', the proposed invasion of Great Britain, autumn, 1940.

Opposite page, top: Men of an assault pioneer Company of 1st Gebirgs Division carrying their rubber assault boat to the River Drau, Yugoslavia, 1941.

Opposite page, bottom: A bunker in the Metaxas Line after it had been stormed and captured by Gebirgsjaeger, Greece, 1941.

Above: On a pathway in the mountains of Greece, men of a pioneer Company prepare satchel charges for use against Greek pillboxes in the Metaxas Line, Greece, 1941.

Below: Jaeger of 4th Gebirgs Division advancing out of Bulgaria into Yugoslavia at the outbreak of war with that country. 9/10 April 1941.

Above right: Helma Oswald, née Auer, who saw Gebirgsjaeger march through Gnas to take part in the campaign against Yugoslavia in 1941, and witnessed a public execution in the same village in May 1945.

Above: An incident during the campaign in Greece, 1941. Men of a Gebirgsjaeger unit scaled Mount Olympus and raised the German war flag on its summit. This picture shows the Jaeger unfolding the flag preparatory to its hoisting.

Below: Jaeger marching through the Pass of Thermopylae during the closing stages of the campaign in Greece, 1941.

Above: Gebirgsjaeger preparing to raise the German war flag on the Acropolis hill in Athens, 1941.

Opposite page, top: Men of Ringel's 5th Gebirgs Division waiting to emplane on a Greek airfield. Their destination was Crete. May 1941.

Right: A caique, the type of vessel in which battalions of Ringel's 5th Gebirgs Division sailed from Greece to Crete. May 1941.

Above: Gebirgsjaeger of 5th Division with their General, Julius Ringel. Crete, 1941. General Ringel.

Below: General Lanz holds a battlefield 'O' Group, during the opening stages of Operation 'Barbarossa'. Eastern Front, 1941.

Right: A Gebirgsjaeger patrol leaving the shelter of an anti-tank ditch during the fighting in the Stalin Line, autumn 1941.

Above: The anti-tank ditch at Timoshevka which was taken by Gebirgsjaeger on 20 September 1941.

Left: A bunker in the Stalin Line, knocked out and captured by Gebirgsjaeger, autumn 1941.

Above: Viktor Luetze, Chief of Staff of the SA, congratulating the Gebirgsjaeger team that won the messenger relay event in the Winter Sports competition in Garmisch-Partenkirchen, 20–28 February 1941.

Below: Jaeger of 5th Gebirgs Division building winter positions on the River Wolkov sector of the Eastern Front, winter 1941/2. The slit trenches are covered with a tent which in turn is covered with branches. In snowy weather this soon becomes indistinguishable from the surrounding landscape.

Opposite page, top: The standard beast of burden in Gebirgs units was the horse or mule. In the Caucasus the Bactrian camel was often used to supplement a unit's Train.

Left: Mountain guns of 4th Gebirgs Division's artillery regiment on the march from the Kluchor Pass to the valley of the River Klisch during the advance in the Caucasus, summer 1942. The artillery pieces (7.5cm mountain guns) have been broken down and loaded on to pack-animals.

Above: A scene during the advance into the Caucasus in 1942. Here a column of Jaeger and HIWIS (Russian volunteers) bring rations up to the front line.

Above: A machine-gun of the High Alpine battalion in action during the assault on the Dombai Ulgen. The Caucasus, 1942.

Opposite page, top: During the campaign in the Caucasus, in 1942, a combined team of expert alpinists from 1st and 4th Gebirgs Divisions

climbed the highest peak in the range of mountains and left on the summit the German War Flag and the Divisional flags of both divisions.

Right: The climbing group en route to the summit of the Elbrus where they planted the divisional and Reichs flags, 21 August 1942.

Above: A battalion column moving through Lappland in the first months of the war against the Soviet Union, 1941.

Below: Supply train of 1st Gebirgs Division in the River Mius positions, winter 1941/2.

Above: One of the pontoon bridges thrown across the River Liza in Lappland, by engineers of 2nd Gebirgs Division, 1942.

Below: Jaeger of 6th SS Gerbirgs Division 'Nord' moving up the line. Louhi sector, Lappland.

Above: Jaeger of 6th Gebirgs Division, in the Finnish theatre of operations. Although it is winter, the men are still not equipped with winter-pattern camouflage clothing. Lappland, 1942.

Below: Men of 218th Jaeger Regiment, 7th Gebirgs Division, during the retreat from the Oedmark, Lappland, 1944.

Above: Colonel Kreppel (white camouflage jacket) and General Wittmann (dark great-coat) during the latter's visit to the HQ of 3rd Gebirgs Division in Nikopol. Winter 1943/4.

Below: A battlefield conference on the Dnieper, winter 1943/4. Schoerner, on the right, commanding XXII Corps, discussing the situation with Wittmann, GOC 3rd Gebirgs Division.

Above: General Konrad, GOC XXXXIX Gebirgskorps Corps (left) and General Kress, commander of 4th Gebirgs Division.

Below: An 'O' Group. Left to right, Phleps, Brigadeführer Carl von Oberkamp, Otto Beyer and Kumm.

Above right: Officers of the German and Italian armies planning an operation. The SS officers are from 'Prinz Eugen' Division. Yugoslavia, 1943.

Right: Artur Phleps, the officer with the moustache in the front rank, with the officers of 7th SS Gebirgs Division 'Prinz Eugen', after taking command of the Division.

Above: The point unit of 'Prinz Eugen' Division comes under fire from partisan forces. Yugoslavia, 1943.

Below: Jaeger of 7th SS on anti-partisan operations in Bosnia, 1943/4.

Above: The type of country through which 7th SS Gebirgs Division 'Prinz Eugen' fought on anti-partisan operations in Yugoslavia.

Below: Jaeger of 7th SS Freiwillige Gebirgs Division 'Prinz Eugen' on anti-partisan operations in the mountains of Bosnia.

Opposite page, top: A column of 7th SS Gebirgs Division 'Prinz Eugen' during operations in Bosnia (Operation 'Black'). May 1943.

Above: This machine-gun post manned by Jaeger of 7th SS Gebirgs Division conforms to the two principal demands of such a position; concealment and a good field of fire.

Opposite page, bottom: The weapons with which 7th SS Gebirg Division 'Prinz Eugen' were issued were not standard in the German Army. This weapon, being operated by Jaeger near Ripac, is a Czech ZB53 machine-gun. Yugoslavia, 1944.

Below: Walking wounded of 7th SS Gebirgs Division 'Prinz Eugen' outside the regimental aid post. Yugoslavia, autumn 1944.

Above: Officers of the 'Prinz Eugen' Division interrogating a brigade commander of the partisan Chetnik organization. Yugoslavia, 1944.

Below: Towards the end of the war the German divisions were reduced to using oxen to pull guns and supply carts. Yugoslavia, 1944/5. 7th SS Division.

Above: The Grand Mufti of Jerusalem shaking hands with an officer of 13th SS Gebirgs Division 'Handschar' during an official visit to the division.

Below left: Jaeger of 15th SS Gebirgs Division 'Handschar' operating in the mountains of Bosnia. Although the division recruited both Muslims and Christians, all ranks wore the fez head-dress.

Below right: Fredi Scheucher, a Gebirgsjaeger who served with 3rd Division.

Left: The Riegersburg in the Ossteier, which was captured by the Russians in their first thrust into eastern Austria in March–April 1945, and retaken by German troops under the command of General Ringel.

Left: The type of terrain in which fighting was conducted in the last months of the war in Obersteier, the northern sector of the Steiermark, where 1st and 9th Gebirgs Divisions fought.

Left: The German military cemetery on the Semmering in Austria, in which lie, mostly, the dead of 9th Gebirgs Division.

Below: The German military cemetery for paratroops and mountain troops, on Crete.

pursuit of the shattered Soviet forces. At the level of Army Group the main emphasis of that pursuit lay with Sixth Army, which was driving towards a major objective; Kiev, the capital of the Ukraine. Supreme Stavka ordered the city to be held at all costs and drew units for its defence from all the Soviet armies in the immediate area. The weakening of these neighbouring armies left them incapable of withstanding the massive blows which Army Group rained upon them. Von Kleist, aware of the reduction in strength of the Soviet host confronting his 1st Panzer Group, promptly launched a massive armoured thrust which shattered and scattered the Russian forces. His panzers roared through the enemy's ruptured front and raced towards the Dnieper, leaving the infantry armies, Sixth on its left and Seventeenth on its right, to come forward as best they could, held as both were to the pace of the foot soldier. Soon, the spearheads of von Kleist's Panzer Group had penetrated so deep into Soviet territory that they formed a long and vulnerable salient, but despite their vulnerability Stavka did not attack this in force. Rather did they, unwittingly, aid von Kleist by issuing the uncompromising order that Kiev was to be held to the last. Indeed the Soviet High Command continued to pour more and still more troops into the Kiev area and that great mass of immobile formations was quickly bypassed by the fast-moving 1st Panzer Group on the one side and, eventually, by the slower-moving Seventeenth Army on the other. Within a short time their advances had created a pair of pincers. If their jaws met they would enclose, west of the Dnieper bend, at least two Red Armies. More than 100,000 trapped Russians would face death or captivity. Let us anticipate the outcome of the Battle of Uman and learn that some Red Army units made good their escape. This admission only serves to underscore the achievements of XLIX Gebirgskorps whose marches and counter-marches across the wide and open Ukrainian steppe land were able to hold within the southern side of the pocket the greatest number of Red Army units and prevent their escape.

The participation of the Gebirgs divisions in the encirclement Battle of Uman was determined by an Army Order dated 19 July which read, 'Now that the fighting for Vinnitsa has ended, XLIX Corps is to regroup and to prepare to advance with its right wing directed towards Nemirov and its left wing at Ilinche.' This set the Gebirgskorps marching towards Uman and into one of the most bitter battles that its divisions were to experience. Another Army Order dated 25 July directed Corps to fling back the Russian rearguards and continue the advance towards Uman.

All the divisions of Corps were now pursuing an enemy who was pulling back and the line of the Soviet retreat would bring its formations marching directly on to the guns of von Kleist's panzer divisions surrounding Uman. The Russian host, fifteen divisions of which were armoured or motorized, was nearly completely surrounded with the only real hope of escape through Uman to Kirovgrad. The panzer divisions of von Kleist's Group now formed a solid wall to prevent the escape of the Red Army to the Dnieper at Kremenchug. With the panzers blocking the eastern and northern routes, the infantry of Seventeenth Army in the south could begin operations to constrict the Uman pocket. But those infantry and Gebirgsjaeger formations already in position were insufficient in number. More were needed to thicken the ring around the enclosed Russian forces.

To meet this need 1st Gebirgs Division and 125th Infantry Division were released from their duties in the Bug bridgehead and force-marched to catch up with 4th Gebirgs and 97th Division. Corps ordered 1st Gebirgs to capture and advance up the road from Vinnitsa to Neminov. General Kuebler stressed the need for speed and Lanz, commanding the 1st, created from his division a mobile group and a marching group. The mobile detachment consisted of Jaeger in trucks, the reconnaissance battalion, some artillery batteries and the PAK. The task of the battle group was to open the road for the marching group, 99th Regiment, and to keep the road clear so that the marching Jaeger met little opposition en route to Neminov where they would take up their positions in the battle line. The 99th marched down the road, then along the western bank of the River Yatran, captured the bridge at Neminov and then headed eastwards to Dukova, while the fast battle group headed south-eastwards towards Brazlov. Opposition to the division's advance, which had been light to moderate to begin with, then hardened, proof that the 1st was entering a sector which the Red Army was determined to hold. The terrain favoured the defence, being hilly and extensively wooded. In the valleys between the hills, the innumerable tributaries of the River Ssed had created swamp-like conditions. The one good, all-weather, road across this difficult region was the predictable route, the one which the Germans would have to take, and the commanders of the Russian rearguard were determined to hold the highway which was vital to their defence of the sector. Most of my correspondents who wrote of events at that time remark that the weather began to change from long, hot, sun-filled days into days of driving rain and frequent thunderstorms. Rural roads, which were often little more than pathways, quickly lost their surfaces, making movement by wheeled transport virtually impossible. The panzers had little-better luck and most of the bogged-down vehicles were forced to wait until a brief spell of clear weather dried the ground sufficiently to liberate them. Although the motorized columns were held fast in the clinging Ukrainian mud, the infantry regiments still continued to march. Life for the Jaeger was an unremitting misery of marching all day long in soaking uniforms and then resting at night in saturated clothing. A correspondent recalled how most mornings, as his battalion grouped to continue the march, there hung above the column a cloud of steam produced by wet clothes drying out on human bodies. The 1st and 4th gained touch and then advanced side by side to areas below Uman, that is to say on the south-western and southern side of the ring around the Russians.

The right wing of 1st Gebirgs gained touch with 9th Panzer Division which was holding the land bridge to the east of the River Ssinyka, but it was only loose touch and much of the area between the inner wings of these two formations was covered only by patrols. The ring was still not yet closed. There was a wide gap in the south between the Rivers Ssinyka and Yatran, and 4th Gebirgs, which had been relieved from the line for a rest, was ordered back into action to close this. The first attacks to cross the Yatran in assault boats were unsuccessful. The Soviets held the ground in too great a strength to be overcome by the action of a single German division, even one as competent as 4th Gebirgs. Yet unless the 4th could fight its way through and reach the river quickly the enemy might expand the existing small gaps and make a mass escape. A line of advance which could bypass the Soviet masses was found when the divisional advance guard captured Polonisstoya and the ford across the River Yatran. The 91st regiment was ordered to cross the river. To do this involved the 91st in a forced march of nearly 30 kilometres, but even when it had forded the Yatran it was given no rest. Instead the battalions were now ordered to catch up with the advance guard which had, by this time, reached a point some 5 kilometres south-west of Podvysokoya and had thus closed another sector of the southern ring. In the dying days of July Army Group South was in a favourable strategic situation. Eleventh Army, its right flank formation, was driving before it a beaten and dispirited enemy. German Sixth Army held fast a number of major Red formations in and around Kiev. Below Sixth Army, Seventeenth Army and 1st Panzer Group had surrounded two Russian armies around Uman.

OKW now directed Army Group South to prevent the escape of the Russian forces across the Dnieper. Von Kleist changed the thrust-line of his Panzer Group from east to south. Along the entire length of his northern pincer arm he had 'dropped off' small detachments to contain, or herd back into containment, those Red Army units that were seeking escape. His remaining formations formed a wall of armour along the northern and eastern sides of the pocket, and on its western side, elements of Seventeenth Army had coalesced to form a firm front. Only in the south and in the south-west was the ring less tight, and the story of the Gebirgsjaeger divisions in those dying days of July and the opening days of August is one of marching and counter-marching; of fighting by day and night to close the gaps in the wall in the south and south-east and to keep them closed.

At OKW level the task of encirclement was considered to have been accomplished and the destruction of the Russian host, now only a matter of time, could be left to the infantry to accomplish. In vain did von Stulpnagel and XLIX Corps commander complain that the infantry were bearing too heavy a burden. OKW was adamant. The armour had to be conserved – the Uman pocket had now become an infantry battle. This may have been the viewpoint at OKW, but it was not one shared by those at the lowest levels of Seventeenth Army. The Russians might be surrounded, but they would certainly make suicidal efforts to break out in the south and south-east where the line was thinnest and which, therefore, offered the most likely avenues of escape. XLIX Gebirgskorps stood on that sector where it was expected the Red Army would make the breakout attempts. Corps' front ran crescent-shaped, north-west to south-east. The left flank was held by 125th Division while below it along the line of the River Yatran was 4th Gebirgs Division. On its right was 1st Gebirgs on whose right flank was, as we have seen, 9th Panzer Division of Kleist's Panzer Group. On the sector held by 4th Division the villages of Peregenovka and Kopyenkovata were those where the Russians were to mount their heaviest attempts. Ternovka was where the main attempt would be made against 1st Gebirgs Division and the village of Podvysokoya was where the final battle would be fought out.

Between the time that XLIX Corps arrived in the area to the southeast of Uman, to the day on which the encirclement operation can be said to have ended, its divisions – or more usually its battalions and even individual Companies – marched backwards and forwards to fight at one threatened break-out point after another. It was a test of endurance. As one man wrote before the offensive began, '. . . whatever happens we must never get tired, but must keep marching . . .'

Even as the units of 4th Gebirgs Division took up their positions between 125th and 1st Divisions they had come under attack. It was soon clear that these early Red Army assaults were more in the nature of probes to test the fighting qualities and defensive abilities of the German defenders, rather than all-out, major assaults. Those were to come later and after hard defensive fighting they were all repulsed. To tighten the divisional front and to gain jumping-off points for the next stage of the offensive, 4th was ordered to take Point 193, a commanding height on the road to Kopyenkovata. The 2nd Battalion, 13th Regiment captured the feature against fanatical resistance which increased as other battalions sought to carry the advance into the village itself. What was planned to be the final attack in the offensive was ordered to open at 10.00 on 5 August. In sober words Corps declared that the operation was to give the *coup de grâce* to the enemy formations. '. . . Tomorrow's battle MUST bring the enemy's resistance to an end . . .' Only the senior commanders knew that there were not enough artillery shells to fight a second battle and no more could be procured.

The objectives for 1st Division were the heights north of Bondaryovka and for 4th Division the villages of Podvysokya and Kopyenkovata. Corps' battle plan was to involve 4th Gebirgs and particularly 13th Regiment, in whose territory both objectives lay, in a struggle whose ferocity became a byword among Gebirgs units. The 13th began its approach march during the night of 4 August, a bright moonlit night, as the War Diary records. There was a gap in Corps' line which the regiment's advance would close when it gained touch with the right-flank neighbour, 91st Gebirgsjaeger Regiment. The village of Podvysokoya seemed to be deserted, but as the leading files of Jaeger drew close it was seen that the enemy was massed in strength around the village as well as in the houses and streets. Reports from Regiment to 4th Division Headquarters stated that the place was crammed with Soviet troops who were clearly determined to hold it. The Russians offered desperate resistance but the 13th's advance could not be held and the Jaeger drove out the enemy, regrouped and began to advance towards the next objective, Kopyenkovata. One who took part in the attack upon that village described the hurricane of Russian artillery fire which crashed down, forcing the advancing Companies to take cover. Its intensity halted the advance but it was not shellfire alone which brought the attack to a standstill. The Red Army units defending the village had had time to construct extensive field works which had been strengthened with barbed wire fences. In support of the Red forces were whole regiments of field and heavy artillery. Reluctantly the Companies withdrew in order to minimize casualties. Reluctantly, because the Jaeger had gone into battle with the certain conviction that they would win the day. But the strength of the trench systems and the artillery fire, backed by machine-gun and rifle fire, much of it coming from defenders only 100 metres' distant, could not be overcome. The Companies went over to the defensive to the east of the village. Both sides were now experiencing the same crisis; failure in the supply system. The almost incessant rain had halted all vehicle movement. The Russian forward units were supplied by occasional air drops, but the Jaeger, in the muddy holes which were their slit trenches, had to wait, hungry and wet through, until a detachment could struggle through calf-deep mud to bring forward cooked food.

During the first week of August the fighting for Kopyenkovata began to reach its climax as the Soviets grouped their forces in the south of the pocket for the offensive that would tear open the German net. This enemy build-up was either not comprehended by Corps, or else was intentionally underplayed for in the SITREP to Seventeenth Army issued during the evening of 6 August, Kuebler stated, '. . . all the Divisions of Gebirgskorps are at this moment going over to a general and all-out assault . . .' This optimistic statement was issued on the same night as the breakout attempts against the thin line of XLIX Corps opened.

'The early part of that terrible night was unusually quiet although a propaganda detachment and 13th Regiment were said to have reported vehicle noises near Kopyenkovata. At 02.00hrs there was machine-gun and rifle fire as on our sector the front suddenly became very active.' A battle report stated, '. . . At about 03.00hrs the sound of engines which had persisted all night, grew louder. In the growing light of day we could see a dense and unbroken column of soft-skin vehicles . . . Towards 05.00hrs the neighbouring regiment halted the Soviet advance and destroyed the tanks escorting the vehicle column. Then we saw another great collection of vehicles and an extensive cloud of smoke on the heights to the south of Kopyenkovata . . . On the road in our sector those columns that had not succeeded in smashing through stood 6 to 8 abreast. The column had driven at top speed through the narrow streets of the village and had been fired upon by anti-tanks guns in position at the exit to Peregenovka. Their fire 'brewed up' the leading vehicles. Then the last truck was attacked and began to burn. The fire spread from truck to truck.

A few escaped back into the encirclement by driving down side streets and across fields. The main breakout attempt had failed but some vehicles had managed to crash through and they, together with their accompanying tanks, were caught in the village of Peregenovka [by the artillery batteries echeloned in depth behind the Jaeger battalions]. Behind the Jaeger slit-trench line the heavy howitzer batteries supporting 13th Regiment reported that they were under infantry attack and then a great flood of Russian infantry swarmed forward and managed to reach divisional headquarters in Peregenovka. It was clear that there had been a breakthrough on some neighbouring sector and that Red units were escaping from the encirclement. Fighting then developed into battles by individual Companies, by artillery batteries and by isolated groups of Jaeger struggling to contain the Russian flood. They fought hard to fling back the Soviet soldiers and they succeeded.'

On another sector 4,000 enemy infantry advanced, marching in step behind a group of tanks. This operation was intended to breach the line and allow the staff of 6th Red Army to escape. The attempt was driven back, but a second attack was made only hours later with the Red Army men storming forward across the bodies of those who had fallen in the first assault. Neither this nor subsequent attacks were able to force a breakthrough. With the collapse of the Russian attacks the commander of the 13th then swung his own main effort to the left flank, determined to capture Kopyenkovata. During the advance the first large groups of Russian troops began to surrender. There were, however, other groups who were determined to fight on, and whose staunch defence prevented the Jaeger from capturing the village. A great number of Russian battalions still tried to break through in mass attacks, advancing time after time into German machine-gun fire. These hopeless assaults were crushed one after the other and the regiment resumed its advance, entered the village, taking care to comb the sunflower fields and the extensive woods which covered the area. More Russian soldiers came in or were taken prisoner. The last flickers of Soviet resistance did not die away until the 14th and even then it required the whole of 13th Regiment to clear the Kopyenkovata woods.

The War Diary of XLIX Gebirgs, describing the scene of destruction, relates how hundreds of Russians, many lying dead in the human wave formation in which they had stormed forward, covered the ground up to the edge of the Jaeger trenches. 'Smashed armoured fighting vehicles and trucks littered the fields, the remnants of the failed break-out attempt during the night of 6/7 August . . . The incinerated and broken bodies of the crews lay amid the wreckage . . . a frightful picture of destruction . . .'

The encirclement Battle of Uman, also known as the Battle of Podvysokoya, was at an end. The Gebirgskorps captured 22,000 prisoners, including three general officers and took one hundred guns and fifty armoured vehicles. It was a splendid victory, but, with only the shortest time allowed for regrouping, Kuebler's Corps was next directed to advance to the Dnieper. Hitler still considered the capture of Moscow to be less important than the seizure of the Crimea, the Donets iron and coal complexes and the cutting off of the Caucasus oil supplies. In pursuit of these objectives, the Jaeger divisions, together with 144th Division, crossed the Dnieper and took part in a series of offensives which gained ground both to the east and in the south. The most bloody of these battles was fought out from 5 to 18 October and has passed into Gebirgsjaeger lore as the battle for Mogila Tokmak. By this time the Jaeger were veterans and had seen death in its most frightening, grotesque and terrifying forms. But the sights seen during the five-day battle near the Sea of Azov, surpassed in horror all that the battle-hardened warriors had yet seen. In his book, *Gebirgsjaeger: The 1st Gebirgs Division 1935–1945*, General Lanz described the battle from the viewpoint of a senior commander and wrote that near Mogila Tokmak a vast rocky hill rose out of the steppe. From the summit of that hill there was a panoramic view of the battlefield, 'on which sights of confusion and disorder on the Soviet side were evident. Between burning villages, disorganized groups of Russian infantry, their officers mounted on chargers, marched to and fro without objective. The enemy artillery, seeking to advance to action, was caught and shot to pieces by our guns. Horses without riders galloped about. Vehicle columns sought to take cover. But this tragedy did not last long. In such a situation even the commissars were powerless. The soldiers began to surrender. One hundred thousand prisoners, numerous guns and tanks fell into German hands. The Russian 18th Army had been wiped out. The 1st Gebirgs Division played a distinctive part in this great victory.'

Kuebler's XLIX Corps then went on to captured Stalino in the Donets basin and fought another battle, almost in isolation, along the River Mius. Both Gebirgs divisions remained in the Mius positions for what remained of 1941, waiting for the early summer of 1942 when campaigning weather would return again.

2nd, 3rd, 6th, 6th SS and 7th Gebirgs Divisions in Lappland, 1941—1945

A T THIS POINT we move geographically from the southern sectors of the vast battle line in Russia to northern Norway, and back in time from the autumn of 1941 to late 1940. At that time and in northern Norway 2nd Gebirgs Division had been put to the tasks of repairing destroyed bridges, erecting new ones and constructing roads. This work was halted towards autumn when orders came for Division to move into the high northern provinces of Norway at the farthest edge of the European mainland, high above the Arctic Circle, where Norway and Finland meet. The 2nd Gebirgs Division was ordered to occupy Kirkenes and the region around that town as far eastwards as the frontier with Finland. One of the principal reasons for the move into an otherwise ungarrisoned area was that British forces had invaded both Greenland and Iceland and OKW was aware of the need to guard the north against British attempts to land in Norway.

The 2nd moved by sea, the small convoy of transports which carried it hugging the coast and arriving at length in Altafiord. The Norwegian province of Finnmark in Lappland, extending eastwards from Kirkenes, was now the divisional operations area. Shortly before the artillery regiment sailed it was able to commandeer sufficient Norwegian 7.5cm pieces to raise two new batteries, Nos. 3 and 6. Anticipating the poor road communications it was likely to meet in the new area, Division also commandeered 600 motorized sledges – inferior to their own Austrian ones in negotiating difficult terrain – but welcome just the same. General Dietl, the Commander of Gebirgskorps 'Norway', decided not to locate his HQ in the small settlement of Alla, with its primitive living conditions. Instead he took over a 500-ton motor-ship, *The Black Watch* and had it brought into Altafiord for use as a mobile headquarters.

Throughout the following weeks tramp streamers plied between harbours in Norway and Altafiord bringing in the supplies which the Gebirgsjaeger would need in the 8-month-long winter that lay ahead. Accommodation for the troops was a primary consideration, and soon small towns had been built to house the units. Together with the construction of living quarters there were other military measures to be met, chief of which was reinforcement. The 199th Infantry Division was ordered up out of southern Norway to join the Gebirgskorps and there were increases in Corps' artillery strength and in the number of engineer road building Companies. The whole force lay quartered in the fishing villages around Varangerfiord and it was in these positions that the units spent the long, dark months. With the end of the winter of 1940/1, a new wave of preparation began.

On 20 April 1941 General Dietl travelled to Berlin and was one of a group of officers at a Fuehrer Conference in the Chancellery. Hitler turned to a map of the far north of Europe and pointed to Murmansk. The importance of that town, he declared, was not only that its harbour did not freeze in winter but that the 1,400-kilometre-long railway line from Leningrad could transport an army which might strike to capture the Finnish nickel ore mines at Petsamo. Germany needed the produce of those mines for her war effort and although Finland was neutral the leaders of the Third Reich anticipated that she would become Germany's ally in a war against the Soviet Union. In that event, it was the prediction of German High Command, that the immediate Soviet reaction would be for the Red Army to advance westwards from Murmansk to capture the Petsamo nickel mines. It was to prevent the loss of these vitally important ore deposits that units of the Army and the Luftwaffe were to be sent to Finland. The imperative for operations by German forces in Lappland were, so Hitler declared, economic and it would be the task of Gebirgskorps 'Norway' to pre-empt any Russian move by striking eastwards to capture Murmansk 100 kilometres away. Dietl was familiar with the Petsamo region and described it to Hitler as looking like the world on the first day of creation with no trees, no vegetation – nothing except bare rock, huge boulders and rushing water. The long winter season, he explained, turned the land into an icy desert with temperatures falling to below 50 degrees of frost. The winter was one long dark night which lasted for eight months. In the short summer the sun did not set and day-time temperatures rose to above 30 degrees. In place of the winter snows rain fell almost continuously throughout the summer, feeding the extensive and groundless swamps. It was a miserable desert both in winter and in summer. 'There has never been a war fought in the high north,' Dietl declared. 'The region is unsuited to military operations. There are no roads and these would have to be constructed before any advance could take place.' He pointed out that if his men were taken to build roads there would be no soldiers to do the fighting. The Gebirgsjaeger general drew the Fuehrer's attention to the lack of prime movers to tow the artillery pieces, to the absence of SP guns and to the shortage of men.

His appreciation of the situation was correct. The future theatre of operations was so forbidding a region that Finnish military authorities declared it to be an impossible place in which to fight a war. Before the onset of the winter season they withdrew all their military forces garrisoning Lappland to areas below the 65th Parallel. The area abandoned by the Finns each winter was more than 800 kilometres wide and stretched from the town of Sumoussalhi on the 65th Parallel to Petsamo in the far north. It was precisely that area to which Hitler had ordered the German Lappland Army. Dietl put forward counter-proposals. For the Gebirgsjaeger to capture Murmansk was not necessary. That town was linked to the rest of Russia by the railway line to which Hitler had drawn attention. If the line were cut to the south of Murmansk no reinforcements could reach it. The Fuehrer first accepted Dietl's proposals but then changed his mind and produced his own battle plan. The Lappland Army would not comprise a single force but would be split into three Corps, each of which would have a separate objective. Dietl's Gebirgsjaegerkorps 'Norway' would still take Murmansk. Nearly 200 kilometres to the south XXXVI Corps was to cut the railway line at Kandaleshka and some 350 kilometres farther south still, Finnish 3rd Corps was to cut the line at Louhi.

Dietl returned to the Gebirgskorps where he discussed preparations for the future campaign with his subordinates. General Feurstein, GOC 2nd Gebirgs Division, expressed serious misgivings on a number of points until Dietl ended the discussion with the brusque declaration, 'I know we are understrength and I am aware of all the difficulties facing us. But if I am given the order to attack I shall do so.' Feurstein, who was perhaps reported as lacking confidence in the German leadership, was replaced by General Schlemmer on 28 March.

Slowly the build-up to the new war began. Maps issued to the senior officers of the Lappland Army were found to be wildly inaccurate when compared to those which the Finnish General Staff had prepared. German cartographers, lacking up-to-date Soviet maps to which to refer, took old maps and used their imagination to interpret both blank areas and Russian map symbols. This was not always successful. They had supposed the double line on Soviet maps to represent a road when it meant only telegraph lines. The German cartographers had also mistaken the lines marking the Finno–Soviet frontier line as a main highway. When the time came for Gebirgskorps to advance, it did so confident in the belief that ahead of it there were good roads. Its commanders and men were soon to be disillusioned; ahead lay only swamp, rock and tundra.

The military preparations then reached down to the level of the rank and file. Leave was stopped and NCOs and men who had been on temporary postings to other formations or who had been away on courses were returned to unit. Their preparations complete, one by one the various detachments of 2nd Gebirgs Division began to move to positions along the Finno–Soviet border. One regiment, the 137th, carried out a cross-country march of 350 kilometres across the tundra of northern Norway as a familiarization exercise. On 18 June the issue of the code-word 'Reindeer' authorized the senior commanders to open their sealed orders. In part these read, 'Gebirgskorps Norway, will advance across the Norwegian/Finnish frontier, occupy Finnish Lappland up to the town of Petsamo, the harbour at Liimanmamaki and the ore mines around Kolosyoksi. The forces will then be disposed tactically so that they are able to defend the area against land, sea and air assault. The issue of the code-word 'Silver Fox' will be the signal for Corps to strike across the Finnish–Soviet frontier and to attack Murmansk . . .'

Three days later, in the sombre, rainy evening of 21 June, Corps began its move and its advance guard had soon reached the Finnish frontier at Boris Gleb. Shortly after midnight the divisional commander arrived and at 02.30 on 22 June, led his men into Finland along the only good road in the whole area, a serpentine one which followed the banks of the River Patsuoki as it flowed towards Petsamo. The division's first objective inside Finland was Parkkina, a fairly large town by Lapp standards and an important one for it housed a number of foreign Consulates. Around Parkkina the division regrouped its regiments ready to lead them into the Soviet Union when the code-word 'Silver Fox' was issued. This did not come immediately. For seven long days the units waited; seven days in which the Red Army had time to prepare its forces and defences to meet the assault which they knew would be made. After a week of frustration the order to march came and the OKW communiqué of 29 June could announce, '. . . German Gebirgsjaeger advanced towards Murmansk, across the snow-covered tundra and by the light of the midnight sun . . .' Dietl's Gebirgskorps had entered the war against the Soviet Union.

The deployment of an entire German army in a region high above the Arctic Circle is one of the lesser-known facts of the Russo–German War of 1941–5. This army was not a huge force. At no time in its brief life did it contain more than six divisions, but it is of interest in the context of this book because many of these formations were Gebirgsjaeger. To use such specialist troops in this region was a misuse of their potential for, although there were indeed mountains in Lappland, the Gebirgsjaeger for the most part did not fight on the high ground but more usually in the swamps and marshes.

The history of the German campaign in northern Finnland is of opportunities lost because Lappland was considered by OKW to be a side-show and not a main battle front. As a consequence the Lappland Army was starved of supplies. The story is of an advance eastwards in the summer of 1941, which went against the basic rules of military offensive strategy; march separately but strike simultaneously. Hitler's rejection of that logical strategy allowed the Red Army to meet and halt the first German assaults in Lappland and follow up with their own counter-offensive during 1942. Thereafter, there were few major military operations until, in October 1944, the Finns abandoned Germany as an ally, and the Lappland Army was forced to withdraw to Norway to avoid being taken prisoner by the Finns, their former allies.

That, in outline, is the course of military operations carried out by the opposing forces in the far north. Before we go on to follow the early battles in detail, let us consider factors which dominated the campaign: The terrain in which thousands of German soldiers were killed by enemy action, by the severity of the climate or by their own hands – for the icy desert which was Lappland induced suicidal melancholia. Let us further consider the size of the new theatre of war, its primitive state and other factors, which gave Lappland its frightening reputation and the undying hatred of those who had to fight there.

In order to present as a complete whole the German Army's operations in that northern theatre of war, the following pages cover the fighting there from the summer of 1941 to the summer of 1944. The retreat of Twentieth Gebirgs Army – the former Lappland Army – during October 1944 is dealt with in a later chapter.

Finland has a low population and long frontiers. Its capital, Helsinki, lies in the south of the country close to the Russian city of Leningrad. In order to protect Helsinki as well as to collaborate with German Army Group North in its operations against Leningrad, the great mass of the Finnish Army was concentrated in the south of the country. Certain sensitive sectors of Finland's central area were protected by a thin screen of troops but the area above the Arctic Circle, where Norway, Finland and Russia met, was not garrisoned at all in the cold weather months. As already explained the Finns considered that no military operations could be conducted in the Oedmark during winter and were also of the opinion that no more than two divisions could be supplied and maintained in that area during the short summer, because of the lack of road and rail links.

The following account by former Oberjaeger Lamm illustrates the difficulties encountered by the soldiers of Dietl's Corps. They were equipped and outfitted for operations in a temperate, central-European climate, but had been sent on active service to a country which experienced violent changes of temperature. 'We had nothing with which to overcome the conditions we encountered when we arrived in the area during July/August 1941. On active service and especially in a combat zone the soldier's first task is to dig in. It was just not possible in our area. The ground was either solid rock or else the top soil was spongy and we met ground water at just one spit down. Digging in was, therefore, impossible and blockhouses made of logs were built on top of the swamp. These were always damp, our uniforms were always wet and our leather equipment was soon covered in mould. In the summer months it never got dark and even at 2 in the morning the sky was so light that it was possible to read a newspaper. The worst things were the mosquitoes and other flying pests which bred in the water and which now had, for the first time in generations, human blood to suck. The mosquitoes moved in clouds and made our lives a misery. Looking back I think that on balance, in the early days, the insects were a worse nuisance than the enemy. For a long time we heard and saw little of the Russian forces and only with the onset of winter did they really become active.'

In a similar vein the situation report submitted by one officer mentioned the almost trackless wasteland where the sparse population lived in isolated villages, set far apart and linked only by the railway. This officer's gloomy report ended with the condemnation, 'If there is a Hell for soldiers, then the Oedmark is it . . .' It was to this mosquito-ridden swampland that Gebirgskorps Norway came in the spring of 1941. Dietl and his men considered the barren and treeless northern Oedmark to be a hell on earth, but much of the southern sector was heavily forested. In some places the deep and silent woods were so primaeval that they could be accurately described as jungle. It was in these jungle conditions that other German units had to fight.

The Lappland Army, soon to be renamed Twentieth Gebirgs Army, and first commanded by General von Falkenhorst, Supreme Commander Norway, was disposed from south to north with 3rd Finnish Corps (3rd and 6th Divisions) on the right or southern flank. In the centre was German XXXVI Corps (169th Infantry and SS Battle Group 'Nord' later to be 6th SS Gebirgs Division 'Nord'). The left or northern flank was held by Gebirgskorps 'Norway' (2nd and 3rd Gebirgs Divisions.) To exercise battlefield control over his three widely spread corps, von Falkenhorst set up Army Headquarters in Rovaniemi, the capital of Lappland, a small town of less than ten thousand inhabitants and positioned just above the Arctic Circle. In that desert region above the 60th Parallel his units prepared for the imminent war with Russia.

The fact that OKW considered Lappland to be a minor theatre of operations and that the war against Russia would be concluded swiftly, is probably the reason why, at least to begin with, little or no consideration was given to the many and varied problems which faced Falkenhorst's army. One of these was unique. The magnetic influence of the North Pole affected both compass readings and wireless traffic and when the seriousness of these problems was at last realized special training course had to be set up and astronomy taught so that, on clear nights, soldiers could move using the stars as a guide. The snow levels in the Lappland winter were appreciably higher than on the other parts of the Eastern Front and a vast number of trucks fitted as snow ploughs had to be employed. This brought the problem that in Lappland's abnormally low temperatures the engine oil used in German vehicles froze quickly into a solid mass and even specially treated, winter grade oils were by and large ineffective. Trucks could not be used unless they were fitted with extra wide tracks to support their weight in the snow and had to have a high ground clearance so that the chassis was not fouled by the high snow carpet.

The question of winter clothing for the troops produced its own problems. The Gebirgsjaeger were familiar with the dangers of frostbite but the rigours of a Lappland winter brought the need for special types of clothing, including a felt balaclava helmet which was pulled down to protect the whole face. Fur-lined garments were essential, and felt-lined jack boots were issued to counter the cold and wet. A white camouflage overall was found to be more practical than the standard issue snow shirt. In summer a type of camouflage balaclava was issued and mosquito nets were essential. Adaptability was the keynote as Oberjaeger Lamm recalled. 'I know that in the Caucasus Gebirgsjaeger used Bactrian camels as draught-animals. We in the Arctic, used, among other forms of transport, sledges, just like explorers, each of which was drawn by twelve dogs. These were quite savage animals, more like wolves than the domestic dogs with which we were familiar.'

When the opening offensive was halted short of its objectives the Germans were forced to accept the Finnish General Staff assessment that the Oedmark region was not one in which major offensive operations could be undertaken. The greatest amount of military activity would therefore be restricted to the three types of patrol: standing, reconnaissance and fighting. As is usual in desert or jungle conditions, reconnaissance and fighting patrols were of deep penetration and might last for anything up to fourteen days. This brought into play the question of how the troops were to be sheltered while away from base since the standard issue tent-half was clearly unsuitable in low temperatures. The troops had to be taught to construct native-style shelters from trees branches and to build snow igloos. Standing patrols, on the other hand, could be accommodated in wooden huts built for the purpose. In Lappland there are no natural food products and all supplies for the German forces had to be brought from outside the area and moved by road because in those days no railway ran north of Rovianemi. The road distances which had to be covered were enormous. The Arctic Sea highway, for example, which ran from Rovianemi to the units in the field, was more than 500 kilometres long. The Lappland Army numbered 100,000 men and needed a minimum supply of at least 5,000 tons of ammunition, food and fuel for each day of battle. Each Gebirgs division had on its establishment 7,000 horses or mules and 100 tons of fodder per day was required by each division. Well might the staff officers of the Lappland Army have echoed the sentiment of their counterparts in the Afrikakorps that, 'a desert is a quartermaster's hell.'

The following chapters dealing with the war above the Arctic Circle describe the first attacks carried out by both Dietl's Gebirgskorps Norway and the SS Gebirgs Division 'Nord' and then carry their story to the middle months of 1944.

The 2nd and 3rd Gebirgs Divisions of Dietl's Corps held the most notherly flank of the German Army on the Eastern Front. Their task was to advance and to cover what Hitler described as the 'laughable 100 kilometres' between the Finno–Russian frontier and the town of Murmansk. The battles to reach that target brought Corps to the River Liza, some 60 kilometres from the objective. The Germans gained little more ground after those first advances and what ground they did capture was very soon lost to Red Army counter-offensives.

For the opening operation Dietl disposed his divisions with 2nd on the left and 3rd on the right flank. The 2nd was to advance with its left wing resting on the Barents Sea. The 3rd was to protect the right wing of 2nd Division in its eastward drive. Between its own right wing and XXXVI Corps away to the south, yawned a gap, hundreds of kilometres wide, which was covered only by patrols of Finnish irregular military units.

Both Divisions of Gebirgskorps Norway spent the 'lost' seven days at the opening of the war against Russia garrisoning the 40-kilometre stretch of tundra between Parkinna and the Finno–Russian frontier, building corduroy tracks into the concentration area of the opening offensive and putting into a useable state the poor country road that ran from Parkkina to the border. The road was in such a state of disrepair that both divisional and regimental war diaries make frequent mention of horses being used to drag trucks out of the mud holes in which they were trapped. And all that road building and road repairing activity was carried on under attack by squadrons of Soviet aircraft. 'We seldom saw our Luftwaffe fighters but were given excellent support by the Stuka squadrons once operations opened and certainly in the early days.'

By 28 June, and despite these difficulties, Gebirgskorps had completed its preparations. Dietl gave orders that the offensive was to open at 03.00 on the following day. The 2nd Division was to break through the Russian defensive positions – lines of massive concrete bunkers which had been set up to defend the approaches to Murmansk. To speed their capture a platoon of 8.8cm guns was to be deployed by firing at point-blank range. During the time that the bunker line was being frontally attacked by one battalion of 2nd Division the main effort was to be made by von Hengl's battle group of 137th Regiment. This detachment, two battalions strong, was to bypass the bunker line on its right or landward flank and seize the bridge across the River Titova leaving the defensive positions to be taken by 2nd Battalion. Shortly before the units were ready to cross their start-lines a bank of sea fog came rolling in. Soon everything was obscured in so thick a cloud that the Stuka attacks had to be cancelled and the artillery observers were forced to shoot 'blind', being unable to direct the fire of their batteries. This was certainly the fog of war in its truest sense and 137th Regiment opened the attack moving slowly through the mist and maintaining direction by compass bearing. The fog screen had the advantage that the two battalions of the outflanking group were able to complete most of their move against minimal opposition. Then at about 04.30 the mist thinning around Point 204, the key position on that sector, disclosed to the Russian troops the line of Jaeger climbing towards the crest. A storm of rifle and machine-gun fire struck the attackers, but they rallied quickly and raced forward in a bayonet charge. The Jaeger stormed over the Russian trench line but before they had a chance to consolidate their gains were involved in fighting off a succession of counter-attacks. Even before the last of these had been crushed, von Hengl's group, with 1st Battalion, 137th Regiment leading, had descended into the valley of the Titova and were streaming forward to capture the river bridge. This was taken and units began to pass over together with other crossings made by detachments carried in assault boats. The Jaeger units on the eastern bank of the Titova concentrated in a small perimeter, preparing to burst out of its confines and carry the advance eastwards towards Murmansk.

Meanwhile, 2nd Battalion, 137th Regiment had opened its attack against the line of pillboxes and the trenches surrounding them. The speed with which this operation was successfully concluded illustrates how hard the Jaeger had trained. Behind assault pioneers who blew gaps in the dense barbed-wire entanglements, other groups went in with flame-throwers and explosive charges. Where the Russian defence was too strong to be overcome by the lightly armed Jaeger, the 88s were brought forward to shoot the bunkers into rubble. By 09.00 the high ground on which the bunkers stood was in the hands of 2nd/137th and every war diary comments that the enemy positions had to be taken out individually and that their garrisons, Mongols and men of other Asiatic races, fought until they were killed or so badly wounded that they could no longer resist. By the morning of 30 June the commander of 137th Regiment could report that the whole bunker line had been taken, the Titova bridge had been captured intact and a bridgehead on the river's eastern bank was held by two of its battalions.

To the north of 137th, the other Jaeger regiment in 2nd Division was advancing towards an objective which Division had designated 'Fishermen's Peninsula'. This sector was to become a running sore which drained the strength of Gebirgskorps for all the time that the Germans held the area. Dietl had too few men to capture the entire peninsula whereas the Russians, with control of the sea and air, could not only reinforce their garrison but could launch attacks at will. Aware of his division's weakness Schlemmer, the general commanding 2nd Division, gave orders to Hake's 136th Regiment to dominate the neck of the land bridge and prevent any Soviet incursion out of the peninsula. The approach march to carry out Schlemmer's order was a terrible experience. The route to the neck of the peninsula lay across fields of chest-deep snow, then over huge boulders and finally through swamp. Hake decided to 'field' only two of the battalions of his regiment for the operation, and to seal off the neck of the peninsula with a single battalion. The second was to make for the Russian base at Titovka at the mouth of the River Titova. The third battalion would be used as porters for stores and ammunition.

Six hours after the Jaeger of the 136th crossed their start-lines they had taken the high ground on both sides of the neck of the land bridge leading into the peninsula. With the first objective gained and firmly in the hands of the one battalion of his regiment, Colonel Hake led 3rd Battalion on a cross-country march towards the base depot at Titovka. Shortly after his departure a crisis brewed on 'Fishermen's Peninsula'. A Russian mass attack sent thousands of Red Army troops climbing the slopes of the high ground to drive the Jaeger from the crests. Soon the Soviets had made a penetration which threatened to turn the battalion's flank. Then warships of the Soviet Navy began to land troops on the sea side, i.e., the westward side, of the land bridge. A Jaeger counter-attack group went in at 03.00 on 1 July, a sea fog hiding the men of the attacking Company as they inched their way towards the summit. The climb was hard but the Jaeger spirit carried them on and the summit was retaken within five hours. Other attacks flung back the Russians on other sectors of the land bridge.

The intensity of the fighting at the neck of the peninsula soon made it clear to Hake, as well as to General Schlemmer, that the task of holding it tightly closed was beyond the capabilities of the single battalion detailed for the task. Hake's entire regiment was now in action on that sector and even these three battalions were barely able to contain the Soviet attacks. Indeed, it was only with the last reserves of men that the several gaps in the line across the neck of the land bridge could be closed – and that with difficulty. However, Corps was still expected to continue with the thrust towards Murmansk. In pursuit of Lappland Army's orders the thrust line of 3rd Gebirgs Division advanced across an area where the Russians had been savagely and repeatedly attacked by Stuka aircraft. The Red Army divisions had broken under this hammering from the air and they had retreated in disorder. Masses of equipment and vehicles lay everywhere and the Jaeger found every type of military hardware abandoned in the Russians' panic flight. The only thing they did not find was the highway they had been told to expect. All they found was a track which the feet of the retreating Soviets had worn in the tundra. Reviewing the future development of the campaign on the Murmansk sector it may be claimed with a certain amount of accuracy that the lack of a suitable, all-weather road determined its outcome. Without such a supply channel any eastward attack was bound to fail. The Jaeger must eventually reach a point beyond which their advance would falter and wither away. And that point was certain to be west of Murmansk and not in that city. Murmansk would not, could not, be taken – at least not by the weak and badly supplied forces of Dietl's Corps.

Even if the lack of supplies was not in itself decisive, the fact that the Russians could and did massively reinforce their units facing the divisions of Gebirgskorps 'Norway', contributed to the eventual failure of the offensive on that sector. It was only the determination of all ranks of both divisions that had pushed forward the defence at all. On 2 July the River Liza was reached and that, to all intents, was the limit of Corps' endeavour. A new offensive to capture the Liza bridges and resume the eastwards drive opened on 5 July and lasted until the 9th. The attack failed to gain its objectives and a new offensive, a thrust on a narrower front, was prepared. It was a shock to the Corps officers when a report came in that the dispatch rider carrying the attack plan had been captured. The operation was compromised and a new plan was produced, employing three battle groups from both divisions. The offensive opened in a week during which the weather changed from unusually dry and sunny to the more usual downpours of rain and bitterly cold nights. The Russian defenders now concentrated in overwhelming strength, were backed by massed artillery. Their defence was staunch and their numerous counter-attacks were well planned and excellently directed. Against such opposition 2nd and 3rd Divisions could make no headway and Dietl broke off the attack on 19 July. A Soviet counter-offensive then opened and when this had been defeated the Corps commander planned a September offensive to take Murmansk. It had as little success as the previous operations and with the arrival of winter the front froze into immobility. Because of the strain to which it had been subjected and the losses it had suffered, 2nd Division expected to be relieved from the line, but it was 3rd Division that was replaced. The 2nd stayed on in the tundra with a new sister division, the 6th, as its partner in Gebirgskorps 'Norway'. Despite Dietl's best efforts his Corps was still a long way from Murmansk.

A very long way south of Dietl's Corps the divisions of XXXVI Corps went into action to cut the Murmansk/Leningrad railway line at Kandaleshka. It is 6th SS Gebirgs Division's first battle we shall follow in this account. The story of its disastrous baptism of fire is recounted because it demonstrates the lack of thought on the part of the Army and SS High Commands in committing to battle undertrained and over-age men and expecting them to achieve military miracles. The men of SS 'Nord' were sacrificed to the uncomprehending attitudes of the High Command.

Before beginning this account of the summer battle for Kandaleshka there is a qualification to be made. At the time in question the SS formation was not a division trained for mountain warfare. It was an infantry battle group which was expected to carry out the tasks of a full-strength Division. In his several reports the first commander, SS Gruppenfuehrer Demelhuber, described his battle group as a division and for the sake of consistency it will be so described in this account. We shall meet it later in this book, in 1944 and 1945, by which time it had become in every respect a Gebirgs division.

In every national army there are formations which are touched with good fortune and become the stuff of military legend. Conversely, there are units which, despite the best efforts of both officers and men, are dogged by misfortune. One of these latter was SS Division 'Nord'. While sailing from Mostoen in Norway to Bettelfiord, the concentration area in the Parsangerfiord in northern Norway, the transport ship *Blenheim*, carrying detachments of 6th SS Regiment, caught fire. There were about 110 killed, of whom 24 were from a battalion HQ group. The bodies of these men, the first casualties suffered by 'Nord' Division, were buried in the cemetery at Banak. For the division it was a sad beginning to the now imminent war against the Soviet Union.

The battle group which was to evolve into 6th SS Gebirgs Division 'Nord', was created through the amalgamation of 6th and 7th Motorized SS Infantry Regiments, a reconnaissance battalion and two batteries of artillery. These units, which were on garrison duty in southern Norway, were formed as a battle group on 1 March 1941 and were placed under the command of Gruppenfuehrer Demelhuber on 17 June. One day later he received orders for his group to take ship for the far north and then proceed to the area of Rauna – Rovaniemi, where it would form part of XXXVI Corps.

Demelhuber took stock of his new Command and was shocked at what he found. His bleak report was passed to XXXVI Corps commander and to the SS Hauptamt and is quoted extensively below to show the parlous condition of the formation he was to lead into battle.

'. . . The Division has recently been formed and in great haste . . . First impressions confirmed that the most basic requirements in individual training . . . and in combat techniques were poor and that no unit training at all has been undertaken. This is no reflection on either the troops or their commanders as they have had no opportunity to carry these out.

'The greatest number of senior and Company commanders are Reserve officers lacking experience of fighting a modern war or of man management. None of the battalion commanders has knowledge sufficient to conduct a modern battle involving infantry and associated arms.

'The artillery has had no experience of co-operation with the infantry . . . Neither the anti-tank detachments nor the mortar detachments have fired live rounds and, to a large extent, neither has the anti-aircraft battery.

'There have been no maneuvres combining all arms and the troops have not been trained for war. The divisional train was only recently raised and at officer level is not ready to meet the demands which would be made upon it in supplying combat units [in the field].

'Mobility is limited because of the many types of vehicle on issue and even in small units there is no single vehicle type. Obtaining spare parts is therefore difficult. Prime movers for the divisional artillery do not meet the standard laid down for a German motorized Division.

'The officers at divisional level must be trained before any attack can be undertaken. The troops are very good and in some cases excellent. The NCOs need training and they lack specialist instruction . . .

'The Division will only be fully operational if it has the opportunity, given to all other newly raised units, to spend two to three months "working up" in a good training area.'

The 6th was not given months or even weeks to work up into a first-class fighting unit. Instead on 20 June it was ordered to march towards the Russo–Finnish frontier and to prepare an attack upon the town of Salla, which lay only a couple of kilometres inside Soviet territory. The nightmare of the march to reach the jump-off area in Finland remains vivid in the memory of those suffered it. The terrain leading towards the border was intensely wooded with trees close together and set about with thick undergrowth. With the exception of a single, narrow, second-class track which ran from Finland to Salla, and thence to Kandalushka, the area was without road communication. Movement on this single track was restricted to wheeled and tracked vehicles. The infantry had to make their way through dense tree masses. 'The whole area was a forest growing on a marsh, through which we could only move along tree-trunk roads.' These corduroy tracks were laid as close to the Russian frontier as was practicable without compromising the German preparations. Deep within the silent woods the corduroy tracks stopped and thereafter the advance to the frontier, ten tiring kilometres distant, had to be made by forcing a way across swamp and through jungle before any attack could be launched. The tree trunks forming the corduroy road sank under the weight of even the light infantry vehicles and rose again coated in slime which formed a greasy surface on which it was exhausting to march. The ground on each side of this narrow corduroy track was bottomless marsh.

The SS regiments struggled through the jungle of trees and undergrowth to reach their concentration areas and on 22 June were told during a briefing session that a state of war existed between the Third Reich and the Soviet Union. Within two days 6th SS Division 'Nord', in no respect ready for active service, received orders to make an attack. This operation, its baptism of fire, would demonstrate the difficulties of fighting a jungle-type warfare; its dangers and its difficulties.

Before XXXVI Corps could capture its final objective, Kandalushka, it first had to take Salla and 'Nord' Division was given that task. Its left-wing neighbour was its sister division in the Corps, 169th Infantry Division, and the right-wing neighbour the Finnish 6th Infantry Division. A wide gap yawned between the Finnish 6th and the 'Nord' divisions and this empty space was swept by Finnish and German patrols. Gruppenfuehrer Demelhuber decided that his division would attack on a wide front, striking for the high ground on both sides of the Kelloselkae–Salla road approximately one kilometre east of the Russo–Finnish border. The infantry regiments were lined up side by side with 7th, which would make the main attack placed on the left, and 6th, whose task it was to protect the sister regiment's flank during its advance, situated on the right. The Russian garrison, of unknown strength, was known to be holding well-prepared and strongly fortified positions protected by anti-tank ditches and minefields. The actual strength of the Red Army units holding the positions had not been established because Corps had forbidden patrols to cross the border in order not to betray the coming attack. It was an unnecessary precaution. That the Germans were about to make an assault could hardly be concealed from the Soviets who themselves initiated operations on the Salla front during the afternoon of 26 June, when Russian aircraft bombed 7th Regiment's form-up positions. The Luftwaffe responded to the challenge on the following day when it sent Stuka squadrons to bomb Salla.

Reconnaissance patrols of the SS which were now allowed to strike across the frontier returned with reports that except for a garrison holding the trench lines the area was otherwise unoccupied. Exploiting the Soviet withdrawal, standing patrols of the SS quickly occupied the positions that the enemy had abandoned. Other patrols which went out to gain touch with the left-wing neighbour returned with the alarming news that new and strong Russian defence works had been erected in the area across which the Regiment's 1st Battalion was to make its assault.

The 7th Regiment's battle plan was for a frontal attack with 1st Battalion, supported by trucks, advancing to capture the high ground known as 'Infantry Fortification'. The Regiment's main effort would be made by 3rd Battalion, in the centre of the line, which would strike along the Salla road so as to gain the northern face of the high ground around

Keskimainen–Saerkivaara. The 2nd Battalion of the Regiment was to advance on each side of the Salla road ready to be switched to support either of the other two battalions. The Corps commander, who had come forward to look at the ground and check the divisional battle plan, decided on a few minor changes, the most important of which was to strengthen the artillery support. Two additional artillery battalions, taken from Corps reserve, were brought in to give covering fire and Stuka attack was ordered to neutralize 1st Battalion's objective.

During 30 June, Russian artillery opened a harassing fire on the Kelloselkae–Salla road and this was followed by a weak infantry attack which collapsed under German defensive fire. There was a longish lull in activities during which 7th Regiment sent out patrols to reconnoitre routes to its objective. From Corps HQ reports were received that enemy strength had increased to three infantry divisions and a cavalry division. Corps also reported that there were no major new fortifications and that those already located and identified were in an incomplete state. This was a fatally optimistic assessment of the situation and one which was to lead to heavy losses.

The attack opened at 14.00 on 1 July with the firing of a preliminary barrage. The first fall of shells set alight the woods with the enemy positions, creating smoke which made it almost impossible for the artillery observers to control the fire of their batteries. At 16.00 the planned Stuka attack went in on the 'Infantry Fortification' and targets to the east of the objective, but again dense smoke made accuracy impossible. The leading files of 7th Regiment crossed their start-lines at 16.25 but the planned support of the artillery batteries was ineffective and even the regiment's heavy weapons detachments could not provide the support that was needed as they too were affected by the thick blanket of smoke covering the whole area. In this, the division's first attack, almost everything that could go wrong did so. The smoke reduced visibility and thus supporting fire. Line communication broke down frequently and the wireless sets functioned either erratically or in most cases not at all.

The 1st Battalion made good progress in the opening stages of its attack even though the approach march was made through the dense forests, but when at last the lines of SS men broke out of the deep woods they found themselves on a wide and open space. This was a killing ground which the Red Army engineers had prepared. Trees had been cut down to give the machine-gunners a clear field of fire, the marshy ground between the tree stumps had been sown with mines and the area had been laced with trip wires. At its edge the SS platoons and Companies formed up but in the face of intense and accurate Soviet fire the advance began to falter. The battalion's heavy weapons group was rushed up the corduroy road to give support and when the road ran out the crews manhandled their mortars and infantry guns along the narrow forest trails to bring them into action. Covered by this supporting fire and using the ground well 1st Battalion's assault platoons began to fight their way forward and at length were close enough to open direct fire upon the bunkers of the 'Infantry Fortification'. The first two pillboxes succumbed to their determined assault, but when Untersturmfuhrer Hering fell, mortally wounded, his men lost the strong control which had guided them and their assault began to fail. The Soviets were quick to sense that hesitation and were no less quick to exploit it. A web of machine-gun cross-fire and a hail of mortar bombs pinned down the Companies of 1st Battalion. Communications broke down and all the men of the assault groups were either killed or wounded. The 1st Battalion's attack on the 'Infantry Fortification' was bogged down with the tank support that had been promised either not coming into action at all or else proving ineffective.

The order was given for some of 2nd Battalion's companies to swing northwards and collaborate with 1st Battalion in its attack. Although the 2nd had been hard hit in its own advance up the Salla road, it had quickly regrouped and swung forward again. The assault of its left-wing Company, one of those ordered to support 1st Battalion, reached to within eight metres of 'Infantry Fortification' while platoons from other Companies took out the bunkers on the south-western side of the objective.

The whole regiment had, as we have seen, advanced shrouded by a pall of dense smoke from the burning trees which had prevented effective artillery support from being given to the infantry spearhead detachments. These then had other crises to overcome. The dense smoke made it hard to identify figures which loomed up unexpectedly so that on many sectors when infantry of both sides clashed it came to hand-to-hand fighting between the determined German attackers and the resolute Russian defenders. At one place in 'Infantry Fortification' the smoke began to clear away and Red Army soldiers, seeing how few in number were the SS men, stormed out of their trenches and bunkers in a hasty but determined counter-attack. Supported by armoured fighting vehicles they charged forward and 2nd Battalion began to waver. It was time for personal leadership and swift action. Obersturmbannfuehrer Schinke, the battalion commander, rallied his men, moved to their head and led them in a charge which drove back the attacking Soviets and went on to roll up the enemy bunker line. In the act of inspiring his men, Schinke was caught by a burst of machine-gun fire from a nearby bunker and fell mortally wounded. With his death died also the inspiration behind the attack, and 2nd Battalion, like its sister battalion, was now halted and trapped under a punishing fire. On its sector, 3rd Battalion had had as little luck, although it must be said its attack was halted less by the enemy than by the burning trees which shrouded its objective.

The attack had not only been halted along the entire divisional front but in several sectors the SS had been forced on to the defensive against assaults by both Soviet infantry and armour. The divisional commander sought to regain the initiative by switching the main effort from the right flank to the left but his efforts had no success. Groups of men began to pull back from the firing line, thinking themselves isolated, cut off and in danger of being wiped out. At 22.30 Demelhuber, realizing that he could not revive the dead attack, ordered his regiments to take up a defensive posture.

That day had been the first one which SS Division 'Nord' had spent under fire and for many of its men the last day of their life. Losses had been heavy and had borne out the divisional commander's gloomy forecast. His half-trained men had been put in against an enemy superior in number and holding strong, prepared positions which were protected by natural obstacles. The result was a foregone conclusion; the division had suffered not just the physical loss of killed and wounded but, more disastrously, a loss in morale. The report by the divisional commander dealing with the first day's operations contains the paragraph, '. . . I found some thirty to forty men from Nos. 1, 2 and 4 Companies, together with the commander of No 1 Company. The men were physically and mentally at the end of their tether. It was clear that the demands made upon them had been too great to be borne by men who were between 30 and 40 years of age. Many were showing signs of battle exhaustion. The CO of 7th Regiment's 1st Battalion, Hauptsturmfuehrer Augsberger, then arrived, intending to take his men back into action. I directed him instead to pull back to his former positions . . .'

Demelhuber was aware that his weakened regiments were not in any condition to resume the attack immediately and when the next assault went in on 4 July, not only could no advances be made but on several sectors Red Army infantry and armour attacks recaptured lost ground. Not until 8 July when the Russians withdrew, could 'Nord' Division take 'Infantry Fortification'. Also during the day Salla was taken – the Russians had fled and the advance was pushed on beyond that town. The German High Command communiqué reported '. . . On the Finnish front during 8th July, an outflanking operation by the Finnish forces enabled German units to capture the heavily fortified town of Salla, after a battle which had lasted for several days. The Soviet Divisions which were fighting there were destroyed . . .'

Summer passed. Autumn came and went, but despite the victories which the campaigning season had brought, it was clear by the end of 1941 that the war against the Soviet Union had failed to produce the Blitzkrieg victory which Hitler had forecast. Worse was to come. Stavka was aware that the German Army on the Eastern Front was materially and climatically unprepared to meet the bitter ravages of winter. When the terrible weather finally halted the German advance, Stalin's generals mounted a wide-ranging winter offensive along the whole battle line. Under its fearful pressure Army Group Centre was forced back from the gates of Moscow and although the Red Army had had less success around Leningrad and in the Ukraine, overall it had achieved a great moral victory; it had broken the myth of German military invincibility. Hitler's war against the Soviet Union had been predicated upon false data and planned with no single military objective. As early as 21 August Hitler had expressed his strategic policy in a Fuehrer Declaration which read in part: 'I see it as most important that before the onset of winter the following objectives be gained. The capture of the Crimea and the coal-producing area of the Donets, the interdiction of Russian fuel supplies from the Caucasus and in the north the isolation of Leningrad and gaining touch with the Finns . . .'

No mention was made of an advance towards Moscow, surely the obvious objective and one which the High Command was continually urging. The die had been cast; Hitler had decided and one consequence of his decision to capture the industrial complexes along the Donets, was the posting of XLIX Gebirgskorps to Panzer Group von Kleist to strengthen that Group's offensive. During the fighting for the Donets XLIV Corps captured Stalino on 20 October and then advanced to the River Mius. Both divisions spent the winter along the Mius until May 1942 when the opening moves were made in the German summer campaign – Operation 'Blue'.

In Lappland, 2nd, 6th and 7th Gebirgs Divisions, together with 6th SS Gebirgs Division 'Nord' and other Army formations, had been struck a severe blow during the great Soviet winter offensive, but despite their superiority in men the Russians did not achieve the destruction of the German forces which had been their intention. The Germans held the Soviet assaults so successfully that the front sank back to the deep reconnaissance patrol activity which had been the principal feature of military operations by both sides. In the spring of 1943, having allowed its tired formations only the briefest of time to retrain, reorganize and regroup, Stavka ordered the dormant winter operation in Lappland to be revived and to become a spring offensive. It was at this time that the Finnish High Command decided to concentrate its forces more tightly and demanded that German and Finnish Divisions should no longer serve in mixed formations, but that each should operate with its own Army. As a consequence German 163rd Division was posted back from 3rd Finnish Corps, 6th Finnish Division was returned to that Corps and 7th Gebirgs Division was shipped across the Baltic to reinforce the Lappland Front. By July 1942 the regrouping was complete and the only Finnish units remaining in the German-held areas were Frontier Force patrols which covered the wide gaps in the German line and intercepted infiltrating Red Army sabotage groups. This massive regrouping had been carried out during the time of the Soviet spring offensive and the difficulties of moving units while conducting active operations can well be imagined. When the reformation had been completed, the Order of Battle of the former 'Lappland Army' now numbered as Twentieth Gebirgs Army was: General Schoerner's XIX Gebirgskorps in the north-west sector around Murmansk; 2nd and 6th Gebirgs Divisions on the landward side with Petsamo Divisional Group and 201st Infantry Division on the seaward front. The 6th Gebirgs Division had come in as a replacement for Kreysing's 3rd Gebirgs Division which on 1 October 1941 began a march from the Barents Sea to the Baltic, but leaving behind its 139th Regiment. The central or Kandaleshka sector was held by General Weisenberger's 163rd and 169th Infantry Divisions grouped as XXXVI Gebirgskorps and in the southern, or Louhi area, General Boehme's XVIII Corps was made up of 7th Gebirgs Division and 6th SS Gebirgs Division 'Nord'.

The failure of Twentieth Gebirgs Army to cut the Murmansk–Leningrad rail link was a severe blow to OKW's plans, but it had not come about because of the Army's lack of will or determination but because the objective had been beyond the power of the under-strength force to achieve. The failure of this first German offensive had been followed by Soviet counter-offensives aimed at driving the Lappland Army back from the railway line and, more importantly, to fling back XIX Gebirgskorps in the Murmansk sector. The Red Army's 1942 spring offensive was a pre-emptive blow and indications that the enemy was building up his strength could not be hidden. Jaeger patrols, operating deep and far in the Russian rear areas, brought back information on the preparations that were being made behind the Soviet front line. These reports indicated that the heaviest enemy blow would fall in the far northern sector, where 2nd and 6th Divisions held post. Twentieth Army, which was now prepared to meet the Soviet spring offensive, did not have long to wait. Stavka opened operations on 10 April 1942 with a thrust against 141st Regiment, 6th Gebirgs Division, and while German attention was being held at that point a land and sea assault was launched on the southern coast of the Motovski Bight as well as in the Liza Fiord. The Soviet intention was to pass round both flanks of 6th Gebirgs, encircle the division and destroy it. A successful operation would not only clear the threat to Murmansk but would also open the way for a Russian advance westwards to Petsamo or for a drive southwards to roll up the German battle line.

When the enemy's operation opened the pressure applied against 6th Gebirgs Division was so great that 2nd Gebirgs, its right-hand neighbour, was asked to help. Detachments were sent and the combined and unshakeable resistance of the force not only met but repulsed the Soviet assaults. It should be remembered that each division of Twentieth Army was holding an area of front quite out of proportion to its strength. Each was operating as an isolated formation to which no reinforcements from the rear areas could be quickly sent because of the poor road network and the terrain difficulties. Front-line units could only be helped by other front-line units; there was no time to wait for troops to come forward from Army reserve. The fighting reached a climax at the end of April 1942 when Stavka carried out another and heavier combined operation, still determined to cut off 6th Division. The Jaeger in the area fought hard but could not hold the thrusts of the Red Army and the Soviet Navy's 12th Marine Brigade. It seemed that now nothing could prevent the division's complete encirclement and destruction. Then nature took a hand and this time aided the Germans. A violent snowstorm blew up and lasted a full three days, paralysing military operations. When the storm died down the Jaeger went over to the attack. Very few of the Russian Marines escaped to reach their boats in the Liza Fiord. By 12 May the battle on the Liza and on the river's eastern bank had ended victoriously for the regiments of 6th Gebirgs Division, but Red Assaults against 2nd Division were still coming in with undiminished fury. Against that division's strong defence the Soviet assault could not prevail and as its attacks ebbed, XIX Gebirgskorps went over to a counter-offensive which drove the enemy back south-eastwards and recovered ground lost in the first days of his offensive. The OKW communiqué dated 22 May 1942 reported that on that northern sector the Soviets had employed, '37 Army battalions which had carried out 125 attacks in the north and 76 on the southern sector. In addition a Marine Brigade of 6 battalions took part in the fighting.'

During 1943 the Lappland front returned to mainly patrol activity, enlivened by local offensives mounted by both sides. Then, in 1944, it was the turn of Boehme's XVIII Gebirgskorps to come under direct and heavy assault as Stavka opened a major new offensive in the southern or Louhi area. Were the Soviets to make a breakthrough there it would allow them a choice of options. They could swing their forces northwards, roll up both XVIII and XXXVI Corps and then advance towards the coast there to trap XIX Corps. Alternatively, Stavka could order a south-western advance to reach the Finnish ports on the northern Baltic and thereby cut off the Finnish Army. The Soviet offensive designed to achieve this strategic penetration was launched in June 1944 and continued for a whole month.

The route which the Russians took in their attack in the Louhi sector was dictated by the terrain. The key to the area was a narrow land bridge between two large lakes. At one end of the land bridge stood the village of Ssemnosero and at the other the village of Yeletyosero. This part of the front was the left flank of the Kienstinki sector where 6th SS Division held post and it was against this sector that the severest blows were struck. In common with the other units, 6th was fielding both its Jaeger regiments and had been holding fixed positions since the winter, the German units having been since that time almost permanently on the defensive. The Soviet blow, although expected, was heavier than anticipated and 'Nord' was attacked by two Red Army divisions. The impetus enabled footholds to be gained in the SS perimeter and heavy fighting ensued at close range and often hand-to-hand until the SS Jaeger regiments regained the initiative and sealed off the penetrations, destroying the Russian formations. The first attack on one sector of 6th's front is of interest for it had been made by Russian storm troops who had waded all night across the marshy ground to reach their attack positions. Waist-deep in the swamp; sometimes chest-deep, the Red Army soldiers had waited throughout the short, summer night and at just before first light had emerged from the clinging mud and gone into a storming charge at the German positions only a hundred metres distant. Although the SS had been surprised by this attack and although at a few places the Jaeger perimeter had been breached, the 6th recaptured the lost trenches in spirited counter-attacks. Then, knowing only too well Soviet military methods, the Companies stood to arms in expectation of a new assault. When it came in it was not so much an attack as a slaughter. The First Russian attack had been made from a point close to the Jaeger positions and the attackers, who had hidden in the marsh, had quickly reached the firm ground on which the SS positions had been set up. But the infantry who now came in opened their attack from nearly a kilometre away and were forced to wade at slow motion pace through the marshy ground to reach the SS positions. These slow-moving lines of brown-coated infantry were easily shot down. It soon became clear that the troops making this suicidal assault had been sacrificed to cover attacks on other sectors by picked assaults units.

The attacks by these storm troops struck into the flank of 6th SS and produced a crisis which only desperate measures could resolve. Corps had no reserve in the accepted military sense, but created one by thinning out its own battle line. That such a thinning out would place an additional burden upon the units left holding their positions was a calculated risk but one that had to be accepted. A Company taken from one less heavily engaged sector joined a second taken from another quieter place, a third came from some other area and so the selection went on. Soon there was a mixed group of Army and SS units. The whole was placed under the command of Standartenfuehrer Schreiber, commanding 12th SS Gebirgs Regiment. His group was facing an enemy whose strength was superior to his own and who was convinced that victory was assured. It was not. Schreiber's group had as its first task to clear the threat to the Corps flank by driving out the Soviets from the dense belts of trees which marked the few islands of firm ground in this region of lakes and marshes. Fighting in dense woodland is a military operation in which the defender, particularly those native to the area, enjoys every advantage. The men of the Red Army units in the Kienstinki sector were familiar with the terrain; hunters, trappers and fishermen who exploited their knowledge of local conditions to the full. It was common for a Russian to tie himself to the upper trunk of a tree from where he was able to inflict a great many casualties before being discovered and killed. The infinite patience of those who live close to nature was also demonstrated by small groups of Russians who hid in the thick undergrowth along a narrow forest path, and were prepared to wait for hours or even days before emerging to ambush and kill a runner making his lonely way or a group of stretcher-bearers carrying one of their wounded comrades away from the fighting.

It must not be thought that the Russians were the only ones with woodmen's skills. By 1944, after nearly three years of positional warfare and deep patrols, the Jaeger's senses were well developed and they were quick to read the noises of night and day; to listen for unusual or prolonged bird calls and to spot on the ground the evidence of recent movement. In the dense belts of trees, in a world of gloom and half darkness, for the sun's rays scarcely penetrated the matted tree crowns, both sides fought a deadly war characterized by silence and slow movement. Throughout these operations Schreiber seemed to bear a charmed life, leading a detachment here, encouraging a group there, inspiring an attack or heading a counter-attack. Around him men fell to the sniper's bullet or were mutilated by the deadly, green anti-personnel mines which the Red Army engineers sowed, it seemed, quite indiscriminately. He survived them all, and like a man inspired infused his joy of combat into the battalions under his command.

His men cleared the enemy from the woods and relieved the danger to the left flank. Immediately, it was given a new task. The Soviet divisions had forced their way into Ssemnosero and it seemed as if the village, small but of great tactical importance, must fall to their battering assaults. Schreiber led his group, depleted in numbers by the battle in the woods, but still of stout heart, into the village and prepared to hold it to the last. His intention to improve the existing defences could not be realized. A massive Red attack swept away the units on either flank and left Battle Group Schreiber surrounded, cut off and fighting for its life. The village had to be held, but Schreiber's group was clearly too weak to do this without reinforcement. A formation had to be found that could either raise the siege or reinforce the defenders. The 139th Gebirgsjaeger Regiment was hastily deployed. Demonstrating their usual élan, the men who had held Narvik stormed towards the village, flung back the Soviet forces around it and gained touch with Schreiber's men. At the height of the battle the commander of 139th Regiment fell in action but undaunted by this loss his Jaeger carried on the attack. Schreiber promptly assumed temporary command of the 139th which, together with his own battalions, destroyed the enemy's initiative on the Kienstinki front.

The recommendation of the award of the Knight's Cross to Franz Schreiber, details three separate operations in which his exceptional leadership was demonstrated. That which dealt with the fighting in the Kienstinki sector reads, 'SS Standartenfuehrer Schreiber played a distinctive part in bringing about the Division's [6th SS Gebirgs] successes during the fighting of June/July 1944, during which one Russian Division was destroyed and a second badly mauled. If the enemy's attempt to outflank the Division had succeeded, this would have led to the collapse of the whole Kienstinki sector, but that attempt was brought to nought. The enormous distances and the swampy, forested conditions made communication difficult and Schreiber had very often to make decisions and to carry out operations on his own initiative.'

Thwarted, both in the north and in the south of the Lappland front, the Russians opened an offensive on the central sector on 30 July 1944. This operation opened with a heavy barrage to which the German guns, although short of ammunition, made a spirited reply. For two days the duel continued between the contesting batteries. Soviet infantry attacks, the first of which came in on 12 August, were held and repulsed. With those defeats the whole front returned to the small actions and patrols which had characterized warfare there. During the time that the front was reverting to minor operations 7th Gebirgs Division had moved into the Kienstinki sector of the Louhi front. There it formed part of XVIII Corps and had as its left-flank neighbour 6th SS. There was no touch with a right-flank neighbour – the nearest Finnish unit was three hundred kilometres or more distant. Within weeks of moving into the Kienstinki sector 7th Gebirgs Division was ordered to launch an operation to capture a line of Soviet blockhouses. This succeeded, but the Russian response was to mount a massive counter-offensive of such power that some units of the 7th were sent reeling back in disorder. It was a standard, German military riposte to launch an immediate counter-thrust before the enemy had had time to consolidate his success and the whole Jaeger line surged forward. At Sukkula there was hand-to-hand fighting as the Jaeger battled to drive back the Soviet formations. Jaeger élan triumphed and the line of blockhouses was firmly in German hands and remained so until Twentieth Gebirgs Army pulled out of Finland in October 1944.

In June 1944 Twentieth Gebirgs Army suffered a severe blow when Dietl, its commander, was killed in an aircraft crash, together with General Engelseer. The post of Army Commander was then taken over by General Rendulic, who was later succeeded by General Boehme who held the post until the end of the war.

Adolf Hitler had anticipated that, as a result of the military reverse suffered by the Third Reich, the time might come when Finland would cease to fight as Germany's ally against the Soviet Union. When that situation arose, as it did in the autumn of 1944, contingency plans which had been prepared were put into operation.

In the earlier chapter of this book which dealt with the outbreak of the war in Finnish Lappland, it was stated that the Finns had concentrated the mass of their army in the south of their country to meet a Russian threat to the capital Helsinki. More than two years of bloody conflict against the Red Army had brought Finland to the end of her manpower resources and her leaders sought a way out of the war against the Soviet Union which the Third Reich seemed certain to lose. By the middle of July 1944 the German forces were everywhere in retreat; not only in Russia but also in western Europe, in Italy and in the Balkans. Germany's deteriorating situation persuaded the Finnish government to open talks with the Soviets. These began in August and within a month a peace treaty had been signed between the two nations.

Generaloberst Rendulic, commanding Twentieth Gebirgs Army, prepared his forces in accordance with the contingency plans that had been drawn up. His most important task was to hold the ore mining areas for as long as possible, and when the time eventually came and the Army had to pull out, the southernmost divisions would withdraw first, swinging in a reverse turn out of central Finland until they had gained touch with XIX Gebirgskorps. Then, with the three Corps concentrated, they would march out of northern Finland to reach positions in north-west Lappland. It will be recalled that the only land route between Lappland and Norway, ran across the high north of Norway. Neutral

Sweden was a barrier and because Hitler was not prepared to violate that neutrality, the German forces in Lappland would be faced with the need to undertake a northward march parallel with the Swedish frontier in order to reach the east-west road which ran below North Cape and followed the line of the coast into northern Norway. The logistical problems to be overcome in moving that number of troops and equipment along a single highway were enormous and were complicated by the fact that the Finnish troops had passed from being Germany's allies to becoming her enemies and their patrols attacked Rendulic's formations as they marched through the gloomy forests in the dark, bitter weather.

Operation 'Birch', involving the retreat of the three Corps of Twentieth Army, began on 5 September 1944. The Army Order of Battle was: XVIII Corps, with 6th SS Gebirgs Division 'Nord', the 'Krautler' Divisional Group and 7th Gebirgs Division. XXXVI Corps had two infantry divisions on establishment, 163rd and 169th, both of which, although not 'Gebirgs' in name, were equipped for mountain warfare. The XIX Corps controlled 2nd Gebirgs, 6th Gebirgs and 210th Infantry Divisions.

'Birch' was planned as a two-stage withdrawal. In the first XXXVI Gebirgskorps would pull back down the so-called 'Arctic Sea' road to a point to the south of Ivalo and would there gain touch with the right wing of 19th Gebirgskorps. XVIII Gebirgskorps was to move along the Rovaniemi–Murmio road towards Skibotten and take up positions north-east of the Swedish border in the area of Karaguendo. The second phase of the operation, the retreat into Norway, would depend upon the weather.

The difficulties of conducting a long withdrawal march in terrible weather were fully appreciated. Adolf Hitler, in fact, doubted whether the operation would succeed because of the distances which the men would have to make. The task of 6th SS Gebirgs Division 'Nord', for example, was to carry out a retreat of 800 kilometres via Kuusamo–Rovaniemi and thence to Karaguendo in the north-western corner of Finland.

By 13 September the German Army had pulled out of the whole of southern Finland and was moving northwards towards Karaguendo. The record of that retreat is one of long marches through the dark, rainy autumn nights, marches in which the units covered usually 30 or more kilometres and continued this for night after night. During the day the short periods of rest which the exhausted troops were able to snatch were broken by the call to stand sentry-go. One man who carried out that retreat recalled.

'In misty forests we pitched our tents and gathered round fires we had lit. It was dripping with rain everywhere. We dried out our kit as best we could and warmed out stiff limbs. Then we lay down on fir branches hoping to sleep. When darkness fell we took up the march again, heading northwards until we reached the coast of Norway and then followed this.

'As we marched through vast, depressing Lappland inhabited areas became fewer. We marched past shining lakes, across, up and then over bare rock faces, through endless, dense forests which eventually become less dense and whose trees become stunted. On our left is the wide river which forms the frontier between Sweden and Finland. Now we are in the mountains which run close to the roads, oppressive in their size. The columns march as if through a stone doorway beyond which are snow covered peaks rising before us ... We have reached the Norwegian frontier.'

Before that frontier was reached an incident occurred which demonstrates the power and durability of hostile propaganda. Rovaniemi was destroyed by fire, an incident which was promptly denounced by the Soviets as a Fascist atrocity and which, despite all evidence to the contrary, is still widely accepted as being true. During the German Army's retreat 6th SS Gebirgs Division 'Nord' served as rearguard to XVIII Gebirgskorps and its 12th Gebirgsjaeger Regiment garrisoned Rovaniemi. There had been fighting with units of the Finnish Army at the approaches to the small town and this had intensified as more and more Finns entered the battle. Within a short time the SS Gebirgsjaeger Regiment holding Rovaniemi was forced on to the defensive. The subsequent course of events has been described in the history of SS Gebirgs Division 'Nord' by the officer who was Deputy Town Major at the time.

'The retreat was carried out with orders to bypass the town of Rovaniemi. My office was in the barrack hut occupied by the Town Major. The Kampfkommandant, the officer responsible for conducting military operations inside the town, was SS Standartenfuehrer Schreiber, commanding SS Gebirgsjaeger Regiment No 12, 'Michael Gaissmair.'

'German military columns were forbidden to pass through the town centre and MPs were on duty to ensure that that order was obeyed. One night the MPs brought in a Finnish man and girl and also reported that fire had broken out in the town. Whether the pair had started the fire could not be determined. We had no means of putting out the blaze which spread rapidly and was nourished by the wooden houses of the town. I ordered a pioneer unit to blow up a number of houses to make fire gaps and thus to isolate the conflagration.

'In the railway station there was an ammunition train. As no locomotive was available I used several panzer to pull railway trucks out of the station and into open country. Then, by some mischance which I have never been able to determine, the ammunition train was pushed back into the station. I received a telephone call from the RTO that the train might blow up at any moment and asking what he should do. There was still no locomotive and the panzers had now been sent away, so that train had to be left where it stood.

'The flames had now reached it and as I made my way to the station, the first trucks blew up. A wheel landed in the door of the Town Major's office less than two metres from me. Then, one after the other, explosions occured and continued for more than two hours, damaging more houses. The Corps Ia was in a slit trench with me. He had come to check on the destruction of the town hotel and was witness instead to a giant firework display. The greatest number of railway wagons had been loaded with artillery shells, signal rockets and mines.

'A report in a Swedish newspaper, printed some twenty years after the event, spoke of the destruction of 41,000 houses in Rovaniemi. The population was 3,000 people, most of whom had already left the town. The so-called planned and brutal destruction of Rovaniemi can thus be seen to be not merely an inaccuracy, but a lie repeated for over three decades after the event.'

Rovaniemi was evacuated on 16 October, and only a few kilometres west of the town the advance guard of 6th SS Division 'Nord' struck Finnish troops who had cut the road to Muonia. When such situations had arisen on earlier occasions SS officers had been able to discuss the matter with their Finnish counter-parts and thereby avoid a bloody confrontation. On this occasion such a compromise was not possible. Red Army commissars were insisting that the Finns attack the Germans. It came to a fight and the SS cleared the first roadblock by frontal attack. The mass of the vehicle column then passed through, but a hail of fire struck and halted the trucks of the final detachment. The Gebirgsjaeger took cover while the divisional artillery commander, who was riding in the same truck as the CO of 12th Regiment, brought one of his guns forward and fired at the Finns over open sights. Covered by that little barrage the men of 2nd Battalion stormed forward and drove the enemy back.

On 28 October, in the area of Muonia, the road to the Swedish frontier was reached and there 11th and 12th Gebirgsjaeger Regiments halted to regroup. Almost immediately both came under surprise assault but an immediate counter-attack flung back the enemy. It was the last attempt by the Finns to interfere with the retreat of 6th SS, and the Gebirgs division reached Karaguendo. Its participation in the campaign in Finland was at an end.

1st and 4th Gebirgs Divisions on the Eastern Front: Caucasus, 1942–1943

T HE 1ST AND 4TH GEBIRGS DIVISIONS, together with the Celere Division of the Italian Army, held the line of the River Mius for nearly seven months. During that period the 1st was temporarily detached from Corps to take part in an operation around Kharkov.

Winter was over and gone. The notorious *Rasputitsa*, the mud produced by the spring thaw, had dried out. The ground was firm. It was the time when mobile operations could begin again – that is from the German point of view – *their* mobile operations. Any major aggressive Soviet move was discounted, until a sudden and completely unexpected Red Army advance towards Kharkov produced a crisis. To overcome this Army Group South drew crack formations from all its subordinate Commands. One division selected to confront the Russians offensive was 1st Gebirgs Division. This formation had, by this time, gained for itself a formidable reputation for aggression in assault and tenacity in defence. Its marching prowess could not be matched. It was, in all respects, the type of first-class unit that was needed to help master the Kharkov crisis. For lack of space its achievement must be reduced to just a few sentences. As part of III Panzer Corps it smashed back the advance of two Soviet armies, penetrated 45 kilometres through the Soviet front and helped to surround the Russian hosts and destroy them. General Lanz described in his book *Gebirgsjaeger* how the Russian infantry, apparently stupified with drink, had stormed forward with linked arms trying to break out of the encirclement. They had attacked almost as if they were robots and at those places where they broke into the German positions the Jaeger dead were later found to have had their skulls split open or to be mutilated in other ways. The Russian infantry were killed in such huge numbers that the dead formed heaps where they had fallen and Lanz, who had fought in the Great War, could not recall seeing death or destruction to compare with that which he saw on the Bereka battlefield.

By the time that 1st Division returned to XLIX Corps, Army Group South's own pre-summer offensive had obtained 'jumping-off' points for Operation 'Blue', the major German offensive of summer 1942.

We have seen in earlier chapters how Hitler rejected the strategic necessity of striking with maximum force at a single target and instead selected a number of objectives so widely spaced that his attacking forces were unable to give mutual support when a crisis developed. In the summer of 1942 he once again ignored the restrictions of time and space upon his strategic plans and rejected the inevitability of diminishing returns. In that summer he launched an offensive using two Army

Groups. One was to drive eastwards for Stalingrad; the other was to thrust southwards into the Caucasus. Had his assaulting divisions been at full strength, had they been fresh, had they launched their attacks against a weak and uncertain enemy and had the terrain conditions been favourable, Hitler's plan might have succeeded. But the German Army on the Eastern Front in the summer of 1942 numbered a quarter of a million men fewer than in the summer of 1941. The shortfall in numbers could only be made good by employing the armies of Germany's allies; good soldiers, perhaps, but not of the calibre of the men of the German Army.

The German's opponents, the Red Army, had suffered disastrous human and material losses during the summer and autumn of 1941 but its winter offensive had gained certain successes. Despite these, its failure to destroy Hitler's armies and drive them from Russian soil had been a blow to Red Army morale. Shaken by manpower losses and low in morale, the Soviets needed, in the opinion of its senior commanders, a long period of rest before they could undertake any major offensive operations. Stalin was of a different opinion. He had infused fresh troops into combat-shattered formations and had, thereby, made good the manpower losses of the previous year. The rigid doctrines which had governed both tactics and strategy were reappraised, new tank types had been brought into front-line service and the Red Air Force was re-equipped. By the early summer of 1942, the Red Army was, once again, a strong and powerful force, numerically and materially superior to its enemies. As a result the German Army was facing a strong and resolute enemy.

The considerations of terrain and weather in the planning of Hitler's new offensive to seize the Caucasus area were of vital importance. The region into which one of the German Army groups had been ordered to advance featured the highest mountains in Europe and the campaigning period to seize these was measured in weeks only. The proposition was that Hitler's weakened armies, dependant upon unreliable allies, were facing reinvigorated Russian forces who were holding good ground from which they had to be driven before the onset of winter. It was a daunting prospect.

If the Red Army leaders had pleaded for a period of recovery and rehabilitation, their pleas had been no less urgent than those of the commanders on the German side. Following on from the catastrophe of the winter of 1941/2, both OKW and OKH had hoped for a whole year in which to rebuild the shattered Army. Hitler, like Stalin, would have none of it. The Fuehrer was certainly aware that the German Army no longer had the numerical strength to mount simultaneous offensives by each of three Army Groups, as it had in 1941 for Operation 'Barbarossa'. Accordingly, he deployed the greatest part of his available strength in the south; the front which he was convinced would win victory for Germany in 1942. Fuehrer Directive No 41, named the undertaking Operation 'Blue' and stated that the principal aim of the offensive was the final destruction of Russia's military forces. In Hitler's opinion the Red Army was at its last gasp while, to Stalin, the German enemy was ready for the death thrust. Both dictators demanded action. The Red Army struck first and the Russian offensive, undertaken against the advice of the generals, was halted by a combination of the *Rasputitsa*, the thick and clinging mud, and superior German strategy. Although the Soviet offensive had failed, it had demonstrated that the new tanks and aircraft were first-class and that the newly introduced tactics had been successful. Only the rigid battle plans insisted upon by Josef Stalin had failed to meet the challenge. There then followed on both sides of the battle line a brief period of relative calm, a calm enlivened by patrols, attacks with limited objectives and assaults to gain tactically important pieces of ground. Army Group South then launched a minor offensive along its southern wing and its success reinforced Hitler's mistaken belief that the Red Army was finished as a fighting force and that only weak elements of Timoshenko's army had escaped the German encirclement. This belief coupled with the fear that Soviet troop reinforcements might strengthen the enemy in the Caucasus or in the Stalingrad area, decided him. The location of Operation 'Blue' and its opening date had been determined. With the initial offensive successfully completed, the Fuehrer could now enter into the final stages of planning this new, major and, as he hoped, final offensive in Russia.

His Directive No 45, dated 23 July 1942, laid out the strategy of an eccentric attack, against the Caucasus and Stalingrad for which he divided the massive Army Group South into two smaller Army Groups. Operation 'Edelweiss', employing List's Army Group 'A' was to encircle and destroy the fleeing enemy forces south of Rostov and then go on to drive down the east coast of the Black Sea so as to deprive the Black Sea Fleet of its bases. Using all available Gebirgs and Jaeger divisions the River Kuban was to be crossed and the high ground around Maikop and Armavir was to be captured. The Directive went on: 'The western area of the Caucasus is to be taken in a fresh advance . . . The Grozny area is to be reached, the Ossetian and Georgian military roads are to be cut at the summit of the passes and, finally, a thrust along the Caspian Sea is to capture the Baku region . . .' An Italian alpine corps could be expected to be added to Army Group's establishment. In Operation 'Fischreiher', von Weichs' Army Group 'B' was to drive for Stalingrad, capture the city and hold the land bridge between the Don and the Volga. It was then to send mobile units along the Volga to block the river at Astrakhan.

Operation 'Blue' cannot be seen as an ambitious plan. It can not even be considered as an over-ambitious plan. It was military madness, because when Army Groups 'A' and 'B' approached their respective objectives, the distance between them would be 4,000 kilometres and this vast gap would increase as 'A' drove deeper south and 'B' drove farther east. It was a scenario for disaster on a grand scale.

This chapter is concerned with the advance of Army Group 'A' into the Caucasus. Stalingrad is referred to only because the disaster which occurred there forced the withdrawal of Field Marshal List's forces in the middle of the winter and in a region lacking road and rail communications.

Hitler's Directive had ordered that all the Gebirgsjaeger divisions were to be deployed. There were only two on the strength of Army Group 'A'; 1st and 4th Divisions of XLIX Gebirgskorps, part of Seventeenth Army on the right flank. There were, at the opening of Operation 'Edelweiss', two other armies under List's command: First Panzer Army, which held the centre, and Fourth Panzer Army which held the left or eastern flank. Within a week of 'Edelweiss' opening Hitler detached Fourth Panzer Army from List's command and sent it racing to the Stalingrad front nearly 4,000 kilometres away. What had been a very difficult operation for the three armies under List's command became an impossible task when his Forces were reduced to two armies. They contained between them only sixteen divisions, and the Caucasus region between Rostov and Zimliansrata on the Don comprised more than 100 kilometres of front which would widen to more than 1,000 kilometres as the advance was pushed home towards the Caucasus mountains. Were everything to be committed to a single battle line, each division would have to cover a width of front of well over 60 kilometres. There was no prospect of reinforcement and even when the promised Alpini Corps eventually arrived it was removed almost immediately and rushed to Stalingrad.

If XLIX Gebirgskorps was pleased that it had at last been given the task for which it was trained, to attack and to capture mountains, its commanders were less happy. There were certain negative factors. To begin with there was a distance of 400 kilometres to be covered – on foot – before fighting for the mountain passes could begin. Corps was without a proper train and Seventeenth Army had had no air transport squadrons allotted to it. There was, however, an overriding sense of relief among the Jaeger that finally the Gebirgs divisions were to be given the opportunity to demonstrate their ability. It was a challenge which they anticipated with pleasure although the Caucasian mountain wall ran for more than 1,200 kilometres on a general north-west/south-east line. The highest peaks were in the central massif and four of these were in excess of five thousand metres. The range on its western [i.e., European] side had peaks that were covered by tree growth of jungle density while on the eastern [Asiatic] side the slopes were bare rock. The region could, in 1942, be truly described as *terra incognita* and aware of this deficiency in his Intelligence sources, Engelseer, commanding 4th Gebirgs Division, dispatched a staff officer to Munich to carry out research in the city's libraries. He found little up-to-date information. Most of the reports dated from well before the First World War and were, therefore, only reliable when they described the region's terrain features or climatic conditions. The foothills of the Caucasus range extended as far northwards as the Rivers Kuban and Terek, that is to say, the approach march which the Jaeger had to make would be across a country better suited to defence than to attack. The heavy rainfall, 400 centimetres was standard and turned into snow when it fell upon the northern slopes of the mountains on the Black Sea side. Above the 3,500-metre line was a region of perpetual snow and ice and of thick cloud masses which formed quickly and dispersed with equal speed. The pre-First World War guide-books mentioned the several passes which pierced the mountains and remarked on the few roads and poor communications in the region. The military road to Sukhumi ran through the 2,800-metre-high Klukhor Pass and could be used by motor transport. There were seven other main passes all of which, according to those old guide-books, had good roads. These passes were the Pseaskha, Adzapch, Chmakmaro, Maruklhsky, Nahmhar, Chiper and Azau.

It is a cliché that the Alpinist's reply to the question 'Why do you climb mountains?' is 'Because they are there'. It was that compulsion which drove the men of XLIX Gebirgskorps to send out a team to climb the 5,633-metre-high Mount Elbrus, the highest peak in the Caucasus, and to plant the Reich's war banner on its summit. That it was an excellent demonstration of Gebirgsjaeger ability cannot be doubted, but it was, in military terms, a pointless exercise. In Hitler's eyes it certainly was and he ranted on about these 'stupid mountaineers who should have been court-martialled'.

It was the task of XLIX Gebirgskorps of Seventeenth Army to drive down the western side of the Caucasus. The operation carried out by Lists's Army Group 'B', with which XLIX Corps was serving, can best be described as a fast drive up a cul-de-sac. Stalingrad was a sore which drained the strength of the German armies in the south of the battle line and when the Red Army's counter-offensive destroyed Paulus's Sixth Army inside the martyred city and then raced westwards, List's Army Group in the Caucasus was forced to retreat to avoid being cut off and destroyed. The Gebirgsjaeger were later to describe their operation as 'the round trip to the Caucasus'. But that lies in the future.

On 6 August Corps' direction was turned from eastwards to southwards. Speed was demanded of the marching columns and within three days, in conditions of oppressive heat and smothered by clouds of mosquitoes, the regiments reached the foothills of the Caucasus. By 12 August 1st and 4th Divisions had captured the passes through the mountains and were striking towards Ssuchumi, that is to say the passes between the Elbrus and the Adzapch sectors. The 1st Division was ordered to reach and seize the 'Old Army' road to the south of Ssuchumi and 4th was to capture the town itself. Although both divisions had broken into the mountains they soon found that they could not advance out of them. Corps' attack to take out Tuapse in the last week of August failed in the face of massive Red Army counter-attacks and with their failure died also the hopes that Hitler had placed upon his battle plan.

Army regrouped and created, in addition to XLIX Gebirgs, a Corps of Jaeger (light infantry). A special temporary Gebirgs detachment, Gebirgs Division Lanz, was built around 13th and 98th Regiments and given the task of capturing a Soviet defence line made up of more than two thousand bunkers and other field fortifications. This crack group captured the entire objective as well as Mount Ssmaschcko, but against increasing Russian resistance and the masses of *matériel* and men which the Red Army put into the defence, could not bring the advance forward. It was the farthest southerly point that the Gebirgsjaeger reached. With winter weather only weeks away and aware of the difficulties of supply that this would mean for the fighting troops who lay on the far side of the mountains, i.e., the southern side, Field Marshal List ordered a withdrawal across to the northern side of the range. Hitler, infuriated by the Field Marshal's action, removed him from command and assumed command himself. His forward HQ was more than 1,000 kilometres away from the battle area and he also was in command at Stalingrad and on every other battle front.

While the Fuehrer sought to direct all the battles that were being fought, Stavka concentrated its efforts at driving in the perimeter held by 'Lanz Division' and of forcing Konrad's XLIX back up the Caucasus to the Don. As early as the first week of November 1942 Lang reported that three Soviet corps and a number of independent brigades were massed against the rapidly diminishing strength of his division. Permission for his men to pull back was refused. As we shall see in the account of 100th Regiment in the Volkhov sector, lack of moral fibre by senior commanders condemned the Jaeger to face unequal odds and to fight and die in conditions of such misery that they cannot be imagined. Sentries died of exposure if they were not relieved within half an hour, and the bitter cold even loosened the fillings in the soldiers' teeth. Rations came forward irregularly and always in insufficient quantities. On 1 December Lanz reported that two men had died that day of exhaustion and that ten others had collapsed. Each day sixty pack-animals died. Only one day's rations for the men remained. There was no fodder for the animals. He reported that it was no longer possible to evacuate the wounded and that road communications had been destroyed by floods, so no ammunition was coming through to the forward positions. And still those in authority would not permit a withdrawal of Lanz's shattered regiments. Rations were cut by half. The front-line strength of one unit fell from 170 men to just ten.

It was eventually realized, even in Fuehrer HQ, that a retreat was inevitable and this was conducted over the next three months; two of which were the coldest months of the year. The difficulties that had to be overcome beggar description. With most of the draught-horses dead, the heavy guns could not be moved except by tractors and Corps had only ten of these. Some machines broke down from constant use in the appalling road conditions. There were instances where artillery pieces had sunk so deep into the mud that three tractors had to be used to drag them free. A deterioration in the weather brought heavy rain which produced floods and when these waters froze, the tractors could not get a grip on the icy surfaces of the mountain roads. Despite the conditions XLIX Gebirgskorps brought out all its guns as well as those batteries which had been seconded to it from Seventeenth Army. The guns were towed; the Jaeger, of course, retreated on foot. After months of campaigning, of fighting against an enemy superior in numbers and equipment, with their ranks decimated by casualties, covered with lice and with empty bellies, the Jaeger marched and marched. XLIX Corps did not form the rearguard for this retreat, but, covered by units of 46th Infantry Division, moved into new positions in the swamps of the Kuban. The Kuban bridgehead, where the Jaeger of 1st and 4th Divisions fought in swamp and marsh conditions, was held until the autumn of 1943.

5th Gebirgs Division in the Volkhov Sector: Leningrad, 1942–1943

WHILE IN THE SOUTH OF RUSSIA 1st and 4th Gebirgs Divisions had played their parts in the destruction of Soviet forces around Uman and had then advanced to the River Mius, another group of Gebirgs divisions serving with Army Group North had been fighting south-east of Leningrad.

Hitler's strategy had not been to capture the city. He had no intention of losing men in street fighting. Rather did he intend to surround it with a ring of military units. The inhabitants would be starved into submission and the buildings smashed by artillery and air bombardment. In time Leningrad must surrender. That the city did not capitulate was due in part to the fact that Leeb's Army Group which had advanced to the south of the city was never able to gain touch with the Finns to the north-west so that the city was never completely cut off. If for no other reason than that the fall of Leningrad would be a blow to the morale of the Soviet people, the Russians could not allow the city to fall into German hands and Stavka mounted a series of vast and costly offensives to drive back Army Group North and thus raise the siege. Although these attacks had begun in the late autumn and had continued throughout the winter, by the spring of 1942, these efforts had achieved nothing and had cost the Red Army heavy and terrible losses.

The most sensitive sector of the whole Leningrad front was in the east; along the River Volkhov. Every Red offensive in that sector had as its principal aim the forcing back of the German forces so that the Volkhov and Leningrad forces could gain touch, break the German ring and thereby raise the siege. So bitter and protracted was the fighting for this river/swamp that Volkhov has been compared to Verdun or the Somme in the Great War, or to Stalingrad in the second. The Gebirgs divisions which fought in these wasteful battles and in these appalling conditions were the 5th, which arrived from Crete in April 1942 and remained with Eighteenth Army along the Volkhov until November 1943, and the 3rd, which arrived in the line during September 1942 but which was withdrawn within a month to fight on the River Mius in southern Russia.

When Ringel's 5th Gebirgs entered the fight at the end of March 1942, its first task was to prevent the escape of Red Army formations trapped in the Volkhov pocket. This had been created as a result of the local Soviet commanders allowing their units to be lured into a German trap within which they were promptly cut off. The tactics employed by the Soviet commanders to break out of the encirclement showed an inflexibility of thought that resulted in a criminal waste of men. In a great many cases this rigid mentality was nowhere more sadly demonstrated than in the frontal attacks which came in against a prepared, determined opponent. A Soviet head-on assault carried out by lines of men marching stolidly forward into the fire of MG 42s and a bombardment of 8.8cm guns, would collapse and die in that defensive fire. Within a couple of hours a fresh Russian assault would be launched in exactly the same fashion at precisely the same area of the German line, and if that attack too, failed, then a third, fourth and fifth attempt would be made. Ringel's division had been briefed, before it went into action, that this would be the pattern of events and as it had been foretold, so did it happen.

Fighting at this intensity lasted from March to the end of July 1942, and in the densely wooded swamps of the River Volkhov the 100th Regiment, 5th Gebirgs fought a great number of defensive battles chiefly in the bridgehead at Kirishi, as well as carrying out local attacks at Vinjagolovo. When the Volkhov pocket was finally destroyed 33,000 prisoners of war marched into German captivity. Fragments of Red Army divisions which had evaded capture by hiding in the almost impenetrable forests, hoped either to escape capture or else to break through the German lines. The 5th was sent in pursuit of these fragments and was soon involved in fighting a sort of jungle war which was not only costly in lives, but, above all, placed a terrible physical and mental strain on the Jaeger.

The autumn and winter of 1942 passed, with battles of lesser or greater intensity along the Volkhov and then, during the summer of 1943, there was another Soviet offensive, which has passed into military history as the Third Battle of the Ladoga. In its opening phases the Red units came in against 5th Gebirgs at so many different places that the division was soon fragmented and individual battalions had to fight their battles isolated, unsupported and with little direction from divisional headquarters. From the conflicting orders which came down from OKH, it was clear that those at that level of Command had no idea of the conditions in which their soldiers were fighting. An example of how out of touch the generals were can be seen in this report written by Helmut Hermann, commander of 1st Battalion, 100th Regiment during the defensive battles along the Volkhov, an area some 60 kilometres east-south-east of Leningrad during the summer of 1943.

'Towards the end of June I was commanding the battalion in the absence of our CO, Major Wecker. For several weeks we had had to change position, which meant, in the vast majority of cases, that we had to give up well-built trenches and take over less well-constructed ones. The reason for this was that our trench line often marked the place which a counter-attack had reached when we drove back an enemy penetration. Our final move brought us to a sector of the front on which, only a few weeks later, a terrible battle was to be fought.

'The swampy ground was dotted with flat, sandy islands few of which were higher than 5 metres in our sector. On the enemy side the ground rose somewhat. There were also dense belts of trees and clumps of birches. By using the corduroy roads which we had laid, particularly in the rear areas, we were able to cross the marshy regions. Only on the flat "high ground" was it possible to dig-in and construct proper defences.

'Our Companies were positioned in every case with a flank resting on an area of high ground. No 1 Company on the right, No 2 Company on the left and No 3 Company in the rear. We had the 3rd Battalion of our Regiment on our right and the 85th Gebirgsjaeger Regiment on the left flank. Between the Companies as well as between the battalions, there were swampy sectors, many of which were under direct enemy observation.

'During my first tour of inspection through the newly occupied positions a squadron of low-flying and slow-flying Il-2 aeroplanes crossed over us. These were armoured ground-attack machines which seemed impervious to rifle and machine-gun fire. It was clear that their targets were some distance behind us so that this time we had no need to worry, but the thought ran through my head that if their bombs were to fall on our positions then nothing would remain of our strongpoints and trenches. And it was clear to me that such attacks would be certain to precede the offensive which we all knew was coming in. The question was; how could we protect ourselves against the threat?

'I knew that in the battles of the First World War deep dugouts had been built by ramming a frame of pit-props deep into the earth. That is what we would have to do. I asked Regiment and convinced them of the need. Regiment spoke to Division and soon, behind the Front, a saw mill began to produce the necessary props which were brought up each night. Four such props formed a frame and where the ground allowed it we could begin the building of deep dugouts which would be proof against enemy artillery fire.

'No 2 Company's positions were the ones in the greatest danger. On the enemy side the ground rose and in addition the Russians had worked their way dangerously close to our positions. Also the route taken by the Company's ration carriers was across a piece of swamp over which the enemy had observation. Any protection which the dark of night once brought was cancelled out by the bright summer nights. Not only that but practically each night enemy storm troops tried to raid our positions. That they could always be beaten off was thanks to one of the guns of our Infantry Gun platoon. It was fired from the flank directly in front of our own positions. The way it worked was as follows. When No 2 Company realized that an enemy assault group was in the area a flare of an agreed colour was fired. In the gun position a shell would be fired immediately. There was always one gunner on duty with a round up the breach. That way the first shell landed just in front of our trenches even before the Very light had died.

'It was clear that the positions which No 2 Company were holding would be folorn hope when the Russian offensive came in. To me it was absurd that the Company positions should have at their back a piece of swamp which, as a terrain obstacle, should be in front of the positions. A more detailed recce decided me. There was no alternative. The left flank of the battalion would have to be withdrawn behind the swamp where the ground was firm enough to build good defensive positions and which would also give the ration carriers a route which was not under enemy observation. I reached a rapid decision. No 3 Company which lay in the area was ordered to strengthen its trenches because, when No 2 Company was pulled back, these would form the front line.

'No 2 Company was not only suffering from the nightly activities of the enemy assault groups, but also was under heavy bombardment from Russian artillery and mortars. Because the withdrawal of the front line which I was proposing was about 400 metres this could not be my decision alone. I had to ask regiment for permission and because the situation was crystal clear, naturally expected this to be immediately forthcoming. Major Wecker, who was acting regimental commander in place of Colonel Glasl who was deputising for the Divisional Commander, wanted to see the situation for himself. I showed him the exposed 2nd Company positions and he agreed my plan, warning me in advance that he would first have to receive permission from Division because a withdrawal of our front line would affect the neighbouring regiment. Then Colonel Glasl, the acting Divisional Commander, wanted to see the situation. As I took him back through 2nd Company's positions to Battalion TAC HQ, he was shattered by the impossible and dangerous situation in which the Company was placed. He promised that he would advise Corps of my plan – regrettably, he could not make a decision on his own initiative as a recent Fuehrer Order for units on the Eastern Front, forbade even the smallest withdrawal of the front line without express approval. Corps reacted by sending the Chief of Staff, a Colonel. I went with him on a daylight tour of the battalion's positions and particularly those of 2nd Company. The Colonel, while agreeing with my intentions, remarked that because of the Fuehrer Order, etc., he would have to obtain permission from Army. Throughout this time No 2 Company was suffering a continual drain of losses.

'Even Army could not give authority but sent a Lieutenant-Colonel of the Staff who would, they said, make a report. I went with him through the positions, explained the situation and the measures which I proposed. He, too, declared himself completely in agreement with these and promised a favourable report but was not empowered to make a decision. And so it went on. Army reported to Army Group which eventually declared its agreement, but not without stressing that because of the Fuehrer Order it ought not to have agreed and only the seriousness of the situation had caused it to act on its own initiative. Army Group permission came down the chain of command. To us all this was unbelievable. It ran counter to all German concepts of Command and against all common sense. To obtain a decision from that most senior authority had taken three weeks, three weeks during which we had suffered losses particularly in No 2 Company. It was simply unbelievable. The Eastern Front was considered to be an "Heeres" Theatre of Operations and Hitler, who was wracked with suspicion, had taken over the post of Commander-in-Chief of the Army. (Italy, for example, was considered to be a 'Wehrmachts' Theatre of Operation and there was more freedom of action there.)

'Throughout this time the battalion was fully active. No 3 Company was engaged in improving its defensive positions, No 4 Company was driving piles into the ground for heavy machine-gun posts whose fire would enfilade the swampy ground to our front. These posts were constructed so that they could not be attacked from the front. The Pioneers also helped us to lay a 300-metre-long chain of Teller mines at one-metre intervals in the swampy ground. All three hundred mines were then detonated and this created a small earthquake; a dark wall of mud rose skywards, the top soil was ripped off and a muddy, impassable, water-filled trench some several metres wide, protected our front. We were later to learn from Russian deserters that the Reds had considered this explosion to be the detonation of a salvo of their "Stalin Organs". No 1 Company was also busily engaged in constructing dugouts for theirs was to become an important position when the time came for the left flank of the battalion to be moved back.

'The reorganization was completed in such good order that before No 2 Company left its positions it was able to salvage some timber props and bring these back with them. The Company was also successful in deceiving the enemy into believing that the positions were still being held. The major offensive which then opened was preceded by a drum fire which lasted for hours and which was of unimaginable ferocity. A deserter had told us shortly before the attack opened when it was coming in. The date was 22nd July 1943. The Commander of No 1 Company, Lieutenant Rohleder, who had been making an inspection of the Company Train, returned to his men just before the barrage opened. What we had anticipated soon came true. The old positions which No 2 Company had evacuated were ploughed up by shells of heavy and super-heavy calibres. Nobody could have survived that shelling. Then the enemy attacked in battalion strength and stormed across No 2 Company's former positions convinced that nobody could have survived. The assault moved on to exploit, as they thought, the gap which had been created in our line. They rushed instead into our enfilading fire and then struck the obstacles in the swamp.

'For more than two weeks three Soviet regiments flung themselves against the battalion's positions and particularly those of No 1 Company. Each attack was preceded by an artillery bombardment and, usually, the attackers came in at first light. In some cases they were actually caught in their own artillery fire. Because our men could only survive by sheltering in the deepest dugouts, the enemy was frequently able to get into our trenches and then had to be driven out by counter-attack. In those endeavours the defenders were able to use their better knowledge of the positions to best advantage. During the second week an enemy air fleet laid carpets of bombs by night across the whole battlefield extending as far back as the artillery gun line. For the first time we saw "Christmas trees" which were dropped as markers. Night after night the carrier detachments of each Company as well as the Pioneer platoon under the command of Artur Schoepflin, brought up hand and egg grenades, improved trenches which had been damaged and evacuated the wounded and the fallen. The mortar platoon, under its commander, Brunner, often had to dig its mortars out of the ground in which they had sunk. Our signallers went out, during pauses in the enemy bombardment, to find broken telephone lines and to repair them. The stretcher-bearers were, of course, on duty the whole time.

'During the fighting No 2 Company was particularly badly hit and its commander, Lt Schneider, was mortally wounded by a shell splinter as he came out of his dugout to check the situation. When the drum fire of the first day of the offensive ended most of the trees had been reduced to waist-high stumps but by the end of the third day nothing was standing; even the stumps had been ploughed up. The whole landscape was nothing more than a vast cratered area. There was a much better field of fire; twice or three times the former distance but nothing was recognizable any longer. A Lieutenant of the Soviet Guards regiment which had made the final attack deserted to us. When the battalion, now severely reduced in strength, was finally relieved the front line was still intact and in our hands. In this type of battle an old precept was shown to be invalid. Once it had been the case that "A field of fire is more important than cover". Here it was the case that one had to survive the drum fire by finding good cover and then one had to struggle with the enemy in hand-to-hand combat in order to regain the position. Only deep dugouts gave complete protection.

'The battalion was rewarded for the sacrifices it had made when 50 Iron Crosses First Class were authorized and these I distributed immediately. The certificates showing name and citation could be awarded at a later date.'

As a side-light to Helmut Hermann's narrative, when Ringel was ordered to Berlin to have the Oak Leaves to the Knight's Cross bestowed upon him, he told Hitler of the privations that his men were suffering. It may well have been that personal account which decided Hitler to act. Whether or not this was the case, very shortly after Ringel's return to his division the 5th Gebirgs, having spent 20 months in the swamps of the Volkhov region, was withdrawn from the line and sent southwards.

756th Regiment in Tunisia, 1942–1943

THE OPERATIONS carried out in southern Russia during the autumn of 1942, would, had they succeeded, have taken the Gebirgsjaeger into the continent of Asia. Only one Gebirgsjaeger regiment actually served outside the European theatre of operations and that one fought in Africa. This very brief description of its service in Tunisia bridges the gap between the end of 1942, a dramatic year of conflict which opened with The Third Reich at the height of its power and leads into 1943, when Germany's fortunes began to decline.

The Gebirgsjaeger unit which fought in the Africa was 756th Regiment, which was flown to Tunisia during November 1942, to hold the feature which we, the Allies, called 'Longstop Hill' but to which the Germans gave the name 'Christmas Mountain'.

Longstop was a hill dominating the Tunisian town of Medjez el Bab, which was itself the gateway to Tunis. Whoever held Longstop dominated Medjez el Bab and who held Medjez controlled the road to the Tunisian capital. At the start of the campaign in Tunisia, in the first weeks of November 1942, the race to seize the mountain had been won by the Germans who garrisoned it with elements of 334th Division to whose Order of Battle 756th Regiment was temporarily added. The German units quickly fortified Longstop's slopes so that when the Brigade of Guards attacked on 22 December, 2nd Coldstream, which formed the Brigade's main thrust, had a hard and difficult fight. The Coldstream then handed over the feature to 18th US Infantry Regiment which quickly lost it to a German counter-attack. The Guards Brigade went in again on Christmas Eve and again took Longstop, but the US troops to whom they handed over the feature lost it for a second time. The onset of bad weather prevented the Allies from making yet another attempt to seize this important piece of ground and it did not fall until April 1943, only a few weeks before the war in Africa was brought to an end. The attack to seize Longstop on that occasion was mounted by 78th Division and the fury of their assault inflicted such heavy losses on 3rd battalion, 756th Regiment, that the battalion ceased to exist as an individual fighting formation and had to be amalgamated with another unit. The Gebirgs- jaeger regiment lost more than 300 men taken prisoner during 78th Division's assault.

Although the defence of Longstop was the main task of 756th Regiment, it was not its only one. During the time that the Allies were building up their strength to win the war in Africa, the fighting around Longstop died down and this temporary lull allowed part of the Gebirgsjaeger regiment to be detached and used in the German offensive

'Eilbote', a spoiling attack to disrupt Allied plans. With the failure of that major offensive and a number of minor ones, the Axis armies in Africa could do no more to delay their inevitable defeat.

Together with the rest of the German forces in Africa, the remnant of 756th Gebirgsjaeger Regiment passed into Allied captivity during May 1943.

7th SS Gebirgs Division 'Prince Eugen' in Yugoslavia, 1942–1945

A T THE BEGINNING OF 1942, the Third Reich was still the dominant Power in Europe. Although the Red Army's winter offensive had been a serious setback to the plans of OKW and its leader, Adolf Hitler, his action in forbidding the army to pull back to a winter line had prevented a wild rout and had stabilized the German front. Supreme Command was now looking past the immediate difficulties of defence against the Red Army's assaults towards a resumption of its own offensive operations.

What was, by comparison, a seemingly minor problem beset the Wehrmacht in Occupied Europe. This was the growth of resistance movements. Many of these had been formed as early as 1940, but had had an uphill struggle against the German occupiers, collaborators with the enemy and native Communist parties who betrayed the patriots to the Germans. With the invasion of the Soviet Union these Communist parties, which had hitherto denounced the war as an Allied aggression, now proclaimed it to be a people's war. They worked hard to encourage the masses to rise against the Fascist aggressors and demanded every effort be made to hinder and destroy the German forces.

Yugoslavia had not one but two politically opposed guerrilla movements. The first of these, raised after the defeat of April 1941, was Mihailovitch's Chetniks, who supported the King and the government-in-exile. The other was a collection of Communist cells controlled by Josef Tito. Under his brutal and rigid authoritarianism these cells were eventually welded into a national army, although Tito's allegiance was less to the people and nation of Yugoslavia and more to the Soviet regime in Moscow. He was, at that stage in the war, the tool of the Communist International, although by 1945, he and the nation he now led, were beginning to break from that thrall.

At the beginning of 1942, partisan operations in Yugoslavia, whether mounted by the Chetniks or the Titoists, were infrequent in number, small in scope and poorly executed. It was, perhaps, Germany's expectation that the Yugoslav partisans could be subdued and eventually destroyed that led to the difficulties connected with the arming of the formation which was to become the 7th SS Freiwillige Gebirgs Division 'Prinz Eugen.' Hitler selected Artur Phleps as its commander, a man who not only had served in the old Austro–Hungarian Army, but who had also been a regimental commander in the SS 'Viking' Division. Hitler had chosen, without doubt, the right man for Phleps' military career in the years before and during the First World War had taken him to, and made him familiar with, areas of Yugoslavia, principally Bosnia, in which his division was to serve for much of its short life.

The 7th's raising order directed that its personnel were to be Volksdeutsche men living in Yugoslavia. Phlep's original intention to create two brigades each of six battalions, could not be realized after Himmler reduced the divisional recruiting area to the Banat, a Volksdeutsche frontier province of the former Habsburg Empire. With his cachement area thus restricted to a single province which had a low population, Phleps revised his ideas and proposed that the new division be made up of two regiments, each of four battalions. The appropriate SS authority, the Fuehrungsamt, obviously considering that Yugoslav guerrilla resistance would remain weak and divided, promptly deleted from Phleps' proposed war establishment the heavy weapons companies that were standard in all divisions. A 'Freiwillige Gebirgs Division' was authorized on 1 March 1942 and recruiting began. As Phleps had foreseen, his area was too small to attract a sufficient number of volunteers and Himmler was forced to order conscription for all Banat males aged between 17 and 54. Thus there existed the paradox that the greatest number of men to serve in the 7th Freiwillige or Volunteer Gebirgs Division were, in fact, conscripts. Thereby, the number of recruits increased to 15,000 men but there were no trained officers or NCOs to lead them. Phleps called upon his former comrades of the Imperial Army to serve and these men led the platoons, companies and battalions of the fledgling division. There was a shortfall in NCOs which was partially overcome by the cross-posting of suitable men from their parent SS units 'Prinz Eugen'. This proved to be very unpopular and a blow to the morale of the posted men who were taken from senior divisions of the Germanic SS and considered their transfer to an ethnic SS division, made up of conscripts, to be a sort of demotion. To increase the number of trained personnel, another source was used. This was the group of Volksdeutsche NCOs and officers who had been forced to fight in the Yugoslav Army and who had been released from prisoner-of-war camps to join the SS division. Within a month of the raising order being issued the division had received the title by which it was to be known – 'Prinz Eugen' – and was complete with all eight Jaeger battalions, an artillery regiment of four battalions as well as divisional troops including a cavalry squadron, a panzer Company and a cyclist battalion. The gallimaufry of weapons with which the battalions were armed included Imperial Austrian machine-guns, Czech heavy machines-guns, Yugoslav models of German Great War rifles and field and anti-tank guns, taken from the armouries of several countries. The problems of supplying these various types of firearms and artillery pieces with adequate and sufficient ammunition can well be imagined.

Throughout the summer of 1942, the division garrisoned southern Serbia, and 'worked up' towards the time when it could be taken on to the German Army's Order of Battle. Its first military operation was during October 1942, against the Chetniks in the Kriva Reka area and was so successful that by the end of December 'Prinz Eugen' was placed under the command of Twelfth Army, having been found in all respects fit for active service. While 7th SS was working towards combat efficiency the enemy forces had grown in strength and had improved their organization. In particular, Tito's Communist groups were so well organized and so tightly controlled that they deserved the name which they had bestowed upon themselves, Yugoslav Army of National Liberation (JANL). This army now numbered more than 150,000 men, structured in divisions and independent brigades and backed by local partisan detachments. The great weaknesses of JANL were its few heavy weapons, lack of air cover and an assured supplies route. After the Western Allies had landed in Italy during the autumn of 1943, supplies were brought to the partisans by air and in such abundance that the balance of power began to swing and continued to swing in favour of the partisan army.

The German military commanders realized that the flow of Allied money, weapons and supplies would subsidise partisan operations aimed at tying down their occupying forces. Every German division used on anti-partisan activities in occupied Europe was one division that could not be deployed against the Red Army on the Eastern Front. In Yugoslavia the operations carried out by JANL were so successful that they turned first-class fighting formations which might have been fighting in Russia into garrison units fully employed in anti-guerrilla warfare. Clandestine warfare waged in rural regions is generally more successful than in urban areas, if only because it can range over so wide an area that permanent control is impossible. Thus, the German Army in Yugoslavia, soon found that although towns and main roads were more or less firmly under its control, partisan units that had been driven from one rural area soon filtered back and controlled the region again. Time and again German forces carried out offensives to clear certain territories and at the end of each sweep JANL came back. This was to be the pattern of 'Prinz Eugen' Division's life; hard fighting and successful sweeps in Bosnia to clear out the guerrilla forces and then more hard fighting to regain control of the same area only months later.

The first of the offensives in which the new division participated was Operation 'White', from January to March 1943. During the course of this operation in which a Croat, three German and three Italian divisions took part, the 7th moved from its garrison area to the south of Karlovac in Croatia and fought its way down to Mostar in Bosnia. This two-month-long offensive cost the division seven officers and 170 men killed and eight officers and 204 men wounded. Two months later, on 15 May, Operation 'Black' began. This southward sweep along the Bosnian coast at Dubrovnik resulted in the loss of three officers and 107 other ranks with a further four officers and 420 men wounded. These losses give an indication of the bitterness of the fighting as well as the military qualities of JANL. At the end of Operation 'Black', there was a change in command when Phleps left the division to take over a more senior post and was succeeded by Brigadefuehrer von Oberkamp. At lower level the tired

Jaeger were given a short rest from combat duties and served in the occupation army in and around Sarajevo.

The political and military events which occurred in Italy during July 1943, and in the months thereafter, had a direct effect upon the German Army in the Balkans in general and upon 'Prinz Eugen' in particular. In the case of the Division, the area of Yugoslavia adjacent to its own occupation zone, was controlled by 2nd Italian Army. With the overthrow of Mussolini and the surrender of Italy in September 1943, the divisions of 2nd Italian Army abandoned their weapons and went home. Those weapons, ranging from pistols to heavy artillery and tanks, were seized and removed by JANL before the Germans arrived, thus increasing the range and weight of partisan attacks in what had been Italian territory and which had now been added to the area which 'Prinz Eugen' had to administer. A short, sharp operation mounted at this time, Operation 'Axis', was just able to round-up the last remnant of the Italian Army and impose German control over the area which their former allies had simply abandoned.

Not long after Operation 'Axis' came to an end the Jaeger regiments were renumbered to become Nos 13 and 14 on the SS establishment instead of being Nos 1 and 2 on the divisional order of battle. At about that time Phleps was promoted to become GOC of 5th SS Gebirgskorps, whose establishment included not only 'Prinz Eugen', but also 369th Croat, 118th Jaeger and 181st Reserve Divisions, as well as the newly raised 13th SS Handschar Division. Corps area was the province of Bosnia and chief among the difficulties which Phleps' Command suffered was that the main supply route for the entire Corps was a single railway line whose track was frequently blown up by partisans. The re-entry of JANL forces into the Peljasac peninsula necessitated yet another offensive, 'Autumn Storm'. This opened on 23 October and was followed by Operation 'Lightning Ball' on 2 December, which was in turn succeeded by Operation 'Waldrausch' on 18 December. The losses suffered by the division in the three-month period from September to December 1943 amounted to 296 killed and 1,170 wounded. A more alarming statistic was that there were more than 1,592 cases of trench foot in the final two months. Several of the missions had been carried out in snowstorms, others had been fought in torrential rain. There had been few opportunities for the Jaeger to dry out their footwear and in some cases the men had worn their soaking wet boots for more than a week without removing them. Trench foot was the obvious result. It may be asked whether the casualties which the division suffered, the privations which all ranks endured, had been worth the trouble in view of the fact that within days of the Jaeger leaving what was thought to be a pacified area, JANL units had re-entered it and had reimposed partisan and not German law. The battle was an unceasing one which the SS Corps could not win, unless it acted in as vicious and unprincipled fashion as did JANL which at that time shot all prisoners of war. The 7th SS did not.

At the beginning of January 1944, 'Prinz Eugen' received a new commander, Oberfuehrer Otto Kumm, who had been Phleps' chief of staff. Kumm replaced Oberkamp whose health had broken down under the strain of battlefield command. Within 7th SS the fourth battalions of both Jaeger regiments were broken up and the men posted to the other battalions. The 7th SS Gebirgs Division 'Prinz Eugen' had been in action for little more than a year and had in that short time gained a reputation for steadiness in both attack and defence and for special skills in mountain warfare, its particular sphere of military operations. Ahead of it in 1944, lay the testing Operation 'Knight's Move' and then, in 1945, its self-sacrificing actions of the final days of the war.

It has already been stated that over the years the Yugoslav partisan forces grew in size and experience and the chapter of this book which covered the first operations of 'Prinz Eugen' Division described a succession of offensives which had harried the partisans. The climax of the anti-guerrilla operations was 'Roesselsprung', mounted in May 1944, whose chief aim was to destroy the enemy command structure by ground and airborne attack. The operation failed to gain those objectives and, indeed, 'Roesselsprung' ended with the partisans having successfully held the German attacks. Thereafter, with very few exceptions of a local and specific nature, there were no more major German offensive operations in Yugoslavia.

Second Panzer Army, whose operational area included Croatia and Bosnia, passed to XVth Gebirskorps the order it had received from High Command South East. Corps' directive to its subordinate formations, among which was 7th SS Gebirgs Division 'Prinz Eugen', described the planned offensive as a concentric attack to destroy Tito's headquarters in Drvar and the Allied military missions which were known to be in that area. Further, Corps was to take out the supply dumps around Petrovac. The orders pointed out that the RAF and USAAF, flying from bases in Italy, were supplying all JANL's military requirements, including artillery, as well as providing air cover for partisan ground troops. The guerrillas were also known to be equipped with German armoured fighting vehicles which they had captured and were using against their former owners. The operational orders issued by 'Prinz Eugen' Division stated in Paragraph 1, that: '. . . enemy forces, chiefly formations from 1st, 5th and 8th JANL Corps, hold the area Binac – Knin – Kupres – Banya Luka – Prijedor. Inside the enemy-occupied territory, particularly in the Srnetica–Strugica mountains and along the railway line running through the forests, there are major supply dumps. The railway is operational . . . The Red commanders are in radio contact with each other . . . Roads and bridges around the periphery of the area are known to be either mined or destroyed.' Paragraph 3 of these orders stated, '. . . 7th SS, reinforced by the assault battalion of 2nd Panzer Army, will thrust from the area of Mrkonjicgrad–Jaice in a general westerly direction and will strike the enemy retreating eastwards . . .' The divisional orders then went on to detail the operations of individual units. The 13th Regiment, with artillery support, was to advance by forced march from Busovaca to Turbe and that village was to be the start-line for a thrust towards Vinenac using armoured fighting vehicles. The 2nd and 3rd Battalions, 13th Regiment, forming the left wing, were to provide the regiment's main effort and were to attack enemy units holding the villages to the west of Natpolje and then go on to take out Jank; the first objective. The advance was then to continue to capture the second objective; the high ground to the west of Rgolje–Mlinista. Meanwhile, 3rd Battalion, mounted in vehicles, was to fight its way across the Rgolje–Mraca road and gain touch with the other two battalions. The Assault Battalion would open its attack from the south-western edge of the town of Banya Luka. Thus, when 'Roessel-sprung' opened, the three battalions of 13th Regiment would be driving westwards towards Drvar with the right flank of 3rd Battalion covered by the divisional reconnaissance battalion. The 105th SS Recce Battalion was to drive northwards up the Knin road towards Drvar, while from the north-west 92nd Infantry Regiment would strike south-eastwards and across country towards that little town. Over Drvar itself, as well as on the hillside in which Tito's Command HQ was located, 500th SS Parachute Battalion would be air dropped and landed by glider. The 373rd Division, spearheaded by Battle Group Willan, had orders to advance and without fail to relieve the SS para battalion on D-Day, 25 May.

The first advances by 13th Regiment struck the enemy almost immediately. JANL had known in advance that a major German attack was about to break over them and had prepared to meet it by constructing strong trench systems in the most sensitive sectors. The partisans did more than just stand on the defensive. Wherever the attack by the 7th began to lose impetus, that weakening of effort was exploited by the enemy commanders who flung their men into heavy counter-attacks. One important point mentioned in the post-battle reports was that Allied fighter aircraft had been active over the battle area throughout the whole period of the operation and that fighter-bombers had attacked German motorized columns. Air attacks of such frequency and on such a scale were a new and disturbing phenomenon of the war in Yugoslavia. Although the Allied aircraft did not intercept either the first or second air drops on Tito's cave at Drvar, their attacks so upset the military timetable that 373rd Division was unable to carry out its orders to relieve the SS paras on D-Day.

When 7th SS Gebirgs Division re-opened its attacks on the morning of 26 May it found that enemy resistance had hardened and his counter-attacks had become more frequent and more difficult to repulse. German troops in other areas did make progress and touch was gained with the SS paras who had by this time fallen back under attack and were occupying only a small sector of the town and the cemetery area. During the night of 26/27 May, 7th's divisional recce regiment captured Ribnik and under that battalion's pressure as well as that of the Jaeger battalions, the enemy began a general withdrawal so that touch was gained between the

Jaeger and the recce units which trapped and encircled a number of partisans units. By this time Tito and his staff, together with the Allied military liaison officers, had all escaped from the area of Drvar. The JANL divisions, which had been fighting desperately to prevent XV Corps from reaching the town, were ordered to evade the German encirclement and regroup. But these units did not leave the area. Instead, they fought actions which slowed down and even halted the advances of 'Prinz Eugen's' regiments. To Corps it was clear that the enemy was still in great strength in the woods and mountains of western Bosnia and that only the most determined action would smash him. A new order, issued on 30 May, directed that on the following day an extension of 'Roesselsprung' would open. An enveloping attack by one group was to destroy the JANL formations in the deep forests between Unac and Sana, while other German formations were to seek out and to wipe out enemy groups in an area 20 kilometres to the south of Drvar and to comb the woods for partisan detachment seeking to get past the German units.

The formations involved in 'Roesselsprung 3' moved off and 13th Jaeger Regiment had immediate success. In the Pedtoci–Uvala region it seized a great number of supply depots and destroyed the small-track railway as well as laying mines on the runway of the Uvala airfield and burning down the hangars there. All three battalions of the 13th reported successes with many *matériel* gains and the almost total destruction of the partisan bands in the area. The 14th Regiment, which had been operating with the reconnaissance battalions and the Corps assault battalion, had its successes in the Prekaja district where the booty taken included two tanks. During the night Second Panzer Army ordered the pocket around the partisan formations to be closed. By issuing such an order it was clear that Army HQ was out of touch with the situation on the ground as it existed. From operational maps it might certainly seem that the enemy forces were encircled, but Army had not reckoned with the terrain difficulties facing the embattled German units. These troops were fighting in an area of high mountain peaks and valleys that were densely wooded. The problems of fighting in the less extensive woodlands of central Europe were magnified a hundredfold in such wild terrain as was met with in the Balkans. The partisans knew the hidden paths that could be used to evade the pursuing German units and also the ambush positions from which they could inflict the greatest possible losses to the Germans with minimal danger to themselves. Partisan detachments could hide and remain hidden, making no sound, lighting no fires, keeping secret their presence in the woods until the Jaeger had passed them by. In the half-light and deep shadows of the woods of Bosnia and Croatia the Jaeger moved slowly and carefully through the trees, acutely aware that death or wounding lay in wait behind each tree and in each clearing. If a man were wounded there was no certainty that the regimental aid post could be reached. Small groups of partisans who had been bypassed would wait for stretcher-bearers or for runners treading their lonely path between headquarters, taking messages because the closeness of the trees prevented wireless messages being passed. Then in the silence of the forest there would be a flurry of rifle shots, a flashing of knives and the partisans would withdraw into the shelter of the trees leaving the mutilated Jaeger dead to serve as a warning. Fighting in such terrain meant that there could be no such thing as a totally enclosed and encircled enemy. The order from Second Panzer Army was a nonsense which bore no relation to the actual conditions. Indeed, although the JANL units might withdraw on one sector, or seem to be encircled on others, the partisan commanders were preparing to mount a general counter offensive and the first signs of this aggression came as early as 2 June.

The 2nd Battalion, 13th Regiment, which had reached a mountain height some 10 kilometres to the south of Uvala, came under attack by the enemy who stormed forward in regimental strength. Other German units, particularly 'Brandenburg' and the 7th's recce battalion, also came under heavy partisan pressure. Even divisional headquarters, located just outside Ribnik, was attacked, but rallied and in a strong counter-attack forced the enemy back towards Protici. In guerrilla warfare there could be no talk of front lines and rear areas. The front was everywhere.

The fighting in and around the Drvar area lasted until 6 June and the division had the distinction of being mentioned in the OKW communiqué. No less complimentary was a Corps discussion group whose report included the sentence, 'As the only mountain troops employed in the operation, the SS [7th Division and elements from 5th SS Gebirgskorps] carried the heaviest burden of the battle and were responsible for its main successes. Their combat efficiency and élan, shown particularly by Company and battalion commanders, the evidence of good, clear leadership and first-class reporting are particularly noteworthy.' The Corps report claimed that 'Roesselsprung' had been a success in that it had destroyed the Communist heartland by occupying the area and capturing the partisan supply dumps. In addition, two élite divisions of the enemy had been severely mangled and forced to break off the battle. Three other Tito divisions had suffered heavy loss although the report conceded that where the partisans had stood and fought they had done so with unusual ferocity. 'Prinz Eugen' produced its own post-battle report. This opened with the claim that 'Roesselsprung' was so secret that details of it were not disclosed to Division until 21.00 on 24 May, and that the operation was until that time unknown. Such a statement conflicts with that made by Otto Skorzeny, the commander of Germany's special forces, who had come to help plan the SS para battalion's operation. Shortly after his arrival in the combat zone and well in advance of its D-Day, Skorzeny learned from native, civilian sources most of the details of 'Roesselsprung', excluding only the airborne landings. With such lax security it is little wonder that JANL could counter Corps' every move. One aspect of German security took on the elements of farce. Sealed orders were delivered to Division on 29 May – that is to say four days after the operation had opened – describing the signals procedures to be followed and the radio frequencies that were to be used throughout the offensive. These orders were not to be opened until the code-name 'Typhoon' was received. The code-word was never issued to the 7th, with the consequence that it was not until after the offensive had ended that 'Prinz Eugen' knew what wireless procedures it should have been using throughout 'Roesselsprung.

Kumm's report remarked that the enemy had introduced no new tactics or Command procedures, but that the guerrilla forces had once again demonstrated their superior mobility, because of their familiarity with the terrain and because they did not depend upon an unwieldy Train organization. Supplies which JANL units needed were either carried by local civilians or air dropped by the Allies. The ability of partisan troops to march incredible distances was commented upon and also considered worthy of mention were those occasions when the enemy decided to fight a set piece battle. The partisans, in Kumm's words, were masters of screening and holding tactics, that is, they covered their front with a screen of small, mobile patrols which looked for weaknesses in the German front. A weak point found, they would mass their own troops and hold the Germans fast while other guerrilla units worked round the flanks and rear. A general attack would then be launched through the weak sector and by the outflanking detachments. The report drew attention to the increase in artillery, anti-tank guns and heavy weapons in the hands of JANL and rejected as a fairy story the statements that the guerrillas were short of ammunition, drawing attention to the large stocks that were found in the captured supply dumps. Kumm's response to the enemy's greater mobility in the mountains was that his soldiers had to be better trained, armed and led. The will to be superior, to fight and to destroy the enemy had to be drilled into his men and he commented bitterly that these things had been noticeably absent throughout 'Roesselsprung'. Kumm then laid down that the best tactical unit in mountain warfare was a Gebirgsjaeger battalion strongly reinforced with heavy weapons, and stressed, once again, that destruction of the enemy – the chief purpose of any undertaking – could be best achieved by relentless pursuit of the partisan groups. The weaknesses of 7th Division were, in his opinion, the inability of junior commanders to see their units as part of a whole operation. In addition, the lack of aggressive patrolling allowed many enemy units to evade destruction or capture, and he directed that even at the height of battle battalion commanders should hold sufficient men in reserve to carry out patrols. He was particularly forthright on the wastefully high expenditure of ammunition and units were warned against opening fire at too great a distance. The enemy should be allowed to approach to about 400 metres before fire was opened, so that every shot could be an aimed one and would score a hit.

It was a document critical of the Luftwaffe in not flying any mission after the second day of the operation and finding reasons for not taking-off, in contrast to the Croatian air force which always responded to a call.

Following on from 'Roesselsprung', the 7th went in pursuit of 1st Proletarian Division, Tito's finest fighting formation, and was so successful in that enterprise that by 9 July that crack unit had been ordered to escape eastwards into Serbia to avoid total destruction. The 1st Proletarian was only one of several units that had been so badly mauled by the Gebirgsjaeger of 'Prinz Eugen' Division that it was no longer fit to undertake offensive operations. In that sense the German offensive can be seen to have been a partial victory and although neither Tito nor his Command Headquarters had been destroyed, they had been forced to move and the resulting inconvenience had disrupted, but not completely halted, partisan offensive operations. One interesting episode of this time was the PURCHASE in a civilian street market of an MG 42. This most modern type of German machine-gun was not on issue to 'Prinz Eugen' and the men of one battalion clubbed together to buy one. Although the MG was military property and should neither have been sold nor bought, the street market was in Croatia which was nominally an independent state and where German writ did not run.

Operations came to an end in the first week of August 1944, but then radio intercepts indicated that Tito's forces in Croatia were under orders to move eastwards into Serbia. This is an appropriate point to outline the overall situation in the Balkan area. In the middle years of the war, OKW ordered von Weichs, the newly appointed Supreme Commander South East, to redeploy his forces and he appointed Second Panzer Army to defend Greece, Albania and Croatia, leaving the Yugoslavia province of Serbia under his authority. The already precarious situation in the Balkans in the spring of 1944 deteriorated sharply when in the autumn of that year Roumania and Bulgaria changed allegiance. This defection made a withdrawal of the German forces from the Balkans inevitable, but the move was threatened when Bulgaria declared war against Germany on 9 September. The Bulgarian 5th Army was positioned at the back of Army Group 'E' while in Thrace Bulgarian 2nd Corps threatened its flank.

The volte-face of these two former allies brought with it the danger that the Red Army's advance, supported by Bulgarian divisions and corps and strengthened by JANL, now moving eastwards to join its Slav allies, would bring about a total collapse of the German Army's southern flank. To prevent that catastrophe Supreme Commander South East saw his first priority as preventing JANL from moving into Serbia and he launched Operation 'Rubezahl'. This offensive was fought, chiefly by 1st Gebirgs Division and Prinz Eugen's 14th Regiment, although in its opening phases both 13th SS Gebirgs Division 'Handschar' and 21st SS Gebirgs Division 'Skanderbeg' participated. Enemy formations encountered during 'Rubezahl' were hit hard, but the German units had too few men to halt completely the partisans' evasive action. Nevertheless, some successes were achieved. On 22 August a combined operation by 'Prinz Eugen' and 1st Gebirgs Division encircled a large guerrilla force and after hard fighting eventually destroyed it. The level of military aid given to JANL by the Allied air forces should be mentioned here. Before the pocket was eliminated more than 1,000 wounded partisans had been flown out of the encirclement to hospitals in Italy by US and British aircraft.

The enemy strategy was now directed towards the capture of the Yugoslav capital Belgrade, and 7th SS was given the task of confronting and dispersing the advancing enemy formations. Such an enterprise was clearly beyond the strength of a single division and Kumm was given authority over all the troops in the area. Barely had his Command gone into action when 'Prinz Eugen' was ordered to break off the battle and march to take over 1st Gebirgs Division's positions in the Nish area. The 1st, acting in a 'fire brigade' role, had received orders to throw back across the Danube the Red Army units that had established bridgeheads on its banks.

Kumm considered the task his division had to carry out in the Nish area. This was to hold open the Bulgarian/Yugoslav frontier until Army Group 'E', now withdrawing from Greece, had passed through Nish. He would have to hold the town against the Bulgarians advancing from the east and the south; against the Red Army to the north and against units of JANL which were now making frequent and heavy attacks. The battle to hold Nish, the retreat from that city and then the battle for Kraljevo involved 7th Division in its hardest fighting to date. It was a time of order and counter-order, of delays and confusion, and not surprisingly. The division was isolated and holding a length of front of 150 kilometres. The southern or right flank at Leskovac ended on wooded heights which were infested with guerrillas and there was no touch with any German unit south of Leskovac. A similar situation existed in the north where the left wing was in Zajecar and where again no touch existed with German formations. To cover this lengthy front Kumm was forced to disperse his regiments and their battalions in small sub-units and to allot each an abnormally long sector of front. To each he issued the same dramatic order, 'Hold out! There will be no retreat.'

On its left 7th faced 57th Red Army which had crossed the Serbian border and was advancing upon Zajecar. On the right it faced 2nd Bulgarian Army now fighting inside Nish. The 7th, a single division, was locked in battle against two enemy armies and was holding them both at bay. To the north-east of Zajecar it defeated the Red Army's infantry assaults each of which was preceded by heavy artillery barrages. Frustrated by the failure of his infantry, but determined to capture Zajecar, the Red Commander flung in even heavier attacks headed by motorized detachments against the isolated and unsupported units of 'Prinz Eugen'. The reason why 'Prinz Eugen' received no assistance was because an officer in Kraljevo, although not under attack, refused to release either the armoured car squadrons of the 7th's reconnaissance battalion or its pioneer battalion. The struggle for Zajecar had seemed on the face of it to be an unequal one, but Jaeger morale and fighting spirit made up in great measure for the lack of men and *matériel* and the Soviet were fought to a standstill. But such overwhelming odds have an attritional effect on the defenders, and by 4 October Bulgarian formations had worked their way round the division's southern flank. Then to the north-east Russian pressure grew again and for the first time, 14th Corps of JANL took part in a set piece battle alongside its allies. Other Yugoslav units acting in a guerrilla role cut the roads behind the divisional front, and patrols from 'Prinz Eugen' had to fight hard to keep these roads open for they were the division's life-lines up which flowed supplies and down which, in time, the 7th would have to retreat.

The situation was now desperate and every day brought new crises, yet there were some German officers in the area who tried to insist on working by the book. One of these was the commander of an arms dump at Paracin who refused to supply a Gebirgsjaeger detachment with hand-grenades and rifle ammunition, both of which were urgently needed in the firing line. The Ordnance officer was adamant. He could issue no supplies as the dump was to be blown up and he had already remitted a return stating the amount of arms and ammunition that he was intending to destroy. Were he to issue ammunition to the 7th Division's Jaeger it would make a nonsense of his Ammunition State. Such bureaucratic logic did not impress the men of 'Prinz Eugen' who threatened to shoot the officer if he did not issue the stores they needed. He complied. Every detachment of the 7th SS was now fighting in isolation and many were surrounded by the enemy and cut off. Such a situation could have only one outcome. Despite his own order that there would be no retreat, Kumm had to bow to the inevitable and issue orders to his units to break off the battle, disengage themselves from the enemy and withdraw.

A report issued by Army Group 'E' laid out in bald and sober terms the events of the autumn of 1944, and the reader can see for himself the struggles, the hardships and the losses which are implied in these words.

'Until the middle of October our understrength forces on the eastern borders of Serbia, which had been offering the most determined resistance, were scattered and forced to abandon the roads and to move into trackless mountains. They sought, and some managed, to escape westwards and to pass through these mountains although having to abandon most of their heavy weapons and a great many vehicles.

'From this time on Army Group 'E' was in effect cut off. Only one road was available for its use and this ran from Skopje via Mitrovica, Kraljevo and Usice to Sarajevo. The last third of this road was in the hands of strong partisan groups. The decisive battle was fought out over the course of the following weeks. Knowing well what successes might be gained the Russians struck from Kragujevac along the western Morava towards Kraljevo which was, to begin with, only weakly garrisoned by our troops.

'Field Marshal Loehr was never for one moment in doubt that the loss of Kraljevo and the road already named would seal the fate of the units under his command. Neither would it be possible to avoid a battle [for the town and for the road] by moving into the Albanian mountains because his troops were unprepared to meet the harsh conditions of the approaching winter. The battle for Kraljevo opened on 22nd October and reached its climax with a Russian encircling movement at Casak, which could only be parried by rapidly extending our thinly held front. The battle was broken off on 2nd November, with the enemy having suffered extremely heavy losses. It was for us a decisive defensive victory. The Kraljevo road stayed in our hands.'

An example of how severe the fighting had been is shown by the 7th SS Division's Strength Return issued on 29 October, which shows that there were only 3,460 all ranks fit for duty. On that day Kumm, the divisional commander, sent the following report to Corps.

'As a result of the past months' defensive fighting in the Nish area against an enemy in overwhelming strength the Division has suffered heavy losses in men and equipment. The greatest number of its vehicles and heavy weapons as well as the majority of its horses have been lost. Division is, therefore, compelled to rely upon unreliabile substitutes for its artillery and signals. Particularly serious is the lack of anti-tank guns. Only in a few isolated cases could the enemy's numerical superiority affect the fighting spirit of our troops. The great mass of the Division remained unshaken. In fact the combat efficiency of the units is higher now than at the beginning of the heavy fighting and this is due to the successes that the Division has achieved both in offensive as well as in defensive battles.'

'Prinz Eugen' held open the road while the main body of Army Group 'E' moved westwards towards Sarajevo, and continued to hold it open until 28 November. This was not, however, wholly a period of defence. Recce and fighting patrols, local attacks as well as cordon and search operations unsettled the enemy and kept him jumpy. It was soon discovered that the Red Army, realizing it could make no breakthrough on 7th's sector, was withdrawing its units and replacing them with Bulgarian or JANL formations, seeking to achieve a victory in some other area.

Still forming the rearguard for XXXIV Corps, the 7th carried out a fighting retreat and then handed over the task to 104th Jaeger Division while it went into reserve in the Ljobovija area. To reach this 'rest' area required the Gebirgs division to march for four days, averaging 33 kilometres each day and much of it through mountainous terrain. At this time the 'Skanderberg' battle group was taken on divisional charge. This formation had formerly consisted of exclusively Muslim SS, but losses had so reduced its numbers, that to bring it up to about the strength of a regiment, German sailors, formerly stationed in Greece, were drafted into its ranks.

Throughout the following weeks Army Group's slow withdrawal through Bosnia and into Croatia continued with 7th SS, once again, forming the rearguard. Partisan activity was now concentrated on delaying the retreat of Field Marshal Loehr's forces so that they could be overhauled and brought to unequal battle by Red Army, Bulgarian and

JANL formations. One attempt at halting the withdrawal was met with at the Drina where the bridge had been blown and the river was in spate. It seemed that there was no way that the mass of troops on the eastern bank could cross to the western bank, but the pioneers of 'Prinz Eugen' were equal to the task. A reconnaissance showed that the pillars of a former bridge at Ljobovija were still standing. Although the distance between the pillars was more than 80 metres the pioneers were determined to bridge the gap. A search for material produced a number of thick wire cables and using these a 12-strand rope-way was constructed and short planks used to form a footway. Throughout the short hours of daylight the pioneers worked and by 9 December, had constructed a crossing whose ropes hung just above the foaming Drina and which swayed with every movement but which was strong enough to hold until all the troops stranded on the east bank had crossed.

Christmas came with the division in action again although one report spoke of Christmas Eve being so quiet that a proper festive dinner could be cooked and enjoyed. In the days running up to the New Year the withdrawal continued and Army Group headed towards the River Save. The year ended, as the divisional history records, with every unit in the division firm, confident as never before, in their abilities, masters of the terrain in which they fought and ready at any time to fling back with heavy loss all the assaults of the enemy. The New Year opened with a massive Red offensive to cut an important rail link. The situation facing Army Group 'E' was a serious one. There was not a single armoured formation on its establishment and yet the enemy's winter offensive was certain to be succeeded by others during the coming months in pursuit of the Soviets' intention to advance along both banks of the Danube. Loehr realized that he must regain the military initiative but that before he could undertake any new offensive he had first to clear his back. This he would achieve by removing the JANL threat to the railway and road communications running northwards from Sarajevo to Brod as well as the routes between Brod and Zagreb (Agram). There were very few formations upon which he could call. The XV Gebirgskorps was under pressure on the River Lika and there were other crises in Smyrnia which his Army Group's diminishing strength was too low to master.

A new crisis arose. A gap was yawning between the left wing of Army Group 'E' and the right wing of Army Group South. A front needed to be formed to close the gap and a Corps attack opened along the whole of its line in order to seal it. A successful conclusion would also relieve pressure on Second Panzer Army of Army Group South which was fighting on the north bank of the Danube. 'Prinz Eugen' bore the main burden of the counter-offensive, code-named 'Spring Storm', which opened on 17 January. If in the past the division had fought well, in this operation it fought as if inspired so that when the 7th was transferred the Corps Commander's Order of the Day was filled with words of praise for what 'Prinz Eugen' had achieved. The deeds which the Corps Commander were praising included the storming assault from Otok which tore the town of Nemeci from the hands of the enemy and the gaining, albeit temporarily, of a bridghead at Buzot.

At this time Brigadefuehrer Kumm left to take command of 1st SS Panzer Division 'Leibstandarte' and was succeeded by Brigadefuehrer Schmidhuber. The 'Skanderbeg' battle group, whose strength had now been reduced to that of a battalion, was taken on charge of the 7th, and became 2nd Battalion, 14th Regiment.

A new German offensive, code-named 'Wehrwolf' opened on 4 February and 'Prinz Eugen', now serving with LXXXXI Corps, took part in this. The operation lasted three weeks and at its end 7th SS was transferred to Army Group reserve. There its task was to serve as a sort of 'fire brigade', clearing the enemy out of Bosnia and particularly from the tactically important Zenica area.

During the time that Army Group 'E' was launching a new operation to reach the River Drau and support Second Panzer Army's participation in a massive offensive in Hungary, 7th SS was en route to Trnovo, near Sarajevo, to take out the partisan forces there. Once again the élan of the 7th was too much for the JANL units which were dispersed and which fled into the mountains. But such local victories could not change the overall picture of defeat which loomed over Germany. On every front her armies were being forced back as the Allied hosts closed in to deal the death blows. On the southern front, in Yugoslavia, the Red forces were still some distance from the frontiers of Germany but they were pushing closer and the loss of every town and village brought them nearer. On 20 March Sarajevo had to be evacuated, a move long overdue, because Army Group 'E' had now only the one road to Brod along which it could withdraw and that road was under constant partisan attack. With only months of the war still left to run, there remained tasks ahead of 7th SS Geibrgs Division 'Prinz Eugen' to undertake and complete.

By the end of 1944 the Yugoslav Army of National Liberation (JANL) was no longer just a partisan force. Over the course of three years it had grown from being a number of scattered bands and this growth had not just given it parity with the German forces. It was now so qualitatively and quantitatively superior to its enemies that Field Marshal Loehr's Army Group 'E' had been forced into fighting a defensive campaign. This is not to say that his hard-pressed formations mounted no offensive operations. This they certainly did and among the most aggressive units in the Balkan threatre of operations was 7th SS Gebirgs Division 'Prinz Eugen.'

The story of the formation during the last months of the Second World War is a bewildering kaleidoscope of furious attack and staunch defence as the whole division or its individual regiments were detached to be rushed from one crisis point to another. That 'Prinz Eugen' was the formation so frequently called upon was due to the fact that towards the end of the war there were very few crack units anywhere in the German Army that were capable of withstanding massive enemy assaults, or leading daring assaults. The 7th SS Gebirgs Division was one such formation and its prowess in conducting 'fire brigade' operations meant that it was selected time and again to stiffen a battle line that threatened to rupture or to spearhead a berserker charge in some short-lived but reputedly vital mission. And those who called upon the 7th knew that it would never fail to respond to the call.

In the last week of February 1945, orders dispatched the 7th back into Bosnia where it was to reach and hold the area around Zenica, a town to the north of Sarajevo. The reason for the urgency was that JANL forces had already begun to encircle the German units in the town and if they were to succeed they would have cut the retreat line for all the German forces in the south of Yugoslavia. It was imperative that Zenica be reached and the road northwards between Sarajevo in Bosnia and Zagreb in Croatia be kept open for the withdrawal to flow freely. The task was not an easy one for by the time that the division had been taken by train from central Yugoslavia southwards to the objective, partisan detachments had already cut the railway line north of Zenica. All movement by train was paralysed until a battle group of the 7th SS moved into action and cleared the railway line, allowing traffic to pass again. The whole division was then committed to battle against an enemy who was no longer content to fight guerrilla operations, but who was armed, equipped and organized to a scale that allowed him to conduct conventional warfare. Against standard German units JANL could more than hold its own, but when it came up against units of the calibre of 7th SS, the high level of proficiency of such formations proved superior to that of the Yugoslavs. In the battles around Zenica the men of 'Prinz Eugen' demonstrated all their fighting skills and had soon driven the partisans away from the town and restored the situation. The 'fire brigade' had little time to rest after this victory. The Croatian 369th Infantry Division, which was retreating from Mostar, was trapped and surrounded to the south of Sarajevo. Field Marshal Loehr did not have the resources to commit an entire division to this new relief operation and it fell upon 'Prinz Eugen's 13th Jaeger Regiment and some artillery to go out and, by breaking the partisan ring, allow the Croat division to escape. The 13th returned to its parent division and then another alarm call came in to rescue 181st Infantry Division which was surrounded and in danger of being destroyed. The JANL formations encircling the 181st were too strong to be dealt with by a single regiment and for this relief operation the whole of the 7th was committed, although the main burden of the assault would be carried by the Jaeger of 14th Regiment.

The plan produced by the commander of that regiment was for his battalions to carry out a long outflanking march so as to come behind the partisan formations and to cut their line of retreat. Then the SS regiment would scale the snow-covered, 1,500-metre-high Igman Mountain and go on to capture the Treskavica Panina which was more than 2,000 metres high. The difficulties of the operation can best be imagined when one reads in post-battle reports that because of deep snow the regimental

Train could not keep pace with the Jaeger. The mules could not make their way through the drifts so the heavy weapons, infantry guns and mortars were unloaded. The Jaeger Companies continued their ascent of the first objective, the Igman, carrying their heavy weapons, and so tiring was the climb that the leading Companies did not reach the summit until after last light. The attack planned for the morning of 23 March opened at first light and in swift fire and movement operations the Jaeger advanced with such élan that by midday they had not only cut the road that was the partisans' escape route, but had also captured the small town of Trnovo which dominated it. Some determined and hard-fighting JANL formations withdrew into the mountains where they concentrated around a dominant, bare and open peak. They could not be allowed to hold the peak and the FOO of the division's artillery regiment, marching with one of the leading groups, promptly brought his guns into action. Covered by their fire, 14th Company moved forward at a jogtrot out of the woods below the crest, advanced up the open hillside in the face of machine-gun and mortar fire and in a desperate assault using machine pistols and hand-grenades, thrust Tito's troops off the summit. The peak was now in the hands of the men of 7th SS Division, but it was a short-lived victory. Barely had the exultant Jaeger consolidated their position on the crest before the enemy artillery opened fire. Yugoslav infantry came storming forward out of the thundering barrage and in mass assault swept the Jaeger from the peak. The Jaeger regrouped and went in again, retook the crest, lost it for a second time and then retook it. But it was a wasteful business. Even though the SS men were dispersed across the crest the fury of the enemy fire was such that every enemy shell burst caused fresh casualties. The battalion commander accepted the inevitable and ordered his men to leave the crest and pull back to the edge of the woods lower down the slope. The Yugoslavs had also suffered badly and their commanders, too, unwilling to lose more men in a bloody but pointless battle, withdrew to positions on the lower slope.

Up on the crest the fighting had been bitter, but no less bitter and wasteful had been the battles on the valley floor where JANL had carried out a number of furious attacks in rapid succession. Their troops had stormed forward in close-packed ranks, intending by force of numbers to overrun the SS positions. They did not succeed. Each attack was repulsed with heavy loss and a breach was smashed in the enemy's encirclement. Protected by 'Prinz Eugen', 181st Division pulled out of the encirclement and only a few kilometres farther north, in the Drina valley, was promptly trapped in another. Once again the 7th was called upon, and detached 14th Regiment to carry out the relief. To accomplish this the battalions marched via Mokra to reach the Romanja, a dominant feature, and two battalions made their way to the summit along a serpentine road. The partisans fought for every curve in that twisting road and during the time that two battalions were fighting their way forward from one hairpin bend in the road to another, 3rd Battalion worked its way around the mountain so as to outflank the JANL positions. On one prominent spur an isolated house garrisoned by about forty partisans was quickly captured. In their panic flight the enemy left behind a German radio transmitter/receiver still tuned to their brigade frequency. The battalion adjutant, who was bi-lingual in Croat, spoke to a partisan commander and by convincing him that he was in charge of a unit which had had heavy casualties, asked for and was given the location of partisan brigade headquarters. Armed with details of the enemy troop dispositions, the Jaeger battalion opened a silent attack and in a swift assault captured the Romanja and went on to seize the Planina, another important area of high ground. The trapped 181st now had an escape route.

While 14th Regiment was embattled on the Romanja, 13th had been conducting a fighting retreat to the east of Zenica, with orders to hold the region until the whole of XXI Gebirgskorps had passed through and was marching northwards. The 'Prinz Eugen' rearguard left Zenica on 14 April and as it withdrew, fighting against increasingly heavy partisan attacks, it again encountered the unlucky 181st Division which was now fighting hard inside Doboj, a town on the road from Sarajevo to Brod. It was standard practice in the German Army for scattered units to be grouped into a scratch force which would be led by the senior officer present. The 7th assumed commander over all the troops in the Dobroj sector and prepared them for the fighting which they would have to undergo as they withdrew northwards out of Bosnia through Croatia and into southern Austria. These preparations paid dividend when the mass of units reached the River Sava. The town of Brod, across whose bridge the group had hoped to cross, was already in partisan hands. 'Prinz Eugen's commander ordered all the assault boats in each division to be handed over. Using these small rubber craft, a ferry service was operated which brought the whole force across the Sava untroubled by the partisans, although the boats were too light to carry the heavy guns and these were rendered useless and abandoned.

The direction of the march which had been generally northwards changed to north-westerly as the 7th and its associated formations marched up the Belgrade–Zagreb highway. Within a few days the retreating group was close to Zagreb [Agram], the capital of the Yugoslav province of Croatia. 'Prinz Eugen', as the strongest unit, continued to provide the rearguard, holding and fighting off the partisan attacks by day, then marching through the night to gain touch with the main body. The closer that they came to the old frontier with Austria, the greater was the crush of military vehicles on the roads. It seemed as if the whole of Army Group 'E' was using the same route to drive through Croatia and reach the Austrian border on the far side of the Karawanken mountains. At this late stage in the war a common urgency directed the military operations of both sides. The nearness of the border between Austria and Yugoslavia dominated all considerations. In Army Group 'E' the intention was to reach southern Austria so that its formations, by using the excellent road and rail network, could escape the JANL. In Tito's headquarters the fear prevailed that the retreating Germans might succeed in that endeavour, and to prevent this every partisan formation was ordered into the area and by unceasing attack slow down the enemy retreat. Tito's troops carried out forced marches to accomplish their commander's orders and struck the Germans from every point of the compass.

At one point in 'Prinz Eugen's progress up the Agram road it became entangled in motorized columns which had been halted for several hours. Partisans had cut the road and railway and no German unit had been put in to clear the Yugoslavs from the road. This was a situation which the 7th was not prepared to tolerate and it was committed to an attack to clear the way. The key point of the operation was a commanding height on whose slopes and crest the partisans were dug in. The Yugoslav soldiers defending the feature against the Jaeger of 'Prinz Eugen' Division did not just fight bravely; they fought heroically and when their commissar realized the hopelessness of the situation, he shot himself rather than be taken prisoner. This small group of Yugoslav troops had been given the task of delaying the Germans and had succeeded, far more perhaps than they realized. The handful of men had held up the German retreat for nearly half a day and would have delayed it longer had not the Gebirgsjaeger of 'Prinz Eugen' destroyed them. Hardly had the column on the road been set in motion when the division was called upon once again to serve in its now familiar 'fire brigade' role. It was now the last week of April and at this late stage of the war it was clear that Germany was within days of total defeat. At such a time, when it might have been expected that troops and units would seek to save themselves, LXXXXI Corps ordered 7th SS to carry out an attack to the west of Zagreb and smash a breach at Karlovac in the enemy ring of troops through which the main body of Corps could escape. On 2 May, the day on which the German forces in Italy surrendered, 7th SS Division sent its 13th Regiment to take up positions some 4 kilometres to the south of Karlovac. The 7th was still loyal to its oath, but the unreliability of some local units on the flank of 14th Regiment meant that the whole division had to be brought in to replace the wavering Croats.

For the next few days the partisans contented themselves with minor patrol activity, but then, on 5 May, they launched a major attack aimed at cutting the road along which the division would retreat. This assault was beaten off, but the signs of Germany's defeat had now become overwhelmingly clear and Karlovac was given up as 'Prinz Eugen' prepared to begin its march towards and into Austria. During the evening of 8 May, the order was received that a general capitulation was to come into effect on the following day. The imminence of surrender and the realization of what it would mean to be defenceless in the hands of the partisans spurred Corps into immediate action. Its subordinate formations were directed to march with all speed to the Austrian border and as the consequence of a partisan violation of a local armistice agreement the commander of 'Prinz Eugen' Division gave supplementary orders to his men that if the enemy fired upon them they were to retaliate and that the division would, if it became necessary, fight its way through to Austria. There then followed a confused period. The war had ended, but the fighting in Yugoslavia was continuing. The demands by Tito's commanders that the 7th lay down its arms could not be complied with in the face of constant partisan provocation. Corps then came to an agreement with the enemy that JANL commissars would accompany the divisional columns as guides and protectors on condition that the division surrender its arms. One of the 7th's last military actions was carried out on 9 May when the pioneer battalion seized and held the bridges at Rann on the Sava so that the division and the last formations of Army Group 'E' could cross the river. Still furnishing the rearguard, 7th Gebirgs was subjected to bombardment by its own guns which had had to be abandoned as a condition of their unhindered withdrawal. On 12 May, two days after that barrage, the pioneers and 13th Regiment were put into a counter-attack to restore the battle line when a Croat formation was overrun and following that incident the division was given two days' rest because all the roads leading northwards to Austria were blocked by the German Army's columns of vehicles and carts.

For many units of the Division the 12th was the day of their last parades. At many of these regimental bands played and all ranks sang the German national anthem. The divisional commander then released his men from their oath of allegiance and urged them to make good speed to the border. One Company from divisional headquarters marched as an organized formation and crossed into safety at Unterdrauburg in Carinthia. Others that grouped around Krainburg, handed in their weapons and marched through the Wurzen Pass to Villach, the whole length of their march under the fire of and attacks by partisan units. The end was not long in coming. On 16 May the remnant of 7th Waffen Gebirgsjaeger Division 'Prinz Eugen' surrendered and passed into a brutal, not to say murderous, captivity out of which few returned to their homes.

2nd Gebirgs Division and 6th SS Gebirgs Division 'Nord' on the Western Front, 1944–1945

A T THE BEGINNING OF NOVEMBER 1944 6th SS Gebirgs Division 'Nord' was ordered to move from the area of northern Finland/Norway and proceed to Oslo where it was to take ship for Denmark. Division was promised a rest period before it was sent to its new theatre of operations – the Western Front. The journey which 'Nord' made from northern to southern Norway was a long one and fraught with difficulties. At this stage of the war the RAF controlled the skies, the sea was dominated by ships of the Royal Navy, while on land Allied Commando detachments frequently destroyed the single-line railway which connected the north and the south of that country. The delays were such that when the 'Nord' advance party reached Jutland in Denmark the rearguard was still foot-marching through northern Norway.

In the third week of December 1944 the Division's 12th Gebirgs-jaeger Regiment reached Kolding in southern Denmark and was joined there on the 21st of that month by divisional headquarters and a few other units. The promised period of rest and recuperation did not materialize. Instead, orders came for 'Nord' to build a battle group and to dispatch this with all possible speed to the Pfalz where it was to take part in 'Nordwind'. This new operation was another of Hitler's plans to wrest from Allied hands the military initiative in north-west Europe. His other plan, the offensive in the Ardennes, the Battle of the Bulge, had failed to gain the victory which Hitler had prophesied and he had cast about for ways in which the stalled attack might be made to flow again. This, he concluded, could best be achieved by attacking the US forces on another sector of the Western Front and thereby force Eisenhower to take units from the Ardennes to meet the new challenge. The sector in which Hitler chose to launch this diversionary operation was northern Alsace and his choice was influenced by two considerations. The first was that the overstretched and inexperienced US Seventh Army held the ground. The second was that on the west bank of the Rhine a force of 100,000 German troops held a bridgehead around Colmar. If the German Army in the west were to launch two simultaneous blows, one by the troops in the Colmar pocket and the other by the troops undertaking Operation 'Nordwind', the result might not just be the destruction of US Seventh Army but also the recapture of Strasbourg. In any event, 'Nordwind' would relieve pressure on the Ardennes front so that a victory either in the Ardennes or in north Alsace must result.

The 6th Gebirgs Division battle group: 12th Gebirgsjaeger Regiment (minus 1st Battalion), 3rd Battalion of the artillery regiment, signals,

pioneers, Pak and a medical platoon was commanded by Standartenfuehrer Franz Schreiber. The experience gained from years of warfare
meant that the officers and men of the division were ready to meet any
sudden emergency. Thus, when the order came on Christmas Eve,
Schreiber and the hardened veterans of his battle group were ready for
action. But they were to encounter a type of warfare in this new theatre
of operations vastly different from that which they had fought in
Lappland and one for which their years on active service in the high
North had not prepared them. Now they were up against an American
army which might have been inexperienced but which was backed by a
staggering *matériel* superiority. One of the first of the new lessons which
the SS learned was that movement could only be carried out safely at
night. During daylight hours Allied fighter–bombers swept the battlefield,
attacking any vehicle or marching detachment that was foolish enough to
attempt a journey. The 6th found also that there was a shortage of fuel in
the west, amounting almost to a famine, which reduced mobility and
combat efficiency and was to lead, in the weeks and months ahead, to
guns and even tanks being abandoned for lack of fuel.

On 30 December 1944 the first elements of the divisional battle
group reached the Pfalz and moved into a concentration area between
Pirmasens and Eppenbrunn where they came under the command of
361st Volksgrenadier Division, one of the two components in XXXIV
Corps. On the following day detachments of Schreiber's units carried out
a swift and silent attack against American forces in the area. It was an
assault made without artillery preparation and was a success, chiefly
because the US forces had not been expecting an attack, because it was
New Year's Eve. With that first mission completed the two Gebirgsjaeger
battalions were concentrated in thick woods to the east of Melch with
orders to attack and capture the small town of Wingen. D-Day for this
operation was 3 January and the battle group's assault was intended to
give impetus to XXXIV Corps' assault. Corps had been given the task of
crossing the River Moder during the night of 1 January, and then driving
south-westwards through the lower Vosges. Although the opening
attacks by 'Nord' SS battle group on New Year's Eve had opened the way
for Corps' other combat detachments, the terrible road and weather
conditions as well as the opposition put up by the 42nd, 45th and 100th
Infantry Divisions of US Seventh Army, made it impossible for Corps to
gain the objectives which it had been set.

The arrival of the Gebirgs division's artillery during 2 January gave
assurance that there would be strong and active support for the Jaeger
battalions, but the artillery war diary records how different was the
fighting in this theatre as opposed to the Lappland front. 'On New Year's
Day 1945, we received a new year's present as the guns were being
unloaded. Allied fighter bombers attacked with greater precision than the
Red Air Force.' Part of the entry for 2 January reads, 'No 7 Battery was
attacked in a cutting in the woods to the south-east of Egelshardt and
then came under a US barrage which covered not just the cutting but the

whole area. During the bombardment an ammunition wagon containing seventy 10.5cm shells was blown up. There was harassing fire throughout the night.' On 3 January the war diary recorded that the village of Mutterhausen was almost totally destroyed by shellfire and that the TAC HQ of No 7 Battery received a direct hit which killed eighteen men.

The failure by 'Nord' sister Division in XXXIV Corps to reach its assigned objective meant that the SS units that had captured Wingen were outflanked. A withdrawal ordered during the morning of the 8th was carried out during the same evening, but because of vehicle shortages 80 wounded SS men and 140 American wounded had to be left behind. Four hundred other Americans, who had been taken prisoner during the fighting of the past days, marched with the retreating Jaeger and then passed into prison camps. During this period of retreat other fighting echelons of the division reached an area west of Pirmasens where they began to relieve 361st Volksgrenadier Division from the line. When that had been accomplished the divisional front ran from the frontier on the left flank, along the Rothbach to Reippertsweiler. The 12th Regiment held the left flank with 11th on the right and with the divisional recce battalion forming part of the reserve. Another reserve unit was the Army's 506th Panzer Grenadier Battalion and some time later a Luftwaffe field battalion came on to strength. During the morning of 11 January, detachments from 12th Gebirgs Regiment moved through positions held by 1st Company, 506th Panzer Grenadier Regiment and into an attack against the Americans. The Jaeger were caught on open ground and were smothered by an artillery barrage which caused them terrible losses. An idea of just what casualties were being suffered at this time can be gained from the experience of the panzer grenadier Company of the 506th, out of whose positions the SS had attacked. That Company, although occupying defensive positions, was reduced from a strength of 250 to just 90 by the end of the day.

By the middle of the second week of January Operation 'Nordwind' had begun to lose momentum and the American forces, exploiting the German weakness, initiated a series of counter-attacks. One which was launched by 100th Infantry Division penetrated the positions held by 12th Gebirgs Regiment and the intruders could only be driven out by an immediate and spirited counter-attack. Shortly after that potentially dangerous penetration had been closed, 6th SS Division was transferred to XV Corps and given the task of reviving the dying 'Nordwind'. There was little if any chance of that task succeeding. Growing US strength on the ground and in the air meant that the German troops were under constant and almost permanent pressure. It was as much as 'Nord' could do to hold the line against the furious US assaults. The attack against 256th Volks Grenadier, the sister divisions in XV Corps, drove it back from its positions on Point 348 near Melch. Immediately, 1st and 2nd Battalions, 11th Regiment went in to regain the position and found themselves in battle against a strong enemy who was entrenched in the forests. But this was a situation in which the Americans, for all their superior strength in armour, infantry and in the air, were at a disadvantage. Fighting in the pine woods of the upper Alsace was, for the Gebirgsjaeger, a return to the conditions in Lappland and they were able, on this sector of the Western Front, to bring into play against the US troops many of the ploys and strategems they had used against the Red Army. SS snipers worked their way forward through the American positions and once behind the trench lines fired at runners, officers and ration parties. The effect upon inexperienced troops of enemy fire coming from the rear unnerved them and reduced their fighting abilities. US patrols which went out sweeping the area for the elusive snipers were themselves fired upon and forced to ground where they were picked off at leisure. The infantry of 45th Division had a particularly difficult time and were soon so dominated by the Gebirgsjaeger that a whole regiment of that formation allowed itself to be encircled. In a desperate endeavour to break the ring, the US commanders committed armour to the battle. It was a fatal move. Not only were tanks unable to operate effectively in the thick forests, but their opponents, armed with explosive charges and panzerfausts, were aware of the tanks' limitations and attacked the Shermans at close quarters, destroying them all. A Command decision was taken not to make another attempt to free the trapped men of 45th Division and after German loud-speaker detachments had demanded their surrender, groups of them began to come in, their action leading within hours to a general surrender. Four hundred and fifty-six men of the US division were taken prisoner, 26 of them officers. A further 200 had been killed. The SS had lost 26 killed, 127 wounded and twelve missing.

Orders came from Corps for a fresh attack at midnight on 23/24 January, with the objective of retaking the exits from the Zinsweiler and Rothbach forests. The division went in without artillery preparation and the élan of the Jaeger brought initial successes. Then the US defence stiffened and street fighting in some hamlets slowed down and then halted the SS attack. Corps, aware of the almost 50 per cent losses in manpower which the Jaeger regiments had suffered, cancelled the operation and directed the SS division to go over to a defensive posture. Replacements which were needed came in to flesh out the depleted ranks but the men were no longer all Reichsdeutsche (German nationals) but predominantly Volksdeutsche (German from other European countries), whose fighting skills were lower. In view of this reduction in combat efficiency, it was as well that fighting died away on that sector of the front and although it flared up from time to time no major operations were undertaken by either side.

During February division was posted back to XXXIV Corps to take part in an offensive in the Ruwer sector. Its objective in this operation was to recapture Trier; a difficult task for a single division. Nevertheless the Jaeger regiments concentrated in the woods to the south of Hinzenburg ready to carry out the assault for which they were promised unusually heavy artillery support. This was to be fired not only by the division's own battalions but also by the guns of 256th Volksgrenadier Division, those of 2nd Gebirgs Division and some 8.8cm batteries. The opposing forces were tank units of US 10th Armored Division. The two Jaeger regiments crossed their start-lines at 04.00 on the morning of 6 March 1945, and bypassing Hinzenburg, crossed the River Ruwer and reached the Trier–Zerf road. Some battalions were then involved in very heavy fighting for the village of Lampaden, but 1st Battalion, 12th Regiment lost its way in the dark and by the time it entered the fighting American resistance had hardened. Neither SS regiment could reach the initial objective of Dreikopf. Trier was now an impossible goal because on other sectors of the divisional front US troops had gone over from defence to counter-attacks led by armoured units. Some of these assaults were beaten off with heavy losses to the tanks units but then, during the night of 8 March, a shortage of ammunition and a general deterioration in the situation forced Corps to issue a withdrawal order. The Ruwer operation was at an end. It had been a bloody business. The Division had lost 180 all ranks killed in action and 300 had been wounded, but at least 450 Americans had been killed and a further 356 had been taken prisoner.

One tragic episode in the fighting had caused the SS a number of casualties. As the battalions advanced during the night of 6 March, the darkness was so intense that 1st Battalion, 11th Regiment and 3rd Battalion, 12th Regiment struck each other between the villages of Lampaden and Paschel, each thinking the other to be the enemy. Before the confusion could be resolved friend had fired on friend.

On 9 March 'Nord' Division was placed at the disposal of Seventh Army from whom it received directions to assist in the creation of a firm front west of the River Mosel behind which the smashed German divisions on that sector could withdraw to the Rhine. LXXXXI Corps, to which 6th SS was now attached, had been so hard hit in the recent fighting that 'Nord', despite its own weakness, was the only formation capable of carrying out effective action. By this time the rapid US tank thrusts and air strikes by fighter-bombers had all but destroyed the cohesion of the German front. The long exposure to battle, the heavy losses they had suffered and the depressing knowledge that war was now being fought on German soil, had all played their part in reducing the combat efficiency of the German armies in the west. At unit level the fact that no rations were coming forward and that touch was often lost with neighbouring units was of more immediate concern. Another unpleasant surprise for the retreating SS units was to find German villages flying the white flag of surrender. No less bitter was it for the villagers to learn that in some cases the SS Gebirgsjaeger intended to turn their civilian homes into military strong-points. Corps had ordered that 'Nord' was to stand fast in order to cover the retreat of other units across the Rhine, and Division proposed to delay the US advance by defending the villages and hamlets along the American thrust-line. In contrast with the deteriorating situation on the German side, American morale had soared with the successes that were being gained as the units of Seventh Army became more combat experienced. Under ground and air attack the German forces were forced into one retreat after another and 'fire brigade' actions which 6th SS undertook were usually too weak to affect the general situation.

On 18 March, the commanding officer of 12th Regiment, so long without knowledge of the real situation, learned from the Wehrmacht communiqué that a defensive line was being set up east of the Rhine, and decided to march the remnant of his regiment to Worms and to cross the river at that point. He divided his troops into battle groups and gave each commander a hand-written order to concentrate at Worms. The hope that the 12th would be able to reach the Rhine before the Americans was a folorn one. The men of 12th Regiment were foot-marching, slowly now, because they were weak from hunger. There had been no issue of warm food for four days, the iron rations had all been eaten and the SS men were reduced to begging for food from the farmers across whose property they were withdrawing. The Americans, by comparison, were well fed, well armed, were mounted in fast moving vehicles and knew that victory rode with them.

During these escape attempts which 12th Regiment's battle groups undertook, one had an unusual adventure. The River Nahe was an obstacle which could not be waded across and a recce patrol was sent to find a crossing point. A bridge was found which was guarded by an American sentry but one who was so hopelessly drunk that he had fallen into a deep sleep. In a house near the bridge his comrades were celebrating, with wine taken from the cellars of the house as a lubricant to their festivities. Taking advantage of this favourable situation, the men of the battle group began to cross the bridge and twenty had passed over before the drunken sentry woke up and noticed what was happening. He was dealt with – silently. On the river's far bank a new crisis developed. An American armoured car was guarding the brigade's exit, but its crew was listening to a radio programme which was broadcasting dance music. It was clear that the attention of the crew was otherwise engaged. The men of the battle group crept past the vehicle with the leader holding a grenade ready to throw into the open turret in the event of an alarm being raised. The whole group crossed the Nahe successfully and without loss. It had been fortunate. Very few other groups from the remnant of 12th SS Gebirgs Regiment were able even to reach the Rhine. Most were intercepted and taken prisoner as they moved across the open fields on the western bank of the river.

While 12th Regiment was going into captivity the other divisional units had been conducting a fighting retreat along the Mosel to the Rhine and to such good effect that the Wehrmacht communiqué for 16 March announced, 'American attacks between Coblenz and Boppard have been brought to a halt.' For the operations that had stopped the US advance, 'Nord' Division could take most of the credit. Late in that same day Corps ordered the SS division to disengage from the enemy and prepare to cross to the Rhine's eastern bank. The exhausted units endured the delays and false starts that are an almost inevitable element of military movements, but by the night of 17/18 March the crossing had been carried out. A regrouping of the remaining divisional units showed that during the fighting of the past weeks the strength of the division had shrunk alarmingly. It was now only at a quarter strength of its war establishment.

A new defensive front was created on the right bank of the great river, between Eltville and Ehrenbreitstein, but the division did not go into action there but was pulled out of the line on 23rd March, and foot-marched to positions along the River Lahn. The divisional commander found that no firm defensive line existed on the division's allotted sector. Such considerations became academic when American tank forces struck along the Frankfurt autobahn on the 27th and dispersed the German defenders. The shattered fragments of the SS division were pushed eastwards, some sub-units joining with other remnants determined to continue resistance to the American advance for as long as possible. Most were overrun or destroyed as the US armour swept on at a fast pace towards Salzburg. Some small groups of Jaeger who had survived the débâcle were swept away as they struggled to oppose the US tank armada and in those last days of the war, what remained of the 6th SS Gebirgs Division 'Nord' was crushed and vanished as a fighting formation.

A last memory of the confusion of those days needs to be recorded. In every army of the world there are reinforcement or replacement units whose task it is to train men for the firing line and to send these to the front when the need arises. The 6th SS Gebirgs Division 'Nord' had such an Ausbildungs und Ersatz battalion and the following account, covering the period from February to April 1945, was written by a recruit of that battalion. His story was reproduced in the history of 6th SS Division and permission to use it is gratefully acknowledged.

'I reported to the battalion in Leoben (in Steiermark/Austria) on 26th January 1945. Our instructors were mostly Volksdeutsche from the "Prinz Eugen" Division and we carried out training in the Leoben and Donawitz hill country. Few of my comrades were from alpine regions and many had never seen a mountain before, to say nothing of a whole mountain range. Our training was interrupted quite regularly by Allied aircraft . . . one of which, probably a Tito machine, used to fire on the mule trains bringing up our rations, but usually without success.

'On 26th March, the first three platoons of our Company were given orders to go out on active service, while No 4 Platoon was selected to stay behind in Leoben. We all thought them to be the lucky ones but I have since found out that most men of that platoon were killed in action during the fighting on the Semmering. According to rumour we were going into action near Karlsruhe and we set out in goods trucks which by Good Friday had reached Nordheim. There we learned that we were to join the 6th SS Gebirgs Division's recce battalion but we could find no trace of that unit. None of us had any weapons nor had we any rations, and we were given time off to go out and to provide for ourselves. We carried out a foot march that evening to Lauffen, then caught a train which carried us to the Hoeglingen area near Ludwigsburg. We were billeted there and stayed over Easter. Some of our comrades who went out into the streets at this time were rounded up and put into a hastily formed machine-gun battalion. The rest of us, if I remember correctly, marched in the evening of Easter Monday towards Hohenasperg. We were in good heart despite still being without weapons and were then told that we were to defend the Hohenasperg fortress. This would be an impossible task as we were unarmed.

'The rumour proved to be false and we marched through the night northwards from Ludwigsburg. I can remember that the march was longer than 50kms and that we marched without the customary halts. We still were without weapons and swapped our rations and cigarettes for firearms which we obtained from the crowds of soldiers retreating down the road. The farther north we marched, into an area east of Heilbron, the more war material we found abandoned alongside the roads and cursed our keenness in getting rid of food and cigarettes for stuff which we were now finding abandoned in increasing quantities.

'We then went by lorry, I think to Neustadt on the River Kocher and had our first brush with the enemy near Cleversulzbach. We were soon surrounded but managed to slip away during the night through the American lines. It was a sort of cowbows and Indians game carried out in deadly earnest. We reached our own lines again – this was probably the first Sunday after Easter. I think it was 7th April, when we arrived in Oehringen and were able to rest for a short time. Then we boarded lorries and were taken north again to the Kuenzelsaua sector of the Kocher. For the next fourteen days we clashed or battled with the enemy and spent some time in very bitter fighting in the forests in the area east of the River Kocher. Our platoon was frequently cut off in the woods, were shot at by our own mortars or entered villages that were already in enemy hands. We fought the whole of those 14 days without any rations coming forward, living on what we could find. By this time we were very experienced "warriors" but were forced slowly back in an easterly direction. Round about 17th or 18th April, somewhere near Hoerlebach, we came across and joined up with one of the battle groups of the 'Goetz von Berlichingen' Division and with them flung back American attacks with heavy casualties. There were some Cossacks serving with that unit and I was surprised at how they would coolly allow the Americans to get within a few feet of their positions before opening fire.

'On or about 19th April, we were told that we were being taken out of the line to be sent to Prague. We carried out a number of night marches and near Crailheim, at Tiefenbach, were given new orders to take up defensive positions on the banks of the Jagst. The remnant of our platoon, some 30 to 40 men dug in in very bad positions, tactically speaking. We had been given from somewhere an old MG 15 with which we were supposed to stop the Amis from crossing the river. The American tanks positioned on the high ground on the other bank soon picked out our positions and smashed them one after the other. I was one of the few who, in the late afternoon, managed to escape from that killing ground. The platoon was, to all intents and purposes, destroyed there and it was clear that US troops were already in the nearby village and all around us.

'As I retreated southwards I met up with some comrades from my unit as well as men from other units. We made up a small group and continued to move towards Aalen. There we were picked up and taken by truck to Dillingen on the Danube. We hoped we would be given a few days' rest there before going back into action but we were only a few hours in the barracks when quite surprisingly US tanks appeared in the town and once again we had to pull back, this time to the bridge over the Danube which was blown up shortly after the last of us had crossed it. Eventually, I reached Munich and was then posted to the 'Nibelungen' Division which was supposed to be in Ingolstadt. I did not reach that place but was taken prisoner on 3rd May.'

1st Gebirgs Division in Hungary, 1944, and in Steiermark, Austria, 1945

I N ORDER TO TELL THE STORY of the Gebirgs Divisions' last campaign we should go back to the end of 1944 and to Hungary whence we shall be led to the operations conducted in Burgenland and Steiermark, the easternmost provinces of Austria, from March to May 1945. In a sense it is fitting that the story of the Gebirgsjaeger should end in the Steiermark for that province was one of the recruiting areas of the German Army's 3rd Gebirgs Division. (To avoid confusion the battle area described in this account will be referred to as the Steiermark and not by its English name, Styria.)

In December 1944 Stavka mounted an offensive to capture Budapest. Stalin intended that the capture of the Hungarian capital be swift and decisive, before commencing Operations 'Vienna' and 'Berlin'. Stalin insisted that these campaigns be won and the Soviet hold on those cities consolidated, before the Western Allies could interfere with his political plans for post-war Europe.

A few weeks before the Soviet 'Budapest' offensive opened 1st Gebirgs Division was moved out of Yugoslavia and into the area of western Hungary between the River Drau and Lake Balaton (the Plattensee). Its position was carefully chosen for the 1st had a dual role. It was to be both a rock against which the Russian westwards drive would shatter itself and secondly, it would form the eastern bulwark for the defence of Vienna. Although the Red Army failed to capture Budapest in December, it did gain other successes, less spectacular perhaps, but vital for the next stages of the westward advance. Russian armour cut the road between Budapest and Vienna, first isolating and then encircling the Hungarian capital. The Germans lacked the strength to break this encirclement and could now only await the inevitable. A new Russian offensive opened in February and within days Budapest had fallen. Soon Soviet armies were racing westwards and the pace of their advance produced a fresh crisis; this time in southern Hungary. Germany, lacking indigenous natural resources, was now totally dependent on the oil fields and refineries at Nagykanitzsa. These were threatened by the advance of the Red Army's spearhead units which had reached to within 50 kilometres of the vital supplies. Hitler declared that if the Hungarian oil fields passed into enemy hands the German war machine would stop and the war would have to come to an end. He planned an operation that would not only smash the Russian assault and build a strong defensive line east of the oil fields, but would also hold the grain-producing areas of Hungary and protect Vienna. The finest formations of the German Army were ordered to the Eastern Front and chief among these was Sixth SS

Panzer Army which Hitler had selected to take the leading part in 'Spring Awakening', his new offensive. D-Day for the operation was to be 8 March, and H-Hour 04.30. Very few on the German side could have expected that this was to be the last major German offensive mounted on the Eastern Front and that the units fighting it would be bled almost to death trying to achieve Hitler's impossible battle plan.

That was for a combined operation to trap and destroy Tolbhukhin's 3rd Ukrainian Front in the area between the Danube, Lake Balaton (the Plattensee) and the River Drau. Army Group South was to strike southwards across the land bridge between the Plattensee and the Valenczsee while, simultaneously, Army Group South East's Second Army was to advance eastwards.

The impossibility of Hitler's battle plan lay not in its strategy but in his choice of area across which the fighting was to take place. The Plattensee lies in the west of Hungary in an area notorious for its marshy terrain. It was in swamp-like conditions that the German armies fought their unequal battle. The OKW War Diary entry dated 7 March reported that, '. . . 2nd Panzer Army attacked with four Divisions: 71st Infantry, 13th SS [a code-name for 16th SS Panzer Grenadier Division), 1st Gebirgs Division and 118th Infantry Division. Advances were made on the southern flank despite increased enemy resistance. The attack was resumed today although with little support from the Luftwaffe because of bad weather. The terrain is still bad [waterlogged] and in the south the armour is held fast . . .'

It was not long before 'Spring Awakening' was in difficulty. Thick mud prevented the trucks from operating; mud so deep that in some places King Tiger tanks sank up to their turrets. The armour could not move but the infantry could and 1st Gebirgs Division, one of the strongest non-SS formations on the establishment of Army Group South, was ordered to revive the flagging offensive. The division's opening attack was made on the Kaposvar sector, and in a demonstration of their customary élan the Jaeger regiments fought their way through three successive lines of Soviet field fortifications and then went on to capture the town of Csomend on 16 March. This victory was the climax of the division's operations in 'Spring Awakening' for soon even its pace began to falter because of the appalling state of the terrain.

Neither the Jaeger nor the armour could do more to gain the objectives they had been set. In the opinion of the field commanders, Hitler's plan had never had any hope of success and when the Red Army opened its counter-offensive on 21 March, the German line reeled under its massive blows and began to break. The Russian deployment was enormous. The Intelligence Officers of Army Group South had identified forty-two Russian infantry divisions and eight mechanized Corps at the end of the first day's fighting, and they knew that behind that first assault wave was an even larger force ready to exploit the breaches that would soon be made.

The strategic plan worked out by the officers of 3rd Ukrainian Front was that a northern Red Army pincer striking through Burgenland, would be paralleled by a southern pincer striking through Lower Steiermark. The northern arm would split Sixth Army from 6th SS Panzer Army on its left, while the southern pincer would detach Sixth Army from its right-flank neighbour, Second Panzer Army. These two out-flanking thrusts would be followed by a central thrust to fragment the now isolated Sixth Army and create a gap through which Soviet formations could pour into the heart of Austria.

The failure of 'Spring Awakening' and the immediate riposte of a Russian counter-offensive made inevitable the withdrawal of Army Group South out of western Hungary. In a retreat where there is always the danger of total collapse, strong measures are needed to stop panic spreading among the formations, all of whom are seeking to use the same escape roads. The standard military solution is to place across the line of retreat a division of prove ability. Its task is to open its front to allow the retreating formations to sluice through, but then to close it against the advancing enemy thereby forming a shield behind which the retreating formations can be reformed.

Army Group South selected 1st Gebirgs Divisions to be that sluice/shield, but the 1st was locked in battle around the Plattensee and could not disengage itself quickly or easily. Its units could only be relieved from the battle line piecemeal. They were then force-marched to the new combat area and slotted into the defence positions which had been set up on each side of the Szentgal–Janoshaza road. Flooding back along that road were civilians, fearful of the rape and pillage that accompanied the Red Army, and trapped among the great mass of trek carts were military formations tied to the slow pace of the civilian traffic. Above the crawling columns of misery moving westwards towards Austria swept the fighter-bombers of the Red Air Force, cutting swathes of death and destruction on the jam-packed roads. For days the columns flooded past the Jaeger in their slit trenches. Then at last the flood faded to a trickle and then that, too, died away.

Now was the time to close the divisional front and prepare to receive the first assaults of Tolbhukhin's soldiers. These attacks came in, a flood-tide of khaki-cold infantry sweeping out the Bakony forest and storming uphill to gain the summit of the ridge from where the road descends to Devescser. The forward Companies of Jaeger were dispersed on the slope facing the enemy. The remaining Companies were on the reverse slope. The Russian assault came in with a rush, depending upon weight of numbers to overroll the Jaeger battalions. When that first impetuous charge and two succeeding assaults failed to sweep aside the Gebirgs division, the Soviets changed tactics and mounted their attacks more skilfully. But they still made no headway against the staunch Jaeger defence. A unit which holds its positions with such tenacity is aware that the formations on either flank might not be so determined, may weaken and begin to give ground. If this happens, small groups from the staunch defenders – in this case 1st Gebirgs Division – are taken from their own sectors and put in to 'stiffen' the wavering neighbours. This was the situation which 1st Division met and mastered in those mad, March days, to prevent the Red Army's northern pincer from working round the left flank of Sixth Army.

But however determined the defence of 1st Gebirgs Division, the weight of Tolbhukhin's offensive was too much for Sixth Army to hold indefinitely. Wohler, the Commanding General, accepting the situation, ordered a slow-paced withdrawal into Austria, to the Reichschutzstellung, a line of defences which should have been completed – but in many places were not – along the Austro–Hungarian frontier. At this point, as Wohler's formations begin their pull back out of Hungary, let us consider the ground across which that ill-fated Army was to fight its last battle, and the strategic situation on the Eastern Front. The terrain to the south and west of the Great Hungarian Plain rises as it runs towards Austria. At first this is seen as a series of low ripples in the otherwise flat *puszta*. Then, around the western shores of the Plattensee the first foothills are met and these increase in height as the land runs westwards into the Steiermark. For the sake of simplicity it can be said that the northern border of that province rests upon the 2,000-metre-high mountains around the Semmering and that these mountains reduce in height as the land goes down towards the bend in the River Mur at Mureck and Radkersburg, which mark the border with Yugoslavia. On the Slav side of the river the ground again becomes a series of ripples as it rises into Croatia. The principal routes ran on a generally north-south line, following the course of the main rivers, but there were rivers to the south of the Steiermark, principally the Raab which run on an east-west axis.

The strategic picture in March 1945 was that on the left flank of the armies in the east, in the north of Germany, the Russians were about to open their main offensive to capture Berlin. In the centre of the German battle line – between Saxony and Prague – there was no immediate Soviet threat. In Austria, where Army Group South was positioned, the 2nd Ukrainian Front, having collaborated in the destruction of Hitler's 'Spring Awakening' offensive was swinging towards Vienna against the opposition of Eighth Army and Sixth SS Panzer Army, the left wing and central formations of Army Group South. Part of Sixth SS Panzer Army had a weak hold upon the ground to the south of Vienna where a defence line of sorts touched the northern side of the mountain barrier of the Semmering.

Sixth Army was positioned to the south of the Semmering, its front extending across the northern and central area of Steiermark – from the Semmering to the northern back of the River Raab. On the right of Sixth Army, on the southern bank of the Raab, stood Second Panzer Army whose area extended into Croatia. Deep inside Yugoslavia, Loehr Army Group South-East was pulling back towards Austria under the relentless pressure of Russian, Bulgarian and Yugoslav forces. In Austria the military situation could be seen as a simple equation: unless Sixth Army and Second Panzer Army, but principally Sixth, defending the ground between the Semmering and Yugoslavia, could hold Tolbhukhin's 3rd Ukrainian Front, Field Marshal Loehr's forces in Yugoslavia would be trapped and destroyed. So Army Group South's task was to stand fast, if necessary by sacrificing itself, so that the troops in Yugoslavia could pull back in good order. The formation in Army Group South with which we are concerned is Sixth Army [IV SS Panzer Corps and III Panzer Corps]. III Panzer Corps, with which 1st Gebirgs Division served, had in addition three weak battle groups, an SS battalion and a Hungarian fortress battalion. III Corps was the most powerful on the strength of Sixth Army – on paper – and its own strongest formation was 1st Gebirgs Division numbering 12,300 men. The defenders of Steiermark faced a powerful enemy array of 6th Guards Tank Army, 4th Guards Army, 26th, 27th and 57th Infantry armies and 1st Bulgarian Army. The Soviets had ample supplies of artillery and armour, were well, if erratically, fed and had masses of men. The German Army was dying. No replacements were being sent from Depot to take over the positions of those who had fallen in the unequal battles of the last months. The supply situation was critical and there was little ammunition for the worn-out guns. On the face of it the fighting in the Steiermark was a desperately unequal battle, but the German Army on the Eastern Front – in this case Sixth Army – was defending the homeland and that was a powerful incentive to fight to the last.

The war in the Steiermark can be divided into three sectors. The first of these was the lower central front to the east of the provincial capital, Graz, and the valley of the east–west flowing River Raab, one of the classic invasion routes into Austria. 1st Gebirgs Division was in the area for a short time, but it is not with that formation that we deal now, but with a hastily collected group of Jaeger convalescents and invalids whose attacks in eastern Steiermark helped drive the Red Army back almost to the Hungarian frontier. The second sector was the upper central front, that is, as far as the Wechsel mountains in northern Styria, where 1st Gebirgs Division fought from the first week of April until the end of the war. The third sector was on the southern side of the Semmering. That vital area was held by another miscellaneous collection of units, known as 'Battle Group Semmering' and then as 'Battle Group Raithel'. In the final days of the war it was retitled 9th Gebirgs Division.

As the war drew to its close the military situation in Austria deteriorated to a point where Sixth Army was fighting in isolation and where it had only loose control over its subordinate formations. Thanks to their training, its senior officers and their staffs kept the machine running although central supply and replacement systems had all but dried up. It was thanks also to such commanders as General Ringel that the defence of the Raab valley sector, was so spirited and so successful.

When in March news was received that the Red Army had invaded Austria, Gebirgs General Julius Ringel, commander of 18th Military

District, convened a meeting of the senior officers of Army Groups South and South East to co-ordinate the defence of the Steiermark and decide the measures that needed to be taken to ensure the speedy withdrawal of Loehr's Army Group out of Yugoslavia. The need to meet the threat from the Red Army in the east and Tito's forces in the south demanded the setting up of a unified defence structure. But the Russians and Yugoslavs were not the only enemy that the German Army commanders now had to meet and overcome.

In an endeavour to stave off the total defeat, that was now certain, Hitler endowed provincial Party bosses (Gauleiter) with extraordinary powers, superior to those of the generals, and directed that the military was to be subordinate to the political. Under these new powers, Ueberreither, Gauleiter of the Steiermark, sent 13th SS Replacement Battalion into action on the Semmering. He had other and more bizarre plans for the service units in his territory, but Ringel, as senior military commander, had no intention of letting his authority be usurped or of allowing Party hacks to sacrifice the soldiers. Another political person who sought to interfere in military matters was Eigruber, Gauleiter of Oberdonau, who ordered the Dachstein Artillery school into action against the Americans and not against the greater threat posed by the Red Army, now inside Austria. Ringel ignored Ueberreither's political directives or else issued his own orders while concentrating upon building a strong force which would be put into action, first, to hold the line to the east of Graz, and then to mount a counter-thrust against Tolbhukhin's armies.

Working quickly and efficiently, Ringel brought the formations in his Military District to a state of readiness as early as 28 March. Among the miscellany of detachments under his command were units on garrison duty and such establishments as No 18 Replacement Battalion – which trained the drivers of horse-drawn carts. To these few detachments he added convalescents of all ranks and grades, military academy cadets and the men of training and replacement establishments. The greatest number of the men whom Ringel called to serve were combat experienced Jaeger who, although aware that they were ill equipped to meet the overwhelming might of the Soviets, were prepared to pit themselves in the unequal struggle.

Ringel set up his battle headquarters in Graz, the provincial capital, which had excellent road, rail and telephone networks, and the scene of hectic activity in his HQ can well be imagined as a succession of signals came in and streams of orders were sent out. A report which might announce the arrival of a detachment of men would be followed by a directive which would set it marching eastwards to take its place in the battle line. Reports of Red Army thrusts made on one sector were met wih instructions for a unit in that area to counter-attack and destroy them. One who saw at first hand the scene in Ringel's HQ recalled that 'Improvisation was the order of the day' and that many detachments that had been in danger of collapse, were regrouped and led back into battle by determined officers.

The way in which Ringel armed his men demonstrates his methods. As the Eastern Front began to crack, a flood of units withdrew out of eastern Steiermark (the Oststeier) through Graz and the surrounding area. Most of these were base-unit or rear-area detachments made up of men who, although well armed, had never fired a shot in anger throughout their military careers. In Ringel's opinion it was wasteful to allow non-combatant detachments to hold on to weapons when fighting troops had none. The 'base-wallahs' were promptly disarmed and sent on their way, their arms being handed over to the front-line soldiers. Soon the Gebirgs general had combined his disparate groups into Battle Group Kunz. The 18th Training Battalion, the principal formation in the battle group, was converted to an assault unit. Major Kunz formed a squadron of three platoons of convalescents and organized the remaining men into four Companies. Battle Group Kunz was placed in the centre of the fighting line with the remnant of a Galician SS division and 10th Fallschirmjaeger Division on each flank to give Kunz's group the support it would need when it spearheaded Ringel's offensive in the Oststeier. Thanks to the General's initiative and drive, his formations were able to take up a firm line from Radkersburg northwards along a range of low hills to Feldbach and thence, northwards again, into the higher ground above and to the east of Graz. Considering itself in all respects ready for action, the force which Ringel had collected and whose name was soon to change to Battle Group Wolff, prepared itself for the attack.

The assault battalion was taken by train to Gleisdorf and then marched to Kirchberg on 31 March. Its task was to hold that town and the tactically important surrounding area. The battle group forced its way through the flood of German and Hungarian soldiers retreating in front of Soviet 18th Armoured Corps and took up positions on the low hills to the east of the town. The darkness of the night was lit, not by Easter bonfires proclaiming the Resurrection, but by the flames of burning farms and houses in the Oststeier as the Soviets, in an orgy of destruction, burned these to the ground. The situation was that on Easter Saturday, 31 March, the Red Army had entered the Steiermark at Rechnitz. Smashing through the weak German defence lines, the Soviets had advanced up the valley of the Raab and were thrusting for Graz. Post-war literature describes the operation as an armoured raid which took Soviet 18th Corps a distance of 110 kilometres in 75 hours. General Balck describes his attempts to meet and beat the crisis as 'the most difficult I ever had to master. It could have led to a catastrophe of unimaginable proportions . . .' The crisis had arisen because Stavka had found the boundary between Sixth Army and Second Panzer Army, which was located along the Raab, and had smashed a breach 30 kilometres wide. One column of Soviet tanks pressed on towards the market town of Feldbach while a second drove through Fehring and then linked up with the main column. That great tank mass then struck towards Kirchberg, creating a salient.

The 1st Squadron of 18th Battalion reached Kirchberg and took over the positions which had been held by the local Volkssturm units. A civilian who witnessed the arrival of the sick, wounded and convalescents who made up that unit wrote that these men 'who came hobbling forward on crutches and with their limbs wrapped in bandages were greeted with laughter by the other soldiers – but they did their duty to the end.' Late in the afternoon the first Red Army probe came in. This was a column of fourteen tanks headed by a command vehicle and accompanied by truck-borne infantry. Finding the bridge across the Raab destroyed the column turned away. Half an hour later the Soviets returned and mounted a heavy attack which cost 2nd Company, 18th Battalion, twenty-one killed. Under Russian pressure the Company began to give ground, but then 1st Company came into action with panzerfausts and repulsed the Soviet armour. This determined defence clearly surprised the Soviets who made no further attempt to advance in the Kirchberg sector. Ringel could be well pleased with the achievements of the assault battalion of Battle Group Wolff. It had not only stopped the advance of the Russian armoured corps but had destroyed a number of armoured fighting vehicles using panzerfaust, the single-shot anti-tank rocket weapon. With the enemy halted in the Kirchberg sector, the Gebirgs general could now group his forces for a counter-attack against the Soviet salient, an operation which would recapture Feldbach. But before the counter-attack could open one small Russian penetration had to be dealt with. This was at the village and mighty medieval fortress of Riegersburg to the north-east of Feldbach. The Soviet tank raid at first bypassed the Riegersburg, but then Red Army patrols captured the village 'screaming and shouting' according to one eye-witness as they attacked the fortress.

During the second day of their occupation Ringel's counter-attack opened. The battle for Feldbach was short but intense with no quarter asked or given. The bitterness of the fighting can be appreciated from the following accounts. 'We were in a cellar and heard from outside the cry "Forward! Forward!" A mass of men was charging up the street led by a sergeant whose arm had been shattered by shrapnel. He looked terrible. His eyes were wild and despite his wound he led the charge with the cry "Forward! We fight on!" . . .' 'Twenty men in the Waldsberg sector went into an attack which ended in hand-to-hand fighting. One of my comrades had a bayonet wound in the stomach. He asked me to take him with me or else to shoot him, but not to leave him to be taken by the Russians.' . . . 'Another attack was made against the Russians. The Captain, a young, tall and strong man from the Tirol led his men into action. The fighting was bitter. The Russians held their positions and would not retreat one step. Days passed with no let up in the intensity of the fighting. Then the Captain came back, without his horse and without his men. His face was tragic as he spoke the words, "I have lost everything. Most of my soldiers have fallen in action and the survivors have been taken prisoner."'

The fighting was hard but Ringel's counter-stroke had been successful and the Soviet forces on his sector had withdrawn. The Riegerburg
was retaken on 5 April and the Russians, if not driven back into Hungary,
no longer posed an immediate threat to Graz. The Red Army carried out
no further operations in the Oststeier until the last day of the war, but
were content to lie behind vast and extensive minefields, many of which,
being unmarked, claimed civilian victims. 'In the Poppendorf area a girl
and two men were killed by mines and a further seven wounded . . . In
the area there were three Russians mass graves as well as a number of
individual German ones. A great many bodies lay unburied in the mine
fields . . .' Finding themselves baulked in the Raab valley, Stavka
redeployed its forces and swung its main effort northwards to the upper
central sector of the Steiermark; to that area in which 1st Gebirgs Division
was fighting.

It is to be regretted that Ringel destroyed by fire all his papers and
operational orders to prevent them falling into Russian hands. There is,
therefore, no full and detailed account of the fighting in which his men
took part in the last days of the war. Indeed, it is true to say that few
contemporary official records exist of the fighting in the Steiermark as a
whole, and that much of the knowledge which we have has been
produced by local educational groups. The history of 1st Gebirgs Division
has little on the fighting in which it was involved and the only detailed
account is the history of 99th Gebirgsjaeger Regiment and the usual post-
battle reports.

We now move from the Oststeier and into the upper central and,
later, the northern or Obersteier areas, where 1st Gebirgs Divisions fought
its last battle. It will be recalled that we left 1st Gebirgs Division defending
its positions on the Szentgal–Janoshaza road, holding fast while behind it
Wohler, commanding Sixth Army, tried to form a cohesive front with the
few and scattered forces available to him. As an experienced commander
Wohler knew that western Hungary could not be held for long and on
Good Friday, 29 March, ordered a tightly controlled and slow-paced
withdrawal back to the Reischschutzstellung. Three days before that
order was received by 1st Gebirgs, there had been a change of divisional
commander when Lieutenant-General Josef Kuebler was succeeded by
Lieutenant-General Wittman.

The rearward march of 1st Division took it from Janoshaza away to
the north of Szombathely into the Oststeir and towards the town of
Oberwart. As a result of the Soviet tank raid at Feldbach the whole
countryside was flooded with stories of Russian armoured masses
capturing villages and towns. One such rumour was enough to halt the
withdrawal of 99th Gebirgsjaeger Regiment. According to civilian reports
Soviet vehicles driving down the road from Koeszegszerdahely had
crossed the border, captured Rechnitz and were heading south-
westwards in the direction of Grosspetersdorf. A Jaeger motorized battle
group was formed and drove back down the Oberwart road towards
Grosspetersdorf. There was no sign of the Red Army vehicles and Major

Groth was preparing to take his patrol back to Oberwart when Krause, commanding the Steiermark rear area, drove into the main square of the little town and ordered the battle group commander to lead his men into an attack to drive the Russians back to the frontier, some 10 kilometres distant. In view of the situation – the ground had not been reconnoitred and the enemy, of unknown strength, was certain to be holding prepared positions in front of Rechnitz – Groth refused the order. While the battlefield argument was taking place the first Companies of the foot-marching battalions of Groth's regiment entered the town. With them came Wittmann, the divisional commander, who immediately cancelled the attack which Krause had given and issued orders to march back to Oberwart. The 99th Regiment then occupied St Kathrein on the western bank of the River Pinka but had barely had time to prepare the village for defence when units of 26th Red Army mounted the first of a series of attacks.

Reports tell of the amateurish way in which the Russian units tried to cross the Pinka. How some soldiers sat on the ground to remove their boots and foot wrappings before wading into the cold waters of the fast-flowing Pinka. They were shot where they sat and then, when the first of three infantry attacks opened, the Jaeger were astonished to see that the advancing Red Army men did not deploy as seasoned troops would have done, but bunched under fire. It was clear that these were 'green' troops who were undergoing their baptism of fire. It was a bitter baptism and could have only one end. Those Red Army men who survived the rain of machine-gun and rifle fire which the Jaeger of the 99th poured down upon them, broke and ran back into the protective cover of the pine woods. It soon became clear that the Russian infantry had been sacrificed. Their commanders needed to establish the strength and morale of the defenders and the attack of the 'green' troops had established these factors. The Soviet commanders then grouped their artillery regiments to crush the Jaeger and blast a road forward. The fury of the shellfire went on for hours but then ceased abruptly. It was a standard tactic for the Red Army infantry to come in behind the barrage, so the Jaeger stood to arms. But no brown-uniformed masses came storming forward and there was a short lull in the fighting on the sector which 99th held. When the next Soviet assault did come in, late in the evening of Easter Sunday, 31 March, its fury fell not upon the Jaeger of 1st Gebirgs Division, but upon the Hungarian battalion holding post around the frontier town of Deutsch Schuetzen. It was a worrying time for the Magyars. Their families were now under the mandate of the Red Army and the Hungarians knew what that meant – particularly for the women. Concern for their loved ones overrode the military imperatives of loyalty and comradeship. The Hungarians had already begun to desert singly and in small groups, but when the Russian attack came in, late on Easter Sunday, the battalion broke and fled. Their flight uncovered the flanks of 99th. To restore the situation a counter-attack was ordered to seal off the gap. A battle group of the division's Jaeger engineer battalion and flak gunners swung into the assault, flung back the Soviets in disorder and sealed the gap. The battle line was now held by a miscellany of units fighting hard to hold off Soviet assaults which were coming in at every point.

It was at this time that Stavka's intention to isolate Sixth Army began to be realized. Sixth Army began to bend under the Soviet pressure except on the sector held by 1st Gebirgs Division. It was fortunate that, in those first April days, a lull in the fighting allowed a few Jaeger detachments to be sent to stiffen units on either flank. Oberwart fell to the furious drive of Russian 30th Corps and one column of that tide of troops turned southwards down the road from Grosspetersdorf towards Kohfidisch where the headquarters of 99th Gebirgsjaeger Regiment was now located. The confusion of the fighting increased when Jaeger groups fighting off Russian infantry advancing from the east found themselves being attacked by other Red Army units which had broken through on other sectors and were driving in from the west. Kohfidisch was lost, but so determined had been the Jaeger opposition that fighting died down along the whole line running from Kohfidisch to Oberwart and the Soviets made no further effort in that area. This inaction left Sixth Army free to pull out the whole Gebirgs division and move it into Obersteiermark to meet a new threat which had developed in that area. Reconnaissance showed that Stavka had begun to mass units. A new offensive was being planned, one which would aim at forcing a way through the mountain ranges south and south-east of the Semmering. That sector was weakly garrisoned. The majority of the troops there were Volkssturm detachments and Companies of Gebirgsjaeger, the so called 'Gneisenau' detachments, independent bodies of recruits employed on security duties. On the Semmering these men were considered to be on active service although Sixth Army had not anticipated a major Russian military operation in such difficult terrain. The recruits and detachments of old men were stiffened by patrols from 1st Panzer Division. Thanks to the inactivity in the Oberwart sector Army could move 1st Gebirgs up to the Wechsel, immediately south-east of the Semmering Pass, and position it to meet the Red Army's imminent assault. By the time that the 1st was in position, Soviet motorized and cavalry units had opened a drive along the Rabnitz river valley, across the Bucklige Welt and had advanced as far as the Wechsel with the clear intention of reaching the valley of the River Muerz. Were that plan to succeed it would give the Soviets access to central and western Austria, a catastrophe to be prevented at all costs. Only a formation of proven fighting quality, 1st Gebirgs Division, would be able to thwart 26th Red Army, which had been brought up from Feldbach to spearhead the drive through the mountains.

Two significant events occurred at this time. Wohler, commanding Sixth Army, was replaced and was succeeded by Rendulic, a former Imperial officer, who had gained a reputation as being a commander who could knit together a strong defensive front. One of Wohler's last acts was to create a number of battle groups to take over the weakly defended Semmering sector and to gain touch with 1st Gebirgs Division on the

Wechsel. The story of these battle groups which eventually became 9th Gebirgs Division, is recounted below. When the units of 1st Gebirgs Division reached the area which was to be their last battlefield, Soviet penetrations had driven so far westwards that there was the acute danger of a breakthrough to the Muerz. As a first move General Wittmann decided to employ a strong battle group to blunt the Soviet drive and force 26th Army back to the line of the River Lafnitz. This was the first priority because the Soviets on the high ground to the east of the river had observation along the whole length of the divisional front. The second part of Wittmann's counter-offensive was intended to drive the Russians back across the north–south road between Wiener Neustadt and Graz. The task of carrying out that operation was beyond the capabilities of a single division, even one as proficient as 1st Gebirgs, but Wittmann was advised that 117th Division was on its way to Obersteier from Italy. With its arrival in the area, Sixth Army's counter-offensive would go in.

Sixth Army opened its attack on 10 April, but although ground was gained in the Moenichwald sector the operation failed to achieve the results planned for. The assault began to flag and an attempt was made to revive it by committing a two-battalion battle group of 99th Regiment backed by SP guns. The full weight of three Russian corps fell upon the aggressive Gebirgsjaeger group. By a strange turn of fate, although Tolbhukin's 3rd Ukrainian Front had now been ordered by Stavka to go over to the defensive, the Red Army Marshal, confident that he could succeed in breaking through the last mountain range, the Fischbacher alps, continued with his offensive against 1st Gebirgs and 117th Divisions. In the subsequent fighting the Gebirgsjaeger smashed 68th Guards Infantry and 135th Rifle Divisions, while 117th recaptured St Kathrein -- almost the last village before the pass through the Fischbacher alps. More and more Soviet forces were committed to force a breakthrough and by 13 April the Gebirgs division was fighting for its life. Against 99th Regiment, holding an 18-kilometre length of front, Tolbhukin put in massed armour. Under this pressure a battalion of the 99th at first gave way but then rallied and fought back. When last light came and the fury of the fighting had died down, wrecks of Russian tanks were strung out across the meadows and the bodies of the fallen lay everywhere. The regiment lost 180 officers and men on that single day – a blood-letting which if continued would soon reduce it to a remnant. Baulked on the sectors held by the Gebirgs and 117th Divisions, Tolbhukin made a double assault; one attack southwards toward the important road junction of Birkfeld, and one northwards to Gebirgs Division's left flank. Cossack cavalry groups infiltrated into the Sassnitz and Feistriz valleys and soon 5th Guards Cavalry Corps, supported by infantry of 26th Army, had opened a new offensive along the whole divisional front. The fighting in the last weeks of the war, particularly in the Gebirgsjaeger sector, is a succession of days and nights of close, often hand-to-hand combat with only infrequent pauses in the attacks and almost none in the fury of the artillery and Katyusha barrages. To the strain of battle was added the terrible weather; fog, rain and snow whipped into blizzards which swept across the high ground of the Wechsel. Rations were infrequent and monotonous; little ammunition was coming forward and almost no replacements. It must not be imagined that such terrible conditions were peculiar to Sixth Army alone. Prisoner interrogation produced the information that food supplies were not reaching the Russian front-line troops and that may have been one factor in the increasing number of desertions to 1st Division. The reported ration strength of 99th Regiment at the end of April, included 1,688 former Red Army men who were serving voluntarily with the Jaeger, chiefly as porters. Many of the group had been with the regiment for years.

On 19 April the village of Feistritz and the high ground around it fell to a surprise Russian thrust. A counter-attack mounted by 117th Division and the last armoured fighting vehicles of 1st Panzer Division failed to recapture either the village or the heights, and the operation ran into trouble almost immediately when 117th met an oncoming Russian attack and was soon surrounded and cut off. The 1st Gebirgs Division was committed to rescue 117th, but could spare only detachments from 99th Regiment for the rescue operation. All the other divisional units were deeply committed to battle. Jaeger patrols from 99th, moving quietly by night, soon found gaps in the Russian lines through which they infiltrated to gain touch with the men of 117th. At first only small groups were brought out, but within a short time the whole division had been evacuated and taken into the SS Corps area.

The fighting of the following days is recorded in the War Diary with attacks made in the Moenichwald–Hochwechsel sector; of beating off Russian assaults, of increasing bad weather and deteriorating living conditions. Tolbhukhin, whose 3rd Ukrainian Front had been rendered inactive by Stavka order, but who still maintained operations on the front facing the Muerz valley, was suddenly ordered to go over to the offensive again. His troops were to attack relentlessly until the breakthrough to the Muerz had been achieved. The reason for Stalin's change of mind was the fear that an armistice for which the German commanders in Italy had asked, might allow the American and British forces to sweep through Austria and upset his political plans. If his troops could break into central Austria before the Western Allies reached the area, the Russian hold could be consolidated. Released from their inaction, Russian infantry stormed formed and in close-quarter fighting captured part of the Wechsel. It was recaptured by the Jaeger. The Reds swarmed in again and retook it. Again the Jaeger went in and drove the Soviets from its summit. Such was the scale of losses to the Gebirgsjaeger that Sixth Army, now really scraping the bottom of the barrel, sent forward a Fortress battalion of old and infirm men to replace 1st Battalion, 99th. The fortress battalion was unsuited for front-line service, and soon demonstrated that inability. News of the death of Adolf Hitler brought only the questions of who would succeed him and for how long would the war now continue? Unwilling to wait for the inevitable end some Jaeger began to desert.

Many of those who tried to make their way back home fell foul of the SS Flying Courts-Martial and were summarily executed. These executions were not always summary nor were they always carried out in secret. Helma Oswald, née Auer, who had seen the Gebirgsjaeger marching through her home village of Gnas in the Oststeier, en route to fight in the Balkans, was still a young girl when she was forced to witness an execution.

'It must have been one of the last days of the war. During March the Russians had advanced quickly into the Steiermark and their tank columns had reached as far as Feldbach. There they had been counter-attacked and had been driven back almost to the Hungarian frontier, but were still holding a number of neighbouring villages, although not Gnas itself.

'On this particular day all the people left in the village, children as well as adults, were ordered to go to the Hauptplatz. In the village square a sort of gallows had been set up and some people, who they were I do not know, were to be publicly hanged. We were ordered to watch the executions and one was particularly brutal because the rope broke and the victim, who was still alive, fell to the ground. He was picked up and a new rope was fetched. Then he was hanged again. The bodies, I think there were three of them, were left hanging for a whole day.' It is likely that the victims were soldiers of the SS Galician Division who could not, of course, surrender to the Red Army and who had hoped to escape alive from the fighting. Back on the Wechsel, to go forward and surrender to the Russians was a risky enterprise but some took that risk. The remnant of No 3 Company of 1st Battalion 99th Regiment were among those who risked it and went over to the Russians during the night of 1/2 May. The survivors of that Company, together with others who remained true to their soldierly oath, held the line and fought back the attacks which continued to come in against them. Dawn of 3 May opened another day of crisis when out of the darkness the first of a wave of infantry assaults struck the Jaeger line. These attacks persisted all day and each was driven back with heavy loss. Heavy losses were also suffered by the Jaeger Companies and a succession of comb-outs of divisional rear echelon detachments produced only a few more men to add to the front-line strength. Another bizarre attempt at reinforcing the battle-experienced Jaeger was a group of men who were sent forward on 4 May. These were forty army officials, former clerks and storemen and all without experience of combat. As such they were an encumbrance and were sent back without being posted to a battalion.

The armistice in Italy, whose effects upon his political plans Stalin had feared, led to the general surrender which was to come into effect on 8 May. Rendulic, Commander-in-Chief of Army Group South, ordered his troops facing the Americans to end hostilities at that time, but gave no such orders to those facing the Russians. The German leader who had succeeded Hitler had ordered the Eastern Wall be as held as long as possible to enable the greatest number of soldiers and civilians to be evacuated or to escape from the Soviets. The German signatories at the signing of the surrender made it clear to the Allies that those German armies still battling in the East: Loehr's in Yugoslavia, Rendulic's in the Steiermark and Schoerner's in Czechoslovakia, would not lay down their arms until they had fought their way through to German territory or to safety. Rendulic ordered his armies to maintain their positions until the evening of 7 May. At last light on that day they could begin their move westwards. Russian obstinacy gave these German troops grace for a further day. Stalin insisted that the war would end on 9 May, although the surrender document had been signed on the 7th. Thus the German armies in the east had two days in which to retreat westwards and reach the American or British zones of occupation. In Austria the line which the German forces had to cross was the River Enns and they had to be on its western, i.e., American, bank by 9 May. A wild rush for the Enns would produce nothing but chaos and Sixth Army intended an orderly withdrawal. The main body would pull back behind the shield of rearguards drawn from a reliable formation – 1st Gebirgs Division.

In an effort to reduce the numbers who would be retreating and thus filling the roads into central Austria, Rendulic released from service all the Austrians in his army and all the Hiwis, the Russians who had served for so long. The order to begin the retreat would come in a coded message and it was a matter of regret for Rendulic that that code-word was not received by every unit, including 1st Gebirgs Division. Division tried to contact Corps, in an effort to obtain clarification, only to find that the headquarters had already broken up. Wittmann, acting upon his own initiative, decided to stand fast for a short time and then withdraw by bounds to a new defensive line, Auf der Schanz, which 99th Regiment would hold. The commander of that Regiment was ordered to report to divisional headquarters where he was told, not only of the signing of the unconditional surrender in Reims, but also of the situation which now faced the Division and his Regiment. He was confident that his men would continue to obey orders and stand fast. Indeed, they had little choice for even on that last day of the war, 8 May, Russian infantry attacks were still coming in against the Jaeger Companies. One attack overrolled the thin line of trenches killing all the Jaeger defenders and driving on until it reached regimental headquarters. The counter-attack Company rushed into action and restored the situation. At 21.00 the noise of battle died away and in the growing darkness the division began to thin out the battle line, with Jaeger leaving their trenches with just one or two men on watch and moving downhill to meet the guides who would take them to join other groups. The skeleton force holding the trench line kept guard until, at 23.00, the last soldiers to fight on the Eastern Front, climbed out of the slit trenches and slipped away into the dark night. Only hours now remained for them to reach the Enns and safety, but they had held to the last, sacrificing their liberty to hold the line, a strong discipline and the 'Jaeger' spirit enabling them to hold firm in conditions that would have tested the strongest nerve.

Division intended to use the Muerz valley road and railway network, but both were choked with traffic and in the congestion divisional and eventually regimental cohesion was lost. Then, at 09.00, the time by which all German movement was to cease, the Gebirgsjaeger battalions still marching along the river valleys en route to the position Auf der Schanz, saw coming out of the woods on each side of the road, the all-too-familiar silhouette of T-34 tanks. Some men in the battalions broke ranks hoping to escape capture, but the greatest number gave up. It was all over and thus in confusion and uncertainty the active service life of 1st Gebirgs Division came to an end. Divisional headquarters reached Liezen and stayed operational until 12 May, to collect stragglers and process them. Then the American Army closed it down. The history of 1st Gebirgs Division had lasted for just under ten years, six of which the division had spent on active service.

9th Gebirgs Division in Steiermark, Austria, 1945

THE FINAL DIVISION to be included in this catalogue of mountain troops, is one which was not created until the last days of the war. This was 9th Gebirgs Division, a number which was actually given to two different units: first in Narvik and then in Austria. It is with 9th Division in Austria that this concluding account is concerned.

In previous pages it was stated that Sixth Army had not anticipated a Russian thrust through the difficult country around the Semmering and had, therefore, garrisoned the area only with Volkssturm units and a few miscellaneous groups. Tolbhukhin's offensive in the Obersteier produced such a crisis that any available forces had be rushed to the threatened area. The Gauleiter of the Steiermark reacted by dispatching from Leoben the last Companies of the SS Replacement Battalion, while Ringel posted the Dachstein Artillery School and a number of independent Gebirgs-jaeger battalions to that sector. These few groups were sufficient to hold the first Red Army probe, but as Soviet pressure increased reinforcement was necessary and the Luftwaffe's 'Boelcke' Squadron was hastily retrained and converted to Gebirgsjaeger status, together with some Army units and a police detachment. This change of status pleased neither the men of the Luftwaffe nor those of the Gebirgsjaeger. The Luftwaffe squadron saw their new status of a demotion while the Jaeger resented these useless personnel who were totally unfit to hold positions in the battle line. The group of units around the Semmering went through two name changes, from Battle Group Semmering to Battle Group Raithel before, literally, in the last twelve days of the war, being named as 9th Gebirgs Division and having an eventual strength of about 10,000 men.

On 8 April, while still carrying the name 'Battle Group Semmering', one of its units, the newly created 155th Gebirgsjaeger Regiment, was ordered to send a patrol to reconnoitre the village of Rettenegg which was reported to be in Russian hands. The situation on this sector was unclear. It seemed to the Jaeger that the Soviet offensive had either outrun its strength or else the troops engaged in the operation were new to war. They had not advanced beyond the village, but had dug field fortifications outside it and occupied the houses. The small Jaeger recce/fighting patrol moved down from the regiment's positions on the Rettenegg Kogel, a hill dominating the village, through the pine trees and towards the outskirts of Rettenegg. The patrol leader had no need to give orders. He and enough of his men were experienced veterans who had a 'nose' for situations. He gave a swift, all-encompassing glance and then the hand signal to charge. The section commanders passed the order to their men. The Jaeger rose out of the ditches and fields in which they had been lying and raced across the Russian trenches, killing the surprised enemy with quick bursts of machine pistol fire and with hand-grenades. Swiftly they struck into the village and in the small market square saw a 2cm guns whose crew, alerted by the sound of firing, were working frantically to bring the piece into action. A long burst of fire from an MG 42 killed them all. The remainder of the Red Army garrison fled, making a swift retreat across the fields and meadows outside the village. Rettenegg was in the hands of the Jaeger once again; but they were too few in numbers to hold it for any length of time. Still, they did have the prize of an enemy gun and this they dragged back to their positions on the Kogel. This light-weight thrust by a small group of Jaeger brought an end to military operations on this sector until 7 May, two days before the end of the war, when 9th Gebirgs Division made one last attack in the Rettenegg sector.

Such small actions were the norm in those days when the Second World War was coming to its end in Europe. The reason for this was that on the Russian side the military effort had been switched to other sectors where less determined opposition would be met. For the Germans, the waning strength of Army Group South no longer permitted any operations other than small and local attacks. More often it was as much as Army Group could do to hold off Red Army probes to find weak spots in the German battle line. The front was quiet on the Rettenegg sector but farther north, on the Semmering, a massive build-up of Russian forces had been completed and an offensive was in operation. Stavka was determined to break through, but its first infantry assaults were flung back, often in hand-to-hand fighting.

A new major Soviet offensive had been planned and the first thrust came in at dawn on 18 April. At first light the Jaeger 'stood to' and almost immediately a massive artillery barrage fell upon them. For hour after hour shells crashed down and the blood-red smoke trails from the 'Stalin Organs' lit the overcast sky. Flying low over the crest of the Semmering and above its neighbouring peaks, close-support aircraft of the Soviet Air Force swooped and dived, machine-gunned and bombed anything that moved on the German side of the line. Late in the afternoon the Russian guns ceased fire. Those on the German side had long since fallen silent for lack of ammunition. In the silence the Jaeger could hear, borne on the east wind, the sound of engines. Stavka had ordered tank formations to spearhead the punch through the mountain barrier. Slowly the giant steel vehicles worked their difficult way uphill towards the Jaeger, waiting, in their slit trenches. The mountains around the Semmering were not ideal tank country, but earlier attacks by Red Army infantry had failed and the Soviet High Command was determined to break through using armour.

On the German side there were no longer ample supplies of panzerfaust or panzerschreck, the infantryman's close-combat weapons against tanks. Now the Jaeger had to allow the Russian tanks to come within arm's length before attacking them with explosive charges. Such actions were highly dangerous if the Russian infantry were in close support of the armour. But if they could be forced to ground, the tanks were isolated and could be dealt with by resolute men. Soon columns of smoke showed with what success the Jaeger of Raithel's group had dealt with the Russian armoured attack. The Jaeger determination seemed to have blunted Soviet aggression for not only did the 19th pass peacefully but on the Fischbach sector, where the Red Army's advance had made its deepest penetration, the Russians abandoned that village and pulled back eastwards.

The skill and combat willingness of the soldiers was holding back the enemy, but how long could these men, particularly the Gebirgsjaeger, sustain the vastly unequal struggle. No supplies were reaching the front line, there were no replacements and ammunition for small arms and artillery was coming to an end. The Jaeger had the moral superiority, but the Red Army had the *matériel* and theirs was a crushing superiority. The worst possible scenario was anticipated and behind the combat zone small groups of officers from the Gebirgs divisions went out to set up ration points and to mark routes – not main roads but secondary ones and even tracks – along which the Gebirgsjaeger could pass when the time came, as come it must, for them to withdraw westwards.

Meanwhile on the peaks of the Semmering and the Fischbacher alps fighting would flare up and die away. A sudden and heavy Russian barrage would fall upon a single Jaeger Company holding some lonely peak and would cease as abruptly as it had begun, leaving behind the diminishing thunder of explosions reverberating among the peaks and the more painful evidence of its passing – the dead and wounded – men who would not be replaced. And because these casualties were not being replaced the burden of front-line life fell upon fewer and fewer men – the survivors, in many cases of years of battle.

The German Army's early years of victory were long since past. Now the communiqués issued by OKW had to be content with recording a successful defence or the minor victory of a local counter-attack. The communiqué of 18 April, for example, read in part, 'In the area of the Ostmark [eastern Austria] repeated attacks by Bolshevik forces to the south-east of Muerzzuschlag, on either side of Fuerstenfeld and near St Poelten, were driven back and lost ground was recaptured during counter attacks . . .' For the men of Battle Group Raithel the period from 19 to 21 April was one of relative quiet. Relative in the sense that there were no major Russian attacks to withstand nor thundering barrages to survive. This seeming Russian hesitation offered the commander of XII Panzer Corps the opportunity to regain the initiative which had been lost. A Corps battle plan was drawn up and troops were grouped. The Grenadiers and the last tanks of 1st Panzer Division struck forward. On their left flank Gebirgsjaeger regiments carried out a series of short, sharp operations which recovered ground lost weeks before and beat down Russian opposition to their advance. By the end of St George's Day, the Jaeger had penetrated deep into the Russian line and had, in bloody hand-to-hand fighting, repulsed the enemy's counter-attacks. The successes achieved had been won in the face of massive Russian artillery and rocket bombardment and despite heavy snowstorms which swept across the bare mountain tops. Snow and the bitter cold that accompanied it was for the hungry Jaeger just another burden which they had to bear.

By 24 April III Panzer Corps had achieved its objective and the blunt-headed Russian salient in the Fischbacher alps had been wiped out. The enemy commanders, aware that the Jaeger of the 9th and the armour of 1st Panzer Division were too strong to defeat, quickly redeployed their forces and swung their new effort towards the Moenichwald sector where they promptly cut off 117th Division. The rescue attempt by 1st Gebirgs to bring out the trapped division had already been described. The 1st then moved to the Kreuzwith sector on 24 April and relieved the 1st Panzer Division from the line.

At this point we must leave the actions being carried out in the mountains of northern Steiermark and consider the rumour, at once bizarre and improbable, which swept through the troops holding the eastern front. Bizarre and improbable though it was, the rumour was widely believed by Jaeger and generals alike and became almost an article of faith, so readily was it accepted and so deeply was it held. The story was that American military units were advancing swiftly through southern Germany and would soon take their places in the battle line alongside the exhausted Jaeger. That this would mean the Americans could be fighting against their Russian allies seems not to have been either considered nor understood. The Americans must surely realize, so went the rationalization for this wild yarn, that Soviet control of Europe would be terribly dangerous for them. America would change, or perhaps already had changed, her alliance with the Soviet Union and would ally herself to Germany. As if to confirm this belief in an American volte-face, there were stories of German soldiers being allowed to pass through the US lines in order to reach Austria. Such stories had a kernel of truth. The Americans were disarming former soldiers and sending them home instead of putting them into prisoner-of-war camps. A distortion of this fact, or else a complete misunderstanding of the American measure, was enough to bolster Jaeger morale with the belief that US help was on its way and that soon they, backed by the lavish supplies of their new-found ally, would be driving eastwards again to a new invasion of the Soviet Union. Even Rendulic accepted this mad invention and sent emissaries to the US commander asking for medical aid and for food supplies. In his autobiography he still seemed astonished that this – to him obvious – request had been turned down. Even the Soviets seemed to have accepted a version of this preposterous idea and dug defence systems against the supposed American betrayers.

One of the more experienced Gebirgsjaeger formations on the establishment of 9th Division was the SS Replacement Battalion, and an earlier chapter described the actions fought on the Western Front by platoons of that battalion. It will be recalled that those sub-units had been sent to reinforce the divisional reconnaissance battalion. The other Companies which had not fought in north-west Europe were eventually put into action in the Steiermark.

The history of that battalion is interesting. Towards the end of 1944 the Fuehrungshauptamt Inspectorate of Mountain Troops ordered Sturmbannfuehrer Koehler to raise the battalion. Cadres were first set up in Yugoslavia but the raising of the fledgling formation was not completed in that country. The unit was very quickly moved to Leoben. The battalion Order of battle was a Headquarters Company and four Jaeger Training Companies, numbered serially. No 5 Company was the horsed transport Column with pack-animals and carts. No 6 Company contained not only the battalion's convalescents but also the motorized vehicle Column. The 13th recruited its men chiefly from Volksdeutsche enclaves in Yugoslavia, Hungary and Roumania with a leavening of Reichsdeutsche. The battalion was commanded by Hauptsturmfuehrer Gruenwald backed by instructors and Company officers, all of them veterans who had been wounded in action and who were waiting to be posted back to their parent formations. Training in mountain warfare techniques was carried out in the alpine areas north of Leoben; by coincidence the same region in which the battalion was to fight its first and only battle.

During March 1945 the 13th Replacement Battalion was ordered to march out on active service. It will be appreciated that, even under optimum conditions, a replacement battalion will not have a large fleet of vehicles in its mechanical transport column and that at the end of a long war any sort of vehicle group would be a luxury. But a battalion about to go on active service, as the 13th now was, needs trucks, and if the unit officers are ruthless they can obtain sufficient to meet their unit's need. The officers of the 13th were unscrupulous in the methods they used. They knew that with the war's approaching end there would be rear-echelon personnel who would write out for themselves movement orders which would take them from the dangers of active service on the Eastern Front. Many of these malingerers who drove into Leoben and its surrounding villages in motor cars did not leave in them. Hauptsturmfuehrer Gruenwald had given precise instructions to his Transport Officer. Any vehicle which was deemed to be making an unauthorized journey, i.e., was being used to take its occupants away from the battle, was to be commandeered. The Companies of his battalion fighting in the mountains needed the vehicles which were being misused by cowards and traitors. Any protest by the dispossessed was to be stilled by the threat of an SS drumhead court-martial. By such ruthless action the Transport officer of the 13th was able to augment the few vehicles on the battalion's War Establishment.

It is not possible to describe the battles in which the 13th SS Battalion took part in the final months of the Second World War. It was absorbed into a miscellany of units which came together under the command of

Colonel Raithel. A summarized account by Karl Poelzl, which was reproduced in the book *Deutsche Gebirgsjaeger im Zweiten Weltkrieg,* gives an artilleryman's impression of the last weeks of the war.

'My posting was an undeserved piece of luck. At the beginning of April 1945 the Gebirgs Survey Team was absorbed *en bloc* as a Signals detachment into the headquarters battery of a battalion which had been raised in Obertrain. On 3 April we travelled to Kapfenberg where our ranks were filled out with Volkssturm men who had brought along their own artillery pieces and the following day we rolled through the Muerz valley to the front at Semmering.

'We were delayed for a long time in Steinhaus am Semmering. There were unit Trains and headquarters everywhere, a mass of vehicles, cables, telephone wires, soldiers in field grey and Volkssturm men in brown uniforms. The Front was very near. There was a continuous rumbling coming from the battle area. During the night of 10/11 April two of our Signals sections took part in an attack called "Eselstein", a very bitterly fought battle. At dawn the sun had risen blood-red over the Erzherzog Johann hotel. The day proved to be just as bloody . . . The 14th April, was a quieter day with only occasional enemy mortar bombardments. It is a gloomy day and our feelings are as gloomy because of what is happening on the Western Front. Even the news of the death of President Roosevelt does not alter the situation . . .

'On 17th April, at about midday the Ivans made a surprise attack, using strong detachments of storm troops and captured the dominating height, the Sonnwendstein. The sounds of battle are close and there is concern among the headquarters staff. The enemy has now clear observation over the whole area as far as the Muerz valley. Towards evening the battle noises die away and we have recaptured the summit although we have suffered severe losses. The survivors of our OP detachments parade to receive their decorations. The CO finds the right words to say to each man before pinning the Iron Cross on to his jacket. The men stand stiffly to attention; these men whom we have known for years, who even in these hopeless days are buoyed up by the ties of duty and honour. Then they go back again up the line . . . During the next day, the 18th, concentrated fire falls on our sector. Gunfire echoes around the heights. Russian fighter-bombers zoom about and drop anti-personnel bombs along the road through the mountains. The next day, 19th, brings a pause in the fighting. Is the enemy committing his forces on some other rewarding sector? Depressing things happen on our sector and people begin to leave the battle line without orders.

'In this catastrophic situation we are given proof of German organization. The battle group has been renamed, '9th Gebirgs Division' and our battalion has thus become 1st Battalion Gebirgs Artillery Regiment No 56. The GOC is, of course, Colonel Raithel. Whatever happens now, "Good luck to the 9th Division." The Russians fire away as usual but their infantry does not show itself so frequently. Rumours spread that the Americans are closing in, probably coming along the valley of the River Enns. The days pass without any special happenings although in the world a lot is happening. We work out retreat routes . . . just in case . . . Will we manage to get away when the time comes before the Russians can capture us? That is our chief worry.

'On 7th May the first rumours of an armistice spread and during the afternoon we see the Volkssturm men marching away in organized bodies. We strengthen our positions, gain touch with our signals detachments and send out patrols. At 4 am during the night of 8th May, Captain Wolf, the divisional Ic sends away the Volkssturm sentries in front of our hotel with the words. "Go home. Make sure you get away. The war is lost."

'Our GOC arrives in Spital, his face sober and sunburned as usual. He climbs into his staff car and leads the small motorized vehicle column which makes up Gebirgs Artillery Regiment No 56, westwards through the Muerz valley. We pass endlessly long columns of horse-drawn carts. Soon we are separated; individual trucks work their way forward and a comradeship, even one of only a few months' duration, is broken."'

In Leoben, meanwhile, 13th Battalion's Train waited for news from the front. The details which came trickling through were not reassuring and it soon became clear to Hauptsturmfuehrer Bart, the Train commander, that when the time came he would have to act on his own initiative. His report stated that he stayed with the battalion until the last day of the war and had, in fact, given the order for the Train personnel to disperse and make their way home. He was able to evacuate the married families of the battalion and to bring them into safety. They were given sufficient food and drink to last until they reached the US Zone in Austria where they would be safe from the Russians. The unconsumed rations which remained in store were handed over to a local hospital.

Bart's report concluded: 'During the evening of 7th May, I was ordered to report to the senior officer in Leoben. I was told he had set up strongpoints to defend the town against the advancing Americans. This struck me as being pointless. What could our few sick and wounded men do, armed as they were with just rifles and machine-guns, against US units equipped with tanks. By the time I was able to report to him – that was during 8th May – the general capitulation had come into effect and the war had come to an end.'

The Train of the 13th dispersed and the remnants of 9th Gebirgs Division reached Liezen on the Enns, where the units were collected by the Americans and disarmed. For the men of the short-lived 9th their war was over.

Epilogue

THE SECOND WORLD WAR came to an end in Europe during the second week of May 1945, and the survivors of the Gebirgs divisions had time to reflect upon what had been suffered, endured and achieved in sixty-seven months of conflict.

Gebirgsjaeger had served in every campaign conducted by the German Army in the course of the war: in Poland, Scandinavia, France, the Balkans, Russia and Africa. They had established their presence in Greece and in the Caucasus by hoisting their country's war flag on the summits of Mount Olympus and Mount Elbrus. They had fought in climates and terrains as vastly different as the Arctic Circle and the hills of Tunisia. Almost, but not quite, they had taken the war out of Europe and into Asia.

Many of the men in the divisions whose world, after Germany's capitulation, shrank to the area of the barbed wire perimeter around a prisoner-of-war camp in western Europe were lucky. They were sent home within months to work once again on the farms and in the forests they had left to go to war. Others were less fortunate. Those Gebirgsjaeger held by the Soviets or in the hands of the Yugoslavs suffered years of imprisonment, hard labour and often death. The two brothers, Ludwig and Josef Kuebler, both of whom had commanded 1st Gebirgs Division, were shot by the Yugoslavs in 1947, as was Field Marshal Loehr and a number of other Gebirgsjaeger commanders.

In this book we have followed the Gebirgsjaeger arm of service from 1935, when it was only the strength of a single division. We have seen it develop to Corps status in 1938 and then through subsequent enlargements up to and beyond the time when it became a Gebirgs Army. The Gebirgsjaeger expansion matched that of two other élite arms of service in the German forces; the SS and the Fallschirmjaeger and that growth is a measure of the reputation gained by the combat efficiency and fighting spirit of the mountain men. The Gebirgsjaeger expanded because its men were first-class soldiers, and because they were first-class soldiers and serving in élite formations, they had paid in full measure the blood price which membership of such an élite demands.

The Gebirgs Divisions which fought for the Third Reich have passed into history and now all that remains of them are in the cemeteries, and only those set up in western countries. The graves of those Gebirgsjaeger who fell on the Eastern Front or in the Balkans were despoiled and levelled. A memorial commemorates all the Gebirgsjaeger who fell for Germany; those whose graves are known and honoured, like those in the cemetery on the Semmering, as well as those whose graves in the east which were desecrated, or those who, like the men who were drowned off Crete, have no known grave. This memorial, a cross, backed by two huge stone columns, one each for the two world wars, stands on the summit of the Hohen Brendten mountain near Mittenwald in Bavaria, is for them all, for all those who went away but did not come back to the peace of the mountains.

Appendix: History of the Army and SS Gebirgs Divisions

1ST GEBIRGS DIVISION

This formation, the model for all the future Gebirgs divisions of the German Army and SS, was created on 9 April 1938, in Garmisch Partenkirchen out of the Gebirgs Brigade which had been in existence since 1 June 1935. When the division was mobilized on 26 August 1939, it was made up of three – and not two – Jaeger regiments. The 98th garrisoned Mittenwald, the 99th was in Fuessen and the 100th in Bad Reichenhall. The 79th Gebirgs Artillery Regiment was stationed in Garmisch Partenkirchen.

On 3 November 1940 100th Jaeger Regiment, which was surplus to establishment, together with certain artillery units, was posted to help create 5th Gebirgs Division.

In 1943 additional units, High Alpine Battalion No 2 and 54th Replacement Battalion came on strength. The 1st Battalion, 98th Regiment was posted away on 20 November 1943 to become High Alpine Battalion No 3 (Army Troops).

The Division was renamed on 12 March 1945, and became 1st People's Gebirgs Division. The addition of the name 'People's' was a propaganda move by the Nazi Party seeking to emphasise the link between the armed services and the German people.

1st Gebirgs Division saw service in southern Poland as part of Army Group South and received the surrender of the city of Lemberg. It was then posted to the Western Front and fought in the campaign in France, taking a distinctive part in the crossings of the Maas, the Aisne and the Loire. With the end of the fighting in France 1st Gebirgs Division was chosen to be one of the formations preparing to invade Great Britain and, when that operation was cancelled, trained to capture Gibraltar. That mission, too, was aborted.

As part of Second Army, 1st Gebirgs Division moved to Kaernten, the southernmost province of Austria, and fought in the war against Yugoslavia. Together with the great mass of the Army 1st Gebirgs moved eastwards for the war against the Soviet Union which it fought as part of Army Group South, participating in the Uman encirclement as well as the capture of Stalino and Mius. It stayed in the Mius positions from December 1941 until the end of May 1942 when it was posted from XLIX Corps to XI Corps, part of First Panzer Army, and fought in the Donetz region. The 1st was one of the two Gebirgs divisions that took part in the advance into the Caucasus during the German summer offensive of 1942, and stayed in southern Russia until March 1943 when it was moved to Serbia. Then followed other moves within Yugoslavia, Greece and Corfu until April 1944, when as part of the OKH/OKW reserve it was posted to Hungary, only to return to the Balkans in August. The 1st moved back into Hungary during December 1944 and in the first months of the New Year served with Second Panzer Army in the German offensive around the Plattensee. It was during this time that the divisional name changed to include the term 'Volks' ('People's'). In April 1945 German Sixth Army, with which 1st Gebirgs Division was now serving, was fighting in the mountains of the eastern Austrian province of Steiermark and it was there that the mass of the division was taken prisoner by the Red Army when the war came to an end.

2ND GEBIRGS DIVISION

This division was created from the units that had formed 6th Division of the former Austrian Army. When it was mobilized on 26 August 1939 the 2nd was composed of 136th and 137th Gebirgsjaeger Regiments and 111th Artillery Regiment as well as divisional troops. 136th Regiment was stationed in Innsbruck, 137th in Lienz and the artillery regiment in Hall in Tirol.

On 1 April 1940 a battalion of 140th Gebirgsjaeger Regiment was converted to become 2nd Battalion, 136th Gebirgsjaeger Regiment. There were also changes in the artillery composition and a number of cross-postings between units of the 2nd and other divisions.

Upon the outbreak of war in September 1939 2nd Gebirgs Division served as part of Army Group South in Poland before returning to Germany where it stayed until March 1940. Selected to take part in the campaign in Norway, the 2nd fought its way towards Narvik and was then placed on occupation duties, first in northern Norway and subsequently in Lappland as part of XIX Corps in Twentieth Gebirgs Army. It served in that Corps and in that region of Lappland until November 1944 when the German forces withdrew into Norway. The 2nd then came temporarily under the command of XXXVI Corps before reverting again to XIX Corps. In December 1944 the division was ordered to Denmark where it regrouped and rested before being sent to fight on the Western Front as part of LXXIII Corps in First Army (Army Group 'G'). Towards the end of the war the 2nd was posted to XII Corps which was fighting in southern Germany and it was destroyed there, the remnant being taken prisoner by the Americans.

3RD GEBIRGS DIVISION

The 3rd Gebirgs Division was another formation taken over from the Austrian Army in 1938 and placed on to the German Army order of battle. The 5th and 7th Austrian Divisions were amalgamated to become 3rd Gebirgs Division. Upon mobilization on 26 August 1939 the 3rd was made up of the following units: 138th Gebirgsjaeger Regiment, stationed in Leoben, 139th Jaeger Regiment in Klagenfurt and the artillery regiment in Graz.

The 3rd was chosen to form the force to attack the Norwegian iron ore port of Narvik, but before the regiment embarked nearly a half of all the men in each Jaeger Company were left out of battle. These men were later used to create Gebirgsjaeger Regiment No 141, which was then posted to 6th Gebirgs Division. There were other cross-postings at this time and another in November 1940. When the 3rd was withdrawn from Finland, 139th Regiment and a battalion of the artillery regiment remained behind and became eventually, Army Troops. Over the years there were gains and losses to the divisional establishment.

At the outbreak of war in 1939 the division served with XVIII Corps in Army Group South before moving from Poland and the Eastern Front to the Eifel region of the Western Front. In March the 3rd was posted from the Hunsrueck to northern Germany from where 139th Regiment sailed for Narvik. After taking part in the bitter fighting for that port, 3rd Division regrouped and was posted, first to northern Norway and then to the Murmansk area of Finland. A short period of leave and regrouping in Germany was followed by a brief return to Norway and then a move to Reval, and to other sectors of the Eastern Front. By the early spring of 1944 the division, now forming part of the new Sixth Army, was in the southern

Ukraine where it served until October of that year with the Hungarian 9th Corps (German Eighth Army) which was fighting in Hungary. Under Red Army pressure the division retreated into Slovakia where it joined First Panzer Army and was serving with XXXXIX Corps of that Army, in Upper Silesia, when the war came to an end. The remnant of Sixth Army were taken prisoner by Soviet forces.

4TH GEBIRGS DIVISION

In the summer of 1940, with the war against France brought to a successful conclusion, it was decided not to proceed with the raising of new units and in fact, to demobilize certain classes of men. As a result the proposal to create a 4th Gebirgs Division was not completed. The only Jaeger regiment that was formed, the 143rd, was posted to 6th Gebirgs Division.

On 23 October 1940 a fresh attempt was made and this time the regiments available were two that had become supernumerary to 25th and 27th Divisions. Upon conversion to motorized or panzer divisional status, infantry divisions forfeited a regiment. Thus Gebirgsjaeger Regiment No 13 was the former infantry regiment of that number surplus to 25th Division establishment and stationed in Ludwigsburg. Gebirgsjaeger Regiment No 91, was the former 91st Infantry Regiment, 27th Division from Kempten. The artillery component of 4th Gebirgs Division was made up of one battalion from each of the original Divisions.

From October 1940 when it was raised until March 1941, the 4th stayed in the Heuberg training area but was moved in April as part of Twelfth Army, to Bulgaria from where it fought in the war against Yugoslavia. It next saw action in Russia as part of Seventeenth Army in Army Group South. During this time, as one of the divisions of XXXXIX Corps, it took part in the

encirclement battles around Uman and finished the year in the Mius positions, staying in that region until the end of July 1942. For the German summer offensive of 1942, the 4th, together with 1st Gebirgs, struck into the Caucasus but, with the order to withdraw, moved into the Crimea. The division continued to serve on the Eastern Front although it changed Corps and Army several times. By the end of October 1944, as part of XXIX Corps in Eighth Army, the division withdrew across the Carpathian mountains and into Hungary. It fought in the Tatra mountains of Slovakia during January 1945, as part of First Panzer Army and it was with that formation that 4th Gebirgs Division passed into captivity, to the west of Olmuetz, on 9 May 1945.

5TH GEBIRGS DIVISION

The units around which 5th Gebirgs Division was created, were 100th Regiment, which was surplus to the establishment of 1st Gebirgs Division, and the former 85th Infantry Regiment, which became supernumerary when 10th Infantry Division changed its role and became a motorized division. The artillery component of the 5th came from both 1st Gebirgs Division and 10th Infantry Division. Both Jaeger regiments retained their original numbers, i.e., 85 and 100, and the Artillery Regiment was numbered 95.

There was, on 1 November, 1941 an exchange of divisional units with 3rd Gebirgs Division, but that formation could not release its cyclist and anti-tank battalions as, to begin with, they were under the control of 6th Gebirgs Division and then became Army troops. Substitute units freshly raised in Germany were then posted to the 5th.

For the first few months of its life 5th Gebirgs Division remained in Germany but then, during March 1941, it moved into the Balkans and took a prominent part in the war against Greece. In the absence of 22nd Air Landing Division, the 5th was selected to be airlanded in Crete to reinforce the Fallschirmjaeger air assault and then went on to capture the island.

After a rest and recuperation period in Germany from October 1941 to March 1942 the 5th was posted to the Volkhov region south-east of Leningrad and served on that sector of the Front for nearly a year before being posted to Tenth Army in Italy. There it took part in the battles south of Rome and the fighting retreat through the Gothic Line before being sent to fight with the Army of Liguria in the mountainous region that borders Italy and France.

It was in the Turin area that the Division passed into American captivity at the end of the war.

6TH GEBIRGS DIVISION

This Division was created in the military training area of Heuberg on 1 June 1940. The cadre around which the newly raised Gebirgs Regiment 141 was built was made up of men from Gebirgs Regiment 139, who had been left out of battle when that regiment went to fight in Norway. The second Jaeger regiment for 6th Division, the 143rd, had originally been intended for 4th Gebirgs Division. The artillery regiment was made up of battalions or Companies taken from several Gebirgs Divisions; the anti-tank battalion came from 2nd Gebirgs and the reconnaissance battalion from the 3rd.

Because of the speed with which its Jaeger regiments came on to strength, 6th Division was completely raised before either 4th or 5th Gebirgs Divisions and appeared on the Order of Battle of Seventh Army as early as 13 June 1940.

The Sixth spent some time on occupation duties in France before being posted to Twelfth Army in Poland with which it moved south-eastwards when that Army moved into the Balkans for the war against Greece. In that campaign 6th took a prominent part in the fighting to break the Metaxas Line and subsequently in other battles in Greece. At the conclusion of hostilities the 6th stayed on in the army of occupation until the end of September 1941 when it was sent to Norway as part of the Gebirgskorps.

The next move was eastwards to Lappland where the 6th served as part of XIX Corps in Twentieth Gebirgs Army, and it remained in that region until the Gebirgs Army pulled out of Finland and back into Norway. In January 1945 the division became part of 'Narvik' force and surrendered to the British Army in the Lyngenfiord at the end of the war.

7TH GEBIRGS DIVISION

On 15 November 1941 the 99th Light Division was converted to mountain troop status and was titled, 7th Gebirgs Division. The description of the infantry regiments of 99th Light then changed to become Gebirgs Jaeger Regiments 206 and 218 respectively.

In September 1943 the division's replacement battalion, was taken away to be renamed and renumbered as Ski Battalion 82, and a new replacement battalion was created for the division.

The 7th remained in Germany until the end of February 1942 and then moved to Lappland where it served with XVIII Corps of Twentieth Gebirgs Army from July of that year until January 1945, when it was posted from that Corps to become part of 'Narvik' Force. A few weeks later came a new posting to XXXI Corps, which was also stationed in Norway.

In May 1945 7th Gebirgs Division was in the Oslo area and it was there that it passed into British captivity.

8TH GEBIRGS DIVISION

In March 1944 it was proposed to create an 8th Gebirgs Division around the veteran 139th Gebirgs Regiment, but the raising was never completed. The incomplete formation was first titled 'Divisional Group Krautler' and later given the number and description 'Division 140, z.b.V' (special purposes).

A fresh attempt to create 8th Gebirgs Division succeeded in February 1945 through the renumbering of 157th Gebirgs Division, which was serving on the Italian front, to become 8th Gebirgs Division. The component regiments retained the numbers they had carried with 157th Division, i.e., Gebirgs Jaeger Regiments 296 and 297 and Artillery Regiment 1057.

The 8th fought in the mountains around Bologna, as part of XIV Corps. In the retreat across the Po in April 1945, the remnant of the division was overtaken by troops of the US Fifth Army and taken prisoner.

9TH GEBIRGS DIVISION

In March 1945, according to Red Cross records, there were two 9th Gebirgs Divisions on the German Army's Order of Battle, although neither formation is listed as such among the Field Post numbers — the most reliable documentary source of Third Reich formations nor on contemporary battle maps.

The first of the two; 9th Gebirgs Division – Nord, had first been designated Divisional Group 'K' (Krautler) and was later renamed and renumbered as 140th Division z.b.V., in the 'Narvik' Force. It went into British captivity at the end of the war.

The second, 9th Gebirgs Division – Ost, was created in the final days of the war around 'Battle Group Semmering', a formation whose order of battle included the officers and men of the Mountain Artillery School for junior

NCOs in Dachstein, the SS Gebirgs-jaeger Replacement Battalion and Luftwaffe ground crews of the disbanded 'Boelcke' Fighter Squadron. On operational maps 9th Division is usually shown as 'Battle Group Colonel Raithel' forming part of III Panzer Corps in Sixth Army. The commander of Sixth Army had asked for a divisional-sized detachment to fill a gap in the line and the hastily assembled units, detailed above, were committed to action on the Semmering Pass.

With the end of the war on 9 May the division broke up and although some men managed to reach the American zone, the greatest number were taken prisoner by the Red Army.

No divisional orders of battle exist for 9th Gebirgs Division – Ost, but it may be accepted that any formal groupings must have been along the lines of unit attachment, i.e., the SS battalion would have formed one Jaeger group, the Luftwaffe detachment a second and the Junior NCOs' Training school would have made up the artillery component.

THE HOCHGEBIRGS BATTALIONS

It was in 1942 that the decision was taken to create high alpine battalions within the Gebirgsjaeger organization. The personnel for these units were skilled Alpinists who were then trained for operations in the highest mountain peaks. Four such battalions were raised but the need for them did not arise and they were soon disbanded.

Hochgebirgs Jaeger Battalion No 1, was created on 20 July 1942 from the 1st Training Battalion for high alpine troops in Berchtesgaden. The establishment was for five Companies. During the winter of 1942/3 the unit was broken up and its components distributed among 1st Gebirgs Division, which at that time was fighting in the Caucasus.

Hochgebirgs Jaeger Battalion No 2 was created out of the 2nd Training Battalion for high alpine troops in Innsbruck. During February 1943 it was posted to the Kuban bridgehead and amalgamated with No 54 Replacement Battalion to create 54th Gebirgsjaeger Battalion which was taken on to the strength of 1st Gebirgs Division.

Hochgebirgs Jaeger Battalion No 3 was raised on 20 November 1943 from elements of 1st Battalion, 98th Gebirgsjaeger Regiment which was on active service in Dalmatia. It was then reorganized and formed a battalion of four Companies, three of which were Jaeger and the fourth a heavy weapons Company. A battery of mountain guns also formed part of the establishment. The battalion then saw service in Italy and in December 1944 became 3rd Battalion, 296th Gebirgsjaeger Regiment. The war service of the Hochgebirgs battalion included the battles for Monte Cassino.

Hochgebirgs Jaeger Battalion No 4 was raised on 20 November 1943 from elements of 1st Gebirgsjaeger Battalion No 98 which at that time was on active service in Dalmatia. It was then posted to Italy and served as Army Troops, finishing the war with 114th Jaeger Division.

6TH SS GEBIRGS DIVISION 'NORD'

The formation which eventually became 6th SS Gebirgs Division 'Nord' was first created as 'Battle Group Nord' on 24 February 1941 around 6th and 7th SS Totenkopf Standarten and the signals battalion of the SS Division. Additional units were added to battle group strength including SS Infantry Regiment No 9 which came on to War Establishment in April 1941.

The battle group went into action on the Lappland sector of the Eastern Front while in Germany preparations had begun for its expansion to a division. These preparations were completed during the early summer of 1942. The newly raised formations: four battalions of SS Gebirgsjaeger, three mountain artillery battalions and various Train units were posted to the battle group in Finland, which had by this time been upgraded and retitled SS Gebirgs Division 'Nord'.

In October 1943 there was another change of title, this time to 6th SS Gebirgs Division 'Nord' and the formation continued to serve in Finnish Karelia until September 1944. It was then called upon to furnish the rearguard of XVIII Gebirgskorps when, in October 1944, the German forces withdrew through Finland and back into Norway. The first units of 6th SS to reach Norway were shipped to Jutland and in December 1944 were formed into SS Battle Group 'Nord' and put into the Ardennes offensive. The remaining units of the division then reached the Western Front and entered the battle line. After conducting a fighting retreat into Hesse, 'Nord', fragmented under American pressure. Nevertheless, sub-units and even individuals joined up with other SS groups and took part in operations in Thuringia. In Bavaria the last, shattered fragments of 'Nord' surrendered to the Americans at the end of the war.

In May 1941 the establishment of the SS Battle Group was, 6th, 7th and 9th Infantry Regiments, each of three battalions. There were three battalions of artillery and the usual Train units. The establishment remained constant throughout the war.

From June 1940 to the end of May 1941 command was held by Brigadefuehrer Richard Herrmann and he was succeeded by Brigadefuehrer Demelhuber. During the latter's time as commander, three other officers acted temporarily as GOC and then in January 1944 Gruppenfuehrer Lothar Debes took over. The final commander was Gruppenfuehrer Brenner who held command from 1 September 1944 until the end of the war.

7TH SS FREIWILLIGEN GEBIRGS DIVISION 'PRINZ EUGEN'

The order to create a Freiwilligen Gebirgs division was given on 1 March 1942, and it directed that the officers of the new division were to be, principally, men who had held commissions in the Habsburg Army and who were living in the Balkans. The first GOC was a Volksdeutsche officer of the Roumanian Army – Arthur Phleps.

His was no easy task, particularly in the matter of arming and uniforming his men. Weapons had to be borrowed from units of the German Post Office and these were supplemented by other firearms from captured enemy sources. The ill-equipped division went into action in October 1942 against Tito's partisans. By that time it had undergone a name change: SS Freiwilligen Division 'Prinz Eugen'.

During December 1942 the division fought in the Agram–Karlovac region before going on, at the end of May of that year, into operations in western Montenegro. In an effort to control the spread of partisan operations in Bosnia–Herzegovina, 'Prinz Eugen' first sent battalion-sized groups into the Sarajevo area. Eventually the whole division was serving there. Following the collapse of Mussolini's regime in July 1943, 'Prinz Eugen', now designated a Gebirgs division, was involved with the disarming of the Italians in northern Yugoslavia as well as in operations to capture the islands of Brac, Hvar and Korcula, and the Perlyesac peninsula. The months spent on anti-partisan operations culminated, during May 1944, in the operation to capture Tito in his headquarters in Drvar, during which 'Prinz Eugen' smashed the 1st Partisan Division. There was a further name change in February 1944, when the number 7 was added to the divisional name. The advance of Soviet and Bulgarian troops through eastern Yugoslavia involved the division in heavy fighting, particularly in the Nish area where it covered the withdrawal out of Greece of German Army Group 'E'. The division then began its own retreat through Yugoslavia.

Swinging from a defensive to an offensive posture, 'Prinz Eugen' attacked the partisan forces during January 1945, and although successful suffered heavy loss. As part of XXXIV Corps it then pulled back northwards through Agram and Cilli where, in May 1945, the remnant of the division was forced to surrender to the Yugoslavs.

The Order of battle during the summer of 1942 was two Jaeger regiments, a cyclist battalion, a cavalry detachment of two squadrons, a panzer battalion, an SS Gebirgs artillery regiment with four battalions, the Train and a replacement battalion.

In the summer of 1944 there was a reorganization and the division was made up of Gebirgsjaeger Regiment 13 'Arthur Phleps' and Gebirgsjaeger Regiment 14, both with four battalions, together with the standard components.

When the Division was created on 1 March 1942 its first commander was Gruppenfuehrer Arthur Phleps. He was succeeded in July 1943 by Brigadefuehrer Carl von Oberkamp. From August 1944 Brigadefuehrer Otto Kumm held command and he was followed by Oberfuehrer August Schmidhuber, the last GOC of 7th Gebirgs Division 'Prinz Eugen'.

13TH WAFFEN GEBIRGS DIVISION DER SS, 'HANDSCHAR' (KROATISCHE NR 1)

'Handschar' was designated Croatian No 1, to distinguish it from 23rd or 'Skanderbeg', the 2nd Croatian Gebirgs

Division. Orders to raise 'Handschar', issued during February 1943, directed that its recruits were to be Bosnians of the Muslim faith recruited from Croatia. There was so much opposition to the raising of 'Handschar' from senior officers of the Croatian Ustaschi organization, that the area in which the Division was to be raised had to be changed from Croatia to southern France.

The division, known initially as Croatian SS Freiwillige Gebirgs Division, completed its training by the end of January 1944 and was then put into action in northern Bosnia where it fought until the end of September 1944. By that time its name had changed, first, to 13th SS Freiwillige Bosnian–Herzegovinian Gebirgs Division (Croatia) and, finally, to 13th Waffen Gebirgs Division SS 'Handschar' (Kroatische Nr 1).

During the autumn of 1944 the German armed forces began to withdraw from the Balkans and many Bosnian soldiers of 'Handschar' were demobilized and sent home. One part of the division, which was in Hungary, formed a battle group which fought in the southern provinces of that country as well as in the fighting retreat which ended between the Plattensee and the River Drau. The remainder of the division, which had been fighting in Yugoslavia, then moved into Hungary and joined the battle group.

Army Group South's February offensive, 'Spring Awakening', striking out of the Plattensee and Drau areas, failed to halt the Red Army's advance. Army Group South was forced back into the Austrian province of Steiermark and the remnant of 'Handschar' that survived the retreat surrendered in the Steiermark to the British at the end of the war.

The divisional order of battle between summer and winter of 1943 was:

Croatian SS Freiwillig. Gebirgsjaeger Regiment No. 1. HQ and four battalions.
Croatian SS Freiwillig. Gebirgsjaeger Regiment No. 2. HQ and four battalions.
Croatian SS Freiwillig. Gebirgsartillerie Regiment. HQ and four battalions.

There is doubt whether all the following units were raised or whether they did not pass the planning stage: cavalry battalion, motor-cycle battalion, cyclist battalion and panzer battalion.

By February 1944 reorganization had reduced the Jaeger regiments to three battalions and had renumbered them; 27th and 28th Regiments. There were also changes in the number of service units, and an SS Gebirgsjaeger Training and Replacement Battalion No. 13 had been created.

The first commander of 'Handschar' was SS Standartenfuehrer von Obwurzer who was replaced during the middle months of 1943 by SS Bridgefuehrer Sauberzweig. He held command until the middle of 1944 and was succeeded by Brigadefuehrer Desiderius Hampel.

21ST WAFFEN GEBIRGS DIVISION DER SS, 'SKANDERBEG' (ALBANISCHE NR. 1)

The order to create this formation was issued in April 1944, with instructions to raise recruits from the Kossovo area of Albania. The shortage of German personnel coupled with a poor standard of volunteer, insufficient weapons and a lack of equipment delayed the plans to raise the division. Indeed, by September, 1944, only 6,500 recruits out of a total enlistment of 9,275 volunteers, could be accepted for active service.

An increase in the scale of partisan activity in the 'Skanderbeg' area meant that units and sub-units were frequently detached to go out on anti-partisan operations. The effectiveness of these patrols, together with the questionable reliability and combat efficiency of the Albanian soldiers, was frequently called into question. It is a fact that 'Skanderbeg' suffered a loss of 3,500 men by desertion during its brief life.

As a result of the breaking-up of German units during the autumn of 1944, the division, now designated 21 Waffen Gebirgs Division der SS 'Skanderbeg' (Albanische Nr. 1.), received three thousand replacements, chiefly sailors of the Kriegsmarine, from Army Group 'E'. The division, with a greater German presence, was then involved in the retreat through the Balkans, during which time the remaining ethnic soldiers of the division were demobilized. The 21st, now Albanian only in name and seriously under-strength, was then broken up and the main units posted to 7th SS Gebirgs Division 'Prinz Eugen'. The Train was sent to the newly raised 32nd SS Freiwillige Division '30 January'.

The Order of Battle showed two Gebirgsjaeger Regiments: Nos 1 and 2, respectively, later renumbered as 50 and 51 (disbanded during December 1944). Each had three battalions. The artillery regiment had four.

Command of the Division was invested in Standartenfuehrer Schmidhuber until January 1945, and then in Obersturmbannfuehrer Graaf.

23RD WAFFEN GEBIRGS DIVISION DER SS, 'KAMA' (KROATISCHE NR. 2)

During June 1944, in accordance with a Fuehrer Directive, work was begun on the raising of a second division of Croatian/Muslim volunteers to which Hitler had bestowed the name 'Kana'. The recruiting area, which had originally been Bosnia–Herzegovina, was changed to southern Hungary.

Although the officers and NCOs were chiefly Reichsdeutsche, their numbers also included Muslim officers and NCOs who had served in the 13th 'Handschar' Division. The greatest number of the rank and file for 'Kama' were Muslims who had responded to an intensive recruiting drive which brought the division at maximum strength to between 8,000 and 9,000 men.

Before 'Kama' had been fully raised it came under pressure from the Red Army which was advancing through Hungary and Yugoslavia and this continuing advance led to the SS having to accept that the Muslims in the division had to be allowed to return to their homes in Croatia. With the loss of so many men it was clear that the division would never be completely raised and in October 1944 its officers were posted to the new 31st SS Division and those Islamic volunteers, who had chosen to remain serving with the division, were drafted to the understrength 13th Division (Handschar). As a consequence of these postings, 23rd 'Kama' Gebirgs Division was struck off strength in October 1944.

The division had a number of name changes during its short life. From June to September 1944 it was known as Waffen Gebirgs Division SS 'Kama' (Kroatische Nr. 2) and 23rd Waffen SS Gebirgs Division. From September to the end of its life in October it was designated 23rd Waffen Gebirgs Division der SS, 'Kama' (Kroatische Nr. 2). For the whole of its brief life command was invested in Standartenfuehrer Hellmut Raithel.

Under his command he had two regiments: Waffen SS Gebirgsjaeger Regiment (Kroat.) Nos 3 and 4, each with a headquarters and four battalions of Jaeger. These regiments were re-numbered, shortly before the division was disbanded, as Nos 55 and 56.

24TH WAFFEN GEBIRGS (KARSTJAEGER) DIVISION DER SS

This formation was raised during July 1942 upon the instruction of the Reichsfuehrer SS. The original establishment was for a Karstjaeger Company of two platoons, but within four months orders had come in for the unit to be expanded to battalion strength. The term Karst is the name given to the high, bare, rocky mountains between Yugoslavia and Italy and the local men recruited for the unit were chosen for their knowledge of this bleak and desolate area.

The battalion remained in Pottenstein until the summer of 1943 and with the fall of Fascist Italy at the end of July of that year, was moved first to Carinthia in southern Austria and from there to Tarviso where it took part in military operations against the Italian garrison of that town and others in the area. As a result of the general unrest in Italy in the autumn of 1943, the battalion moved to north-eastern Italy and specifically to the Trieste region where it was fully committed to anti-partisan missions.

On 18 July 1944, as a result of successful operations and increases in strength, the Karstjaeger was ordered to expand to divisional strength and was first known as Waffen-Gebirgs (Karstjaeger) Division-SS and then 24th Waffen-Gebirgs (Karstjaeger) Division der SS. Preparations to raise the new formation began during the summer of 1944 and the HQ of the proposed division was located in the Udine area. The majority of the men in the regiments were to be Reichsdeutsche, chiefly from the South Tyrol and Istrian areas, as well as Volksdeutsche and local volunteers. The intention to raise a division of two Jaeger regiments and an artillery regiment could not be realized and on 5 December 1944 the incomplete division was ordered to reduce to brigade size, but even that strength could no longer be reached.

In April 1945 Karstjaeger Regiment, No 59, was engaged in defensive fighting against the British Eighth Army and the partisans in the Julian alps and suffered heavily. The remnant was then absorbed into Battle Group Harmel, a mixed group of Army, police and SS units which fought its way back through the mountains to the German frontier. With the general surrender on 9 May 1945, the formation broke up.

THE WAFFEN GEBIRGS BRIGADE DER SS (TARTAR NR. 1) AND THE EAST TURKISH UNIT OF THE SS

In June 1944, Heinrich Himmler, the Reichsfuehrer SS, ordered a Tartar Gebirgs regiment to be raised in Hungary. The cadre around which the new unit was to be formed was a body of two hundred men of a German police unit who were to be transferred *en bloc* to the SS. That group was then to amalgamate with Tartar volunteers who had accompanied the German Army when the Crimea was evacuated by Army Group South. SS Standartenfuehrer Fortenbacher was named as CO of the new unit.

The German police authority was reluctant to lose its men and the Waffen SS had little faith in the fighting value of the Tartars. These two factors slowed down the raising of the new unit so that it was not until September 1944 that it came on the German Order of Battle. The unit was disbanded in January 1945 and the men were posted to the East Turkish Unit of the SS.

The East Turkish unit, like the Waffen Gebirgs Brigade, was raised in the summer of 1944 and within a short period was given a number of titles and descriptions. East Musselman SS Division; Turkish Musselman Division and Musselman SS Division of New Turkestan. In July there was a name change to 1st East Musselman SS Regiment and in October a name was bestowed which it carried to the end of the War — East Turkish Waffen Verband der SS.

The history of the unit was that in 1943 Himmler had had talks with Major Meyer-Mader, CO of the Army's 480th Turkish Battalion, which produced the decision to raise an East Musselman division. The Grand Mufti of Jerusalem was also involved in the discussions. Meyer-Mader was then transferred to the SS and the formation was raised in Lublin in Poland around two battalions of the 450th Turkish Field regiment and the 1st Battalion of 94th Regiment. Raising of the new division began in the area of Poniatova and continued during August 1944, in Kaposvar (Hungary). The move to Kaposvar was delayed because the unit was involved, as part of the Dirlewanger Brigade, in putting down the Warsaw uprising.

It was realised as early as the autumn of 1944 that it would not be possible to raise a complete Turkestan division and during October Himmler ordered that either a new unit be raised or the original one be regrouped in Slovakia. Details of the new formation cannot be established as documentary material did not survive the war.

The order of Battle of the East Turkish formations was:
1st East Musselman SS Regiment. HQ and three battalions.
The East Turkish Waffen Verband of the Waffen SS:
Group 'Idel Ural'. HQ and No 3 Battalion.
Group 'Turkestan' (No 1). HQ, 1st and 2nd Battalions.
Group 'Crimea' (No details given).
In March, 'Group Adjerbayan' came on to strength.

Commanders of the unit:
January 1944   Sturmbannfuehrer Meyer-Hader.
20 October 1944 Standartenfuehrer Haroun al Rashid.

Map 1: Operations carried out by 1st, 2nd and 3rd Gebirgs Divisions in Poland, 1939

Map 2: The Narvik area of Norway in which Dietl's Group fought during spring 1940

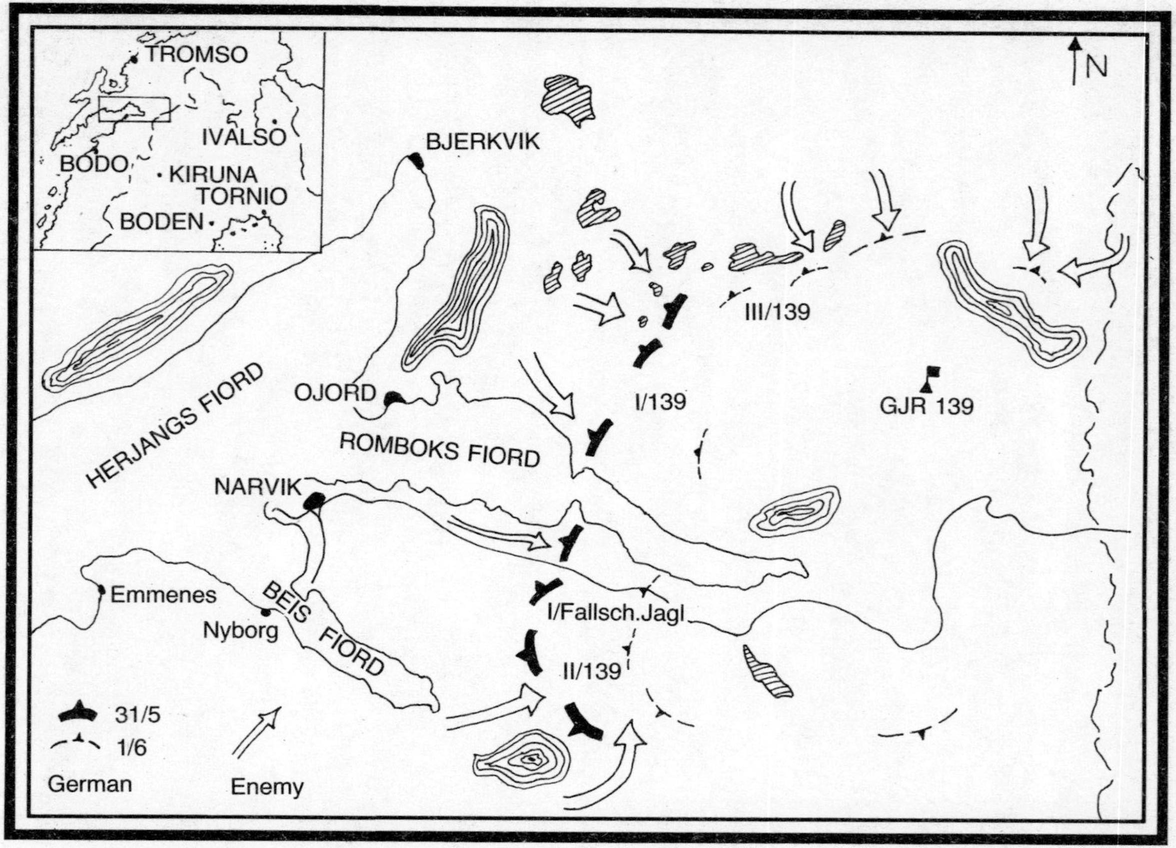

Map 3: The Balkan Theatre of Operations, showing campaigns in Greece, Yugoslavia and the fighting in Crete, 1941

Map 4: Operations carried out by 1st Gebirgs Division during the campaign in Yugoslavia

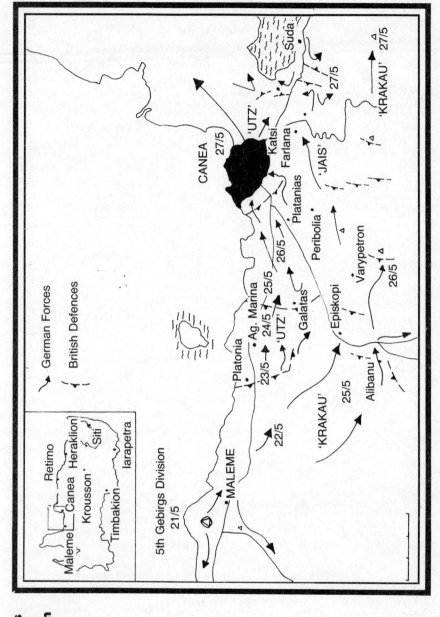

Map 5: Operations carried out by 5th Gebirgs Division in the Canea area of Crete, May 1941

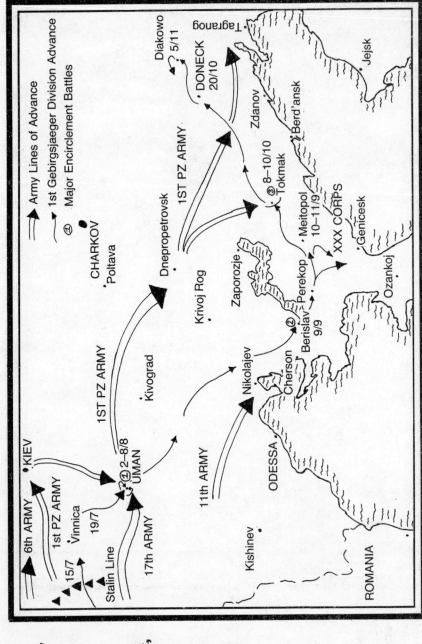

Map 6:
Operations
carried out by
Army Group
South during
the first
months of
Operation
'Barbarossa',
Eastern Front,
1941

Map 7: The Lappland area in which Twentieth Gebirgs Army fought from 1941 to 1944

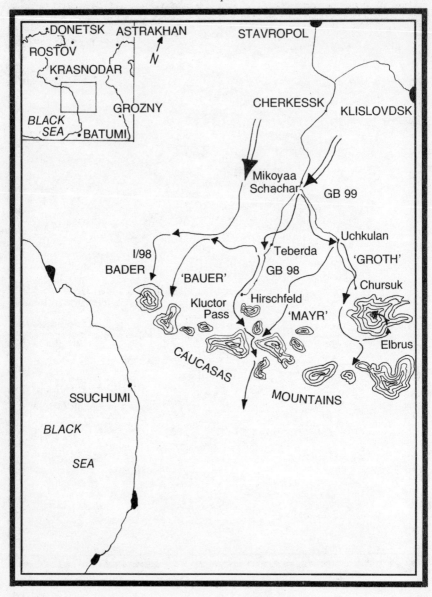

Map 8: The Caucasas area in which 1st and 4th Gebirgs Divisions fought in Autumn 1942

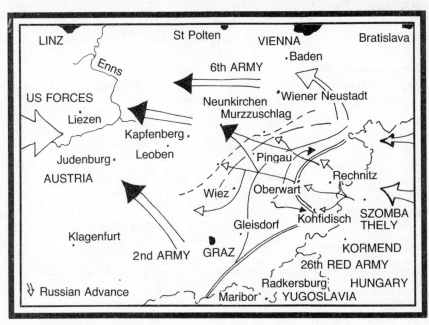

Maps 9 and 10: The final weeks of the war for the Gebirgsjaeger, showing the holding operations fought around Semmering and the eventual collapse in early May 1945

Select Bibliography

Published works:

Braun, J. *Enzian und Edelweiss.* 4te Gebirgs Div. Podzun Verlag, 1955.

Dobiasch. *Gebirsgjaeger auf Kreta.* Limpert, 1942.

Erfurth, W. *Der finnische Krieg, 1941/44.* Lines Verlag, 1977.

Ernsthausen, A. *Balkanerrinerungen.* Meyrsche-Detmold.

Kaltenegger, R. *Schicksalweg und Kampf der Bergschuh Division.* Stocker Verlag.

Kumm, O. *Vorwaerts, Prinz Eugen.* 7te SS Freiwillige Gebirgs Division. Munin Verlag, 1983.

Meyer, K. *Serbien, Griecheland, Kreta feindrei.* Schutzen Verlag, 42.

Nordhaus, G. *Alpenkorps im Angriff.*

Rendulic. *Soldat in stuerzenden Reichen.* 1965.

Ringel, J. *Hurra! Die Gams.* 5te Gebirgs Div. Stocker Verlag, 1956.

Schreiber, F. *Kampf unter dem Nordlicht.* 6te SS Gebirgs Division 'Nord'. Munin Verlag, 1969.

Thuermer, E. *In der Hoelle von Millerovo.* Stocker Verlag, 1986.

Wiesbauer, T. *Im Eis und Tundra.* Vowinckel, 1983.

Unpublished works:

K T B 2te Gebirgs Division. Gefechtsberichte. Gebirgsjaeger Regiment 137.

Jodl Fredinand. Kurzbericht ueber die Kampfhandlungen in Petsamo und Verrrangerraum. 5 November 1944.

K T B 20te Armee. various dates.

A O K 20. KTB. Appendix 3. Baendetaetigkeit und Organisation von AOK 20 (Geb). February 1943

List of Contributors

List of Contributors
Thanks to those who gave special help or contributions:

Beer, Prof. Dr.	Kumm, Otto	Ross, Alexander
Christian, Hans	Lamm, R	Scheucher, Fredi
Flecker, R.	Montemaggi, Amadeo	Schober, Gerd
Hajek, Wilfrid	Oswald, Helma	Spiess, Alfred
Hermann, Helmut	Roesch, Elfriede	Yerger, Mark

Index

A
Aalen, 172
Adzapch Pass, 133
Agia Marina, 79, 80
Agram (Zagreb), 67
Ahr, River, 27, 34
Aishe, River, 40, 41, 44
Albanische Nr. 1 Gebirgs Division der SS, 205
Aliakanu, 78, 79, 80
Altafiord, 104
Armavir, 131
Arpaluki, 52
Auer, Helma: see Oswald, Helma
Auf der Schanz, 187
Augsberger, Hauptsturmfuehrer, 119
'Autumn Storm', Operation, 147
'Axis', Operation, 147
Azau Pass, 133
Azov, Sea of, 103

B
Bagneux, 44
Bahia Castillo, 35
Balaton, Lake (Plattensee), 173, 174, 175
Banat, 145
Banya Luka, 148, 149
Bar, 91
'Barbarossa', Operation: *see* Eastern Front (1941)
Bart, Hauptsturmfuehrer, 195
Bastogne, 39
Bavarian Army, Royal, 14
Bela Spisska, 20
Belgium, 39ff
Belgrade, 48, 68, 154, 161
Belshanitsa Mountains, 61
Beveka, 129
Beskides Mountains, 19, 20, 22
Béthancourt, 43
Bettelfiord, 114
Beyer, General Eugen, 15, 19, 20
Bihac, 67
Binac, 148
'Birch', Operation, 127
Birkfeld, 184
Bjornfell, 31, 33
Bleiburg, 65
Blenheim, 114
'Black', Operation, 146
'Blue', Operation, 129ff
Boehme, General, 121, 122, 125
Boppard, 169
Boris Gleb, 107
Brandenburg special operations group, 45

Brazlov, 98
Bregenz, 15
Brenner Pass, 14
Brod, 157, 161
'Bueffel', Operation, 37–8
Buenos Aires, 35
Bug, River, 18, 21, 93, 94, 96, 98
Bulgaria, 49
Busovaca, 149
Buzot, 158

C
Camels, Bactrian, 109
Canea, 73, 75, 76, 78, 79, 80, 81
Cap Gris Nez, 45
Carinthia, 15
Casak, 156
Caucasus, 129–35
Chasseurs Alpins, French, 33
Chemin des Dames, 41, 42
Chiper Pass, 133
Chmakmaro Pass, 133
'Christmas Mountain', 142
Christoph, Hans, 52
Cilli, 65–7
Cleversulzbach, 171
Coblenz, 169
Colmar, 164
Copenhagen, 34
Corinth, 49, 62
Coucy-le-Château, 41
Cracow, 87
Crailheim, 171
Crécy-au-Mont, 43
Crete, 87, 72–85
Crna, 66
Csomend, 174
Czechoslovakia, 15, 16

D
Dachstein Artillery School, 10, 189
Danube, River, 154, 157
Demelhuber, Gruppenfuehrer, 114, 119
Deraznia, 91
Devescser, 175
Dietl, General, 11, 27, 31–7, 104–13, 125
Divisions, Mountain troops: *see* Gebirgs Divisions
Dnieper, River, 97, 99, 102
Doboj, 161
Doeberitz, 27
Don, River, 134
Donawitz, 170
Donets, River, 103

Drau, River, 65, 173–4
Dreikopf, 168
Drina, River, 157, 160
Drvar, 149, 150, 151
Dunkirk, 41
Dubrovnik, 146
Dukla Pass, 19, 20
Dukova, 98
Dunajel, 20

E

Eastern Front (1941), 86–104
Eastern Front (1942–3), 129–41
Egelshardt, 165
Ehrenbreitstein, 170
Eidelweiss badge, 11
'Eidelweiss', Operation, 130ff
Eifel, 39
'Eilbote' offensive, 143
Elbrus, 133
Elsfiord, 36, 37
Eltville, 170
Elvegadsmoen, 29
Engelseer, General, 125
Enns, River, 187, 195
Epagny, 44
Episkopi, 84
Eppenbrunn, 165
'Erika', 22

F

Fagevers, 30
Falkenhorst, General von, 109
Farm Chatillon, 43
Fauske, 38
Feistriz Valley, 184
Feldbach, 64, 179, 180
'Felix', Operation, 46, 63
Feurstein, General Valentin, 15, 20, 22, 34–8, 106
Finneda, 37
'Fishermen's Peninsula', 112
Flecker, Rudolf, 41
France (1940), 39–45
Frankfurt, 170
Frein, 16
Fresnes, 41

G

Galatas, 78, 79
Galicia, 19
Gebirgs Divisions:
    1st, 198
    2nd, 199
    3rd, 199
    4th, 200
    5th, 200
    6th, 200
    6th SS 'Nord', 203
    7th, 201
    7th SS Freiwillingen 'Prinz Eugen', 204
    8th, 202
    9th, 202
    13th Waffen, der SS, 'Handschar', 204
    21st Waffen, der SS, 'Skanderberg', 205
    23rd Waffen, der SS, 'Kama', 206
    24th Waffen, (Karstjaeger), der SS, 207
Gebirgs Brigades, 207
Glasl, Colonel, 139
Gleisdorf, 179
Gnas, 63, 186
Graz, 16, 63, 178–9
Greece, 47–62, 68, 87
Grosspetersdorf, 181, 183
Groth, Major, 182
Gruenwald, Hauptsturmfuehrer, 193
'Gulasch Cannon', 89
Gurk, River, 67

H

Habedanck, Gert, 55
Hake, Colonel, 112, 113
Hall, 15
'Handschar', 13th Waffen Gebirgs Division der SS, 204
Hapnesbro, 36
Hautuzinche, 92, 93
Hemnes, 36, 37
Hengl, Lieutenant-Colonel von, 37
Hengl, von, 111
Heraklion, 73, 75, 76, 85
Hermann, Helmut, 137–41
Hinzenburg, 167, 168
Hochgebirgs Battalions, 202
Hochwechsel, 185
Hoeglingen, 171
Hohenasperg, 171
Hohen Brendten, 197
Holosko, 24, 25
Hopen, 37

I

Iarapetra, 85
Ida Mountains, 72
Ilinche, 97
India, 71
Ingolstadt, 172
Innsbruck, 15
Istibei, 52
Italy, Surrender of, 147

J

Jagst, River, 171
Jaice, 148
Jank, 149
Janoshaza, 175, 181
Jodl, General, 31
Jura Mountains, 44, 46, 63

K

Kaernten, 16, 62, 63
Kaina, 84
Kalami, 81
'Kama', 23rd Waffen Gebirgs Division der SS, 207
Kandaleshka, 106, 114–16
Karaguendo, 126, 128
Karawanken Mountains, 161

Karlovac, 146, 162
Karlsruhe, 170
'Karstjaeger', 24th Waffen Gebirgs Division der
  SS, 207
Kelkaya, 52, 59, 60, 61
Kelloselkae, 116
Keskimainen, 117
Kharkov, 129
Kienstinki, 122–5
Kiev, 96, 97, 99
Kirchberg, 179, 180
Kirishi, 137
Kirkenes, 38, 104
Kirovgrad, 97
Klagenfurt, 16
'Knight's Move', Operation, 148
Knin, 148–9
Kocher, River, 171
Koehler, Sturmbannfuehrer, 193
Kohfidisch, 183
Kolding, 164
Kolosyoksi, 106
Komarovcze, 92
Kongur, 56
Konivszka, 22
Konrad, 134
Kopyenkovata, 100, 101, 102
Kragvjevac, 155
Krakau, Colonel, 78, 80, 82, 84
Kraljevo, 154, 155, 156
Kremenchug, 97
Kress, Colonel, 40, 65–6, 88
Kreysing, General, 38, 121
Kriva Reka, 145
Kroatische Nr. 1 Gebirgs Division der SS, 204
Kroatische Nr. 2 Gebirgs Division, 206
Kuban, River, 131, 132, 135
Kuebler, General Josef, 181, 196
Kuebler, General Ludwig, 14, 23, 26, 41, 65,
  88, 90, 91, 94, 98, 102, 196
Kuenzelsaua, 171
Kumli, River and valley, 61, 62
Kumm, Oberfuehrer (later Brigadefuehrer)
  Otto, 148, 152, 154–5, 158
Kupres, 148
Kuusamo, 126

L
Ladoga, 137
Lafnitz, River, 184
La Gloire, 42, 43
Lahn, River, 170
Lamm, Oberjaeger, 108, 109
Lampaden, 168
Lang, 65–7, 134
Lanz, General Hubert, 14, 94, 98, 103
Lappland, 11, 87, 104–28
Lauffen, 170
Lavamund, 65
Lavanth valley, 48
Lechfeld, 13
Lemberg, 19–25
Leningrad, 105, 119–21, 136ff
Leoben, 16, 170, 189, 193, 195

Leskovac, 154
Letsita, 52
Lienz, 15
Liezen, 195
'Lightning Ball', Operation, 147
Liimanmamaki, 106
Lika, River, 157
Limoval, 43
Liza, River, 113
Liza, River/Fiord, 113, 121–2
Ljobovija, 156, 157
'Longstop Hill', 142
Louhi, 106, 121, 122
Low Countries (1940), 39ff
Lubotin, 17
Ludwigsburg, 171
Lutra, 52, 85
Lvov: *see* Lemberg
Lyon, 44

M
Maas, River, 40
Maikop, 131
Maleme, 73, 75, 76, 77, 78, 80
Malovanka, 23
'Marita', Operation, 48, 63, 68
Marne, River, 41, 44
Maruklhsky Pass, 133
Medjez el Bab, 142
Mega Chorafiam, 84
Melch, 165, 166
'Mercury', Operation, 72
Metaxas line, 48, 50–2, 61–2, 68–9
Misbach, River, 65, 66
Mitrovica, 155
Mittenwald, 197
Mius, River, 103, 129, 136
Mlinista, 149
Mo, 37
Moder, River, 165
Modion, 77, 78, 79
Moenichwald, 185
Mogila Tokmak, 103
Mokra, 160
Morava, River, 68, 69
Moravia, 16
Mosel, River, 168
Mostar, 146
Mostoen, 114
Mosyoen, 35, 36
Mraca, 149
Mrkonjicgrad, 148
Muerz, River, 183–5, 194–5
Munich, 172
Muonia, 128
Mur, River, 65
Murmansk, 87, 105–7, 110–14, 121
Murmio, 126
Mutterhausen, 166

N
Nahe, River, 169
Nahmhar Pass, 133
Namsos, 35

Narvik, 11, 28–38
Nemeci, 158
Nemirov, 97, 98
Neon Chorion, 81, 84
Nenstadt, 171
Nisch, 68, 70
Nish, 154, 156
'Nord', 6th SS Gebirgs Division, 203
Nordheim, 170
'Nordwind', Operation, 164, 166
Novy Sandec, 20
Norway, 27–38, 87, 104, 107

O
Oberkamp, Brigadefuehrer von, 146, 148
Oberwart, 181, 183
Oeta Mountains, 62
Ofotfiord, 29
Oise–Aisne Canal, 40, 41
Oise, River, 40
Oswald Helma, 63–4, 186
Otok, 158

P
Paschel, 168
Parkkina, 107, 110
Parsangerfiord, 114
Patsuoki, River, 107
Pedtoci, 150
Peregenovka, 100–2
Petrish, 51, 57, 59
Petrohan Pass, 68
Petrovac, 148
Petsamo, 105, 106, 120, 121
Pfalz, 164
Phleps, Artur, 144, 145, 147
Picker, 24
Pinka, River, 182
Pirgos, 81
Pirmasens, 165, 166
Planina, 161
Platanias, 77, 80, 83
Plattensee: *see* Balaton, Lake
Podvyssoya, 87, 99, 100
Poelzl, Karl, 194
Poland, 18–26, 87
Pollein, 65
Polonisstoya, 99
Pont St Mard, 42
Popotlivitsa, 52, 55–9
Poppendorf, 181
Prekaja, 150
Prijedor, 148
'Prinz Eugen', 7th SS Freiwillingen Gebirgs
   Division, 204
Protici, 151
Przemysl, 21, 22
Pseaska Pass, 133
Puechler, Franz, 29

R
Raab, River, 176, 177, 179
Rabnitz, River, 183
Raithel, Colonel, 193, 194

Ramcke, Colonel, 77
Rann, 163
Rauna, 114
Rechnitz, 182
Redl, Alois, 65
Reichschutzstellung, 176
Reippertsweiler, 166
Retimo, 78, 80, 81, 84, 85
Rettenegg, 189, 190
Rgolje, 149
Rhine, River, 169
Ribnik, 149, 151
Ringel, General, Julius, 52, 61, 72, 76–8, 82–3,
   136, 141, 177–81, 189
Rocroi, 40
Roesch, Elfriede, 63
'Roesselsprung': *see* 'Knight's Move',
   Operation
Rognan, 37
Rohleder, Lieutenant, 140
Romanja, 160, 161
Romboks fiord, 31
Rommel, Erwin, 14
Ronenfiord, 36
Rosenberg, 17
Rothbach, River, 166, 167
Rovaniemi, 109, 110, 114, 126, 127
Rudki, 23
Rupel Pass, 48, 50, 61
Rupesco, 52, 55, 56, 58, 59, 61
Ruwer, River, 167, 168

S
St Kathrein, 182, 184
St Vid Pass, 66
Saerkivaara, 117
Salla, 115–19
Salonika, 62
Salzburg, 15, 46, 170
Sambor, 22–3
Sana, 150
Sarajevo, 67, 147, 155–6, 159
Sassnitz valley, 184
Sava, R, 161, 163
Save, River, 157
Schinke, Obersturmbannfuehrer, 118
Schlemmer, Colonel, 15
Schlemmer, General, 106, 112
Schmidhuber, Brigadefuehrer, 158
Schneider, Lieutenant, 141
Schobel, Gerd, 49
Schoerner, Colonel, 22, 24, 62
Schreiber, Standartenfuehrer Franz, 123, 124,
   127, 165
'Sealion', Operation, 44–5, 63
Semmering, 170, 176–7, 183, 194
Sfakia, 85
Signy, 40
Sildvik, 32
'Skanderbeg', 21st Waffen Gebirgs Division der
   SS, 205
Skibotten, 126
Skopje, 155
Skorzeny, Otto, 151

Slovakia, 17, 87
Soerfold, 37
Sofia, 68
Soissons, 44
Somme, River, 41
'Sondermeldungen', 62
Sonnwendstein, 194
Spiess, Alfred, 45–6
'Spring Awakening', Operation, 174
'Spring Storm', Operation, 157
Srnetica–Strugica mountains, 148
Stalin Line, 87–93, 96
Stalino, 103
Steiermark, 16, 173–95
Stettin, 34
Story Shokovec, 17
Struma, River and valley, 49, 50, 52, 54, 59
Strumica, 51
Stylos, 80, 81, 84
Styria: *see* Steiermark
Szentgal, 175, 181
Ssed, River, 98
Ssemnosero, 124
Ssinyka, River, 98, 99
Ssmaschcko, Mount, 134
Ssuchumi, 133
Suda Bay, 76, 79, 81, 83, 84
Sudetenland, 16
Sukkula, 125
Sultanitsa, 52, 57–9

T
Taraldsvik, 30
Tartar Nr. 1, SS Gebirgs Brigade, 207
Terek, River, 132
Ternovka, 100
Thaya, River, 16
The Black Watch, 104
Titova, River, 111, 112
Trapesca, 52
Treskavica Panina, 159
Trier, 167
Trondheim, 28, 30, 34, 35, 38
Tuapse, 133
Tunisia, 142–3
Turbe, 149
Turkish unit of the SS (Tartar No. 1), 207
Tyrol, 15

U
Ukraine, 86
Uman, 87, 95–103
Unac, 150
Unterdrauburg, 65, 163
Usico, 155

Utz, Colonel, 77
Uvata, 150, 151

V
Valenczsee, 174
Varangerfiord, 104
Vardar, River, 62
Varypetron, 80
Vasano, 52
Vensmoen, 37
Vienna, 64
Villach, 163
Vinjagolovo, 137
Vinnitsa, 93, 96–8
Vironya, 59
Vistula, 18
Volkhov Sector of Eastern Front, 136–41
Volkovinche, 91
Vorarlberg, 15
Vosges Mountains, 40, 165
Vramos, 83
Vrases, 83

W
'Waldrausch', Operation, 147
Warsaw, 18, 19, 21
Wechsel, 177, 183, 185
Weisenberger, General, 121
Wecker, Major, 137, 139
'Weygand Line', 41
White Mountains, 72, 77, 82
'White', Operation, 146
Wiener Neustadt, 184
Windisch, Colonel, 28
Wingen, 165, 166
Wittman, Lieutenant-General, 181, 184, 187
Wittmann, Lieutenant-Colonel, 80, 83, 85
Wolfsberg, 64
Worms, 169
Wurzen Pass, 163

Y
Yatran, River, 98–100
Yeletyosero, 122
Yugoslavia, 62–7, 68–71, 144–63

Z
Zajecar, 154
Zagreb, 157, 159
Zboiska, 24, 25
Zenica, 159, 161
Zinsweiler, 167
Znaim, 16
Zuchowice, 25